STUDIES IN EVANGELICALISM
edited by
Kenneth E. Rowe &
Donald W. Dayton

FREEDOM AND GRACE:
The Life of Asa Mahan

by

Edward H. Madden
and
James E. Hamilton

Studies in Evangelicalism,
No. 3

THE SCARECROW PRESS, INC.
Metuchen, N.J., & London
1982

Library of Congress Cataloging in Publication Data

Madden, Edward H.
  Freedom and grace.

  (Studies in evangelicalism ; no. 3)
  Includes bibliographical references and index.
  1. Mahan, Asa, 1800-1889. 2. Evangelicalism--
Biography. 3. Clergy--Biography. 4. Philosophers--
Biography. 5. Educators--United States--Biography.
I. Hamilton, James E. II. Title. III. Series.
BR1643.M34M32   285.8'092'4 [B]   82-5724
ISBN 0-8108-1555-9   AACR2

ACKNOWLEDGMENTS

In writing this biography of Asa Mahan we are primarily indebted to Richard Dupuis and Marian Madden, without whose very substantial aid in research and writing, there would have been no book. Their heartwarming generosity and their constant encouragement are gratefully acknowledged.

For many helpful, indeed crucial, suggestions we are much indebted to Marlene Merrill, Peter H. Hare, W. E. Bigglestone, Joseph L. Blau, Daniel Merrill, and Gertrude Jacob, all of whom critically read the entire manuscript and gave much valuable advice. It is a pleasure to thank them publicly.

All of the archivists and reference librarians with whom we have worked have been very helpful. The two to whom we are most indebted are W. E. Bigglestone of Oberlin College and Frank Lorenz of Hamilton College. Their professional standards are outstandingly high.

We gratefully thank the Institute for Advanced Study, Asbury College, and the National Endowment for the Humanities for their support at various stages of our work. The encouragement and support of Elaine Hamilton, Harold Burchell, and Dennis Kinlaw have been indispensable.

Edward H. Madden
James E. Hamilton

CONTENTS

EDITORS' NOTE

The current resurgence of Evangelical religion has
highlighted the important role of Evangelicalism in the formation of American culture. This series will explore its
roots in the Evangelical Revival and the Awakenings of the
18th century, its 19th-century blossoming in revivalism and
social reform, and its 20th-century developments in both
"sect" and "mainline" churches. We will be particularly
concerned to emphasize the diversity within Evangelicalism--
the search for holiness, the millennial traditions, Fundamen-
talism, Pentecostalism and so forth. We are pleased to
publish as the third volume of "Studies in Evangelicalism"
this biography of Asa Mahan, whose life touched so many
aspects of 19th-century Evangelicalism.

Edward H. Madden received his A. B. and M. A. from
Oberlin College, the institution that Asa Mahan served as
first president. After receiving the Ph. D. from the University of Iowa in philosophy, he began a distinguished career
in the philosophy of science and the history of American
philosophy expressed in several books and many articles.
After long service at the State University of New York (Buffalo), he worked at the Institute for Advanced Studies at
Princeton before taking an early retirement in Wilmore,
Kentucky to pursue his own research and writing.

James E. Hamilton, Professor of Philosophy at Asbury College in Wilmore, Kentucky did his undergraduate
work at Houghton College, Houghton, New York and his theological degree at Asbury Theological Seminary. After receiving an M. A. at Miami University in Ohio, he completed

doctoral work on Asa Mahan with Professor Madden at the State University of New York (Buffalo). Professor Hamilton is also an ordained elder in the Southern Indiana Conference of the United Methodist Church.

Donald W. Dayton
Northern Baptist Theological
   Seminary
Lombard, IL

Kenneth E. Rowe
Drew University
Madison, NJ

PREFACE

Asa Mahan was not a one-dimensional man. Although
nineteenth-century America produced many talented people,
each genuinely significant in his own specific line--Charles
G. Finney as preacher, Mark Hopkins as teacher, James
McCosh as scholar, Charles William Eliot as college president, Theodore Weld as abolitionist, Lucy Stone as champion
of co-education--Mahan, incredible as it seems, was outstanding in all of these roles. He preached widely in America and the United Kingdom as advocate of New Light theology; and as professor of mental and moral philosophy he
taught and wrote effectively at Oberlin and Adrian colleges.
As the first president of each school, he advocated the "new
education" which was eventually established at Harvard College in 1869 by Eliot. He defended the rights of women to
co-education on equal terms with men and engaged in antislavery activity, including many acts of civil disobedience.
His philosophical and religious ideas defined and controlled
his reform activities, and the latter enriched his ever de-
veloping web of ideas.

Mahan began to assume his many roles when he became a trustee of the Lane Theological Seminary in Cincinnati, where he was pastor of the Sixth Presbyterian Church.
The young minister was the most committed supporter of
Theodore Weld and other seminarians in their abolitionist
activity, the result being that he and his family were ostra-
cized by many in the community. When the Board of Trustees denied the right of the students to speak the truth as
they saw it, the great majority of the seminarians, under
the leadership of Weld, left Lane and with Mahan as president and Finney as professor of theology moved to Oberlin,

ix

where the Oberlin Collegiate Institute was re-founded in 1835
to admit black students.   Women had been admitted, though
not on an equal basis, at the original founding in 1833.
Mahan used both Oberlin and Adrian not only as bases from
which he continued to press the claims of emancipation, equal
co-education, and the new curriculum, but also to support
the Liberty, Free Soil, and the Republican parties.   He even
advised President Lincoln on military strategy during the
Civil War, much to the annoyance of Secretary of War Stanton.   He was an early opponent of President Grant and ran
for Congress in Michigan on the Greeley ticket in 1872--a
bitter campaign indeed.

More than any other religious leader in nineteenth-
century America, Mahan consistently attacked Calvinism in
all its forms and developed, defended, and promoted Free
Will Trinitarianism and the doctrine of sanctification (or the
"second blessing," as the Methodists liked to say).   Though
his treatment of each was unique, he worked essentially in
the tradition of John Wesley's notion of Christian Perfection.
Mahan's religious views received much criticism, particularly
during the Oberlin years, from Presbyterian and Congregational sources, but his and similar views of sanctification,
holiness, full salvation, or the second blessing became increasingly important in American Protestantism from 1850
on.   By the latter part of the century they constituted one
of the dominant strands in Protestantism, echoes of which
subsequently receded and swelled as religious fashions came
and went.   Mahan lived in England the last fifteen years of
his long life--one that spanned most of the nineteenth century
--and his views from 1874 on helped spark the success of
the Oxford and Brighton Conventions which led into the Keswick Movement of the evangelical wing of the Church of England.

At both Oberlin and Adrian Mahan was professor of
mental and moral philosophy.   His success as a teacher of
this subject has always been credited with the great emphasis
that Oberlin has traditionally put upon philosophy.   He also
published numerous influential books in all areas of the subject.   Jabez Burns, a Scottish minister, thought the president of Oberlin one of the best philosophers in America and
wrote that Mahan's refutation of Jonathan Edwards' effort to
reconcile determinism and free will was the most effective
ever written.   This estimate of great merit by a contemporary of Mahan--one of many--coincides with the estimates of
recent commentators.   Morris Cohen, a noted American

philosopher, characterized Mahan as having an acute, critical mind; Charles M. Perry, scholar in American intellectual history, has written that Mahan read Kant and his successors with shrewd intelligence and that his Intellectual Philosophy exhibits astounding accuracy and keenness of criticism.

Mahan was an effective advocate of Scottish realistic philosophy, although, unlike many of his contemporaries, he was also influenced by Kant and Cousin. His Critical History of Philosophy, published in 1882 when he was eighty-three years old, is a choice example of this tradition. In recent years a significant amount of interest in the history of Scottish realism in America--in Wayland at Brown, Bowen at Harvard, Mahan and Finney at Oberlin, and McCosh at Princeton--has surfaced, and the original sources have begun to be republished. The reasons for the resurgence of interest are numerous, one being that Scottish concepts of agency and action have become an active influence in the work of numerous contemporary American philosophers.

The activist, religious, and philosophical strands of Mahan's life are far from discrete; indeed, there could scarcely be a life more unified, stringently so, than Mahan's. His philosophical views of agency and freedom helped shape his religious views, and the two together determined in large part his reform activities. "Ought" implies "can." According to Mahan, what a person does, or is, is in some crucial sense "up to him." He is an agent that causes things to happen and not a patient whose action is molded and determined by external causes. All events are caused, to be sure, but some of them are caused by a person. Being an agent and thus having freedom, man is able to accept the gift of salvation offered through God's grace and, in like manner, to ask for the presence of the Holy Spirit in combatting sin, both in oneself and in the world. From these positions it is only one short step to personal reforms such as temperance and to social reforms such as abolition, women's rights, and the new curriculum. Indeed, the link between philosophy and reform held not only for Mahan but for his Oberlin and Adrian students as well: it was his courses in mental and moral philosophy that knit together college life and the world of reform societies and fugitive slaves.

Because Mahan touched so many bases in his work a study of his life helps illuminate numerous strands of American philosophical, religious, intellectual, social, and political history. They converge in his life and take on new meaning in the rich context of his life. However, the man is never lost amidst the cluster of ideas that he helps illuminate. Mahan was above all an impressive person--fiery, heedless of consequences where principles were concerned, unyielding, hard on himself and others, utterly earnest but not without a sense of humor, hopeful but often frustrated, quick witted and intelligent, deeply devout and loving, genial, abrasive, and, as a result of this mixture, genuinely tragic--a person whose life story has abundant interest.

Chapter 1

NEW YORK YEARS

Asa Mahan was born in Vernon, New York on November 9, 1799, the son of Samuel and Anna Mahan. His parents were New England stock and had lived in Worcester, Massachusetts during their early years. Samuel had fought in the Revolutionary War and eventually received a pension which was helpful in his later years. After his first wife had died leaving a young family, Samuel married Anna, a member of the Dana family, who nurtured the children already born as well as the three to come. In addition to their son, Anna and Samuel were the parents of Polly, who lived only three years, and Betsy, who died well before Mahan. The strength seemed to have been concentrated in Asa, who lived to his ninetieth year.

Asa's parents moved to Oneida County, where Vernon is located, sometime in the 1790's, a time when that area of New York State very much counted as a frontier of the young country. Though they were probably members of the Vernon Presbyterian Church or the Vernon Center Church (Anna was a devout Christian), their names do not appear in the records of either church or in any of the histories of Oneida County. All too soon for the Mahans Vernon ceased to be frontier and the call of land without fences came from western New York. In 1811 the family moved to Orangeville, located southwest of Rochester, which at the time was a formidable rival of Warsaw for the location of the Wyoming County seat. When the Mahans arrived, there were forty or fifty families already well established. Samuel and Anna were members of the Presbyterian Church and are

1

mentioned, though not prominently, as charter members of
the church and pioneers of the area in F. W. Beer's History
of Wyoming County. Their names are erroneously recorded
as Samuel and Anna Mehan. Asa was twelve years old when
he journeyed to Orangeville, and he was delighted with the
prospects of adventure in the wilderness and hills around
the thriving hamlet.[1]

Asa Mahan was a spirited and adventurous youth and
was deeply interested in religion as a result of his mother's
influence. His adventures and his religious experiences far
from being compartmentalized were inextricably and sadly
connected. Young Asa had three close brushes with death,
the result being a fear of dying and horror at the thought of
being buried, the intensity of which requires an explanation.

In Vernon Asa and a young friend went to a mill pond
where they had never been before to wade in the cool water.
A tree was felled across an end of the pond and they proposed to jump off the tree into the water. Realizing that
neither of them knew how to swim, Asa decided to wade out
to determine the depth of the water. He waded ten or twelve
feet and then suddenly stepped into a depth far above his
head. He turned in the direction which he hoped was toward
the bank and struggled under water until he reached the shore
in a dreadfully exhausted condition.

On another occasion, soon after the Mahans arrived
in Orangeville, the snow became so deep that deer floundered
in it and were easy prey to hunters walking on their snowshoes. His neighbors and one of his half brothers were successful hunters and Asa, spurred on by such examples, constructed his own snowshoes. Having finished them he started
out late one afternoon, with a gun on his shoulder, following
the tracks of the hunters. Eventually he came to a spot
where on successive days they had gone different ways, and
he had no idea which route they had taken that day. Had
Asa been prudent he would have awaited their return, but
instead he impetuously chose one way at random and continued his journey. He was then three miles or more from
home or any other shelter, and his home-made snowshoes
wholly fell apart. Like the hunted deer he was now at the
mercy of the deep snow around him. He had in fact taken
the right route and the hunters found him upon their return.
After they repaired his snowshoes he managed by late evening, after a tiring struggle through a storm of snow and
wind, to reach home safely, greatly to the relief of his ter-

rified parents.   Asa could not help but think what would have
happened to him had he taken the other path.

A half mile from Samuel's farm in Orangeville there
was a large forest containing a section of dead and rotting
trees.   The trees had been girdled by insects years before
and were so far decayed that in a strong wind high branches
and whole trunks were broken off to hurtle to the ground.
While searching for his father's cows one day, Asa was
tempted to go into the heart of the devastated area to pick
wild berries.   A storm came unexpectedly and quickly, and
the winds with almost hurricane force scattered limbs and
whole trees around the fleeing youngster who, in terror, as
he ran toward a sturdy stand of trees vowed to God that if
He would preserve him just this once he would ever after
lead a new life.   Asa did escape, but he was unable to keep
his vow. [2]

These three close calls, in addition to the death of a
friend at whose funeral he was a pallbearer, raised in Asa's
head a fear of death and revulsion at the thought of being
placed in a coffin and buried in the ground.   The fear and
revulsion remained with him for years to come--indeed,
through college, seminary, and early pastoral days.   The
most trying part of his ministry was officiating at funerals.
Whence the unusual force of this emotional reaction?   It was,
at least to some extent, a matter of his religious training.
He had been brought up a strict Calvinist, which, in his denomination, meant Old School Presbyterian views.   He had
been taught that God graciously saves some undeserving sinners while condemning the rest to eternal damnation.   The
Elect, those who are saved, are just as passive in their behavior as the damned; they are all determined to act in the
way they do, and whether they are saved or damned was
predetermined.   Although Asa never doubted that his mother
was among the Elect, he felt that he was hopelessly barred
from God's love and hence his death meant eternal damnation.

The reason he could not keep his vow to God made
during the forest episode was that he could not rid himself
of the oppressive feeling that what he vowed or did would
not make any difference in any case.   He accepted the notion
that he was religiously passive and had only to wait and see
God's inevitable will enacted.   He entertained no doubt that
he was not one of the fortunate ones already and immediately
saved.   His life seemed hopeless, and he was often near
despair over the grimness of his prospects both in this life

and the life to come.[3]   Had he not been an exceptionally
strong-willed, resilient, and hardy youth he might well have
fallen by the wayside.

It might seem strange that a youth even in an age
far more religious than our own should be so preoccupied
with religious concerns and so deeply indoctrinated in one
view.   The strangeness disappears in part, however, in
light of Asa's early training and the character of his mother.
As soon as he was able to read, the first treatises put into
his hands were the Longer and Shorter Catechisms of the
General Assembly of the Presbyterian Church, the shorter
of which he thoroughly memorized.   Theological debate was
raging among New England Calvinists at this time, and Anna
Dana Mahan was acquainted with the writings of Old School
Calvinists and the variations of Edwards, Hopkins, Bellamy,
and Emmons.   Missionaries from Connecticut sometimes
stopped at the Orangeville farm to discuss theological views
with her, and from his twelfth to his seventeenth year there
was no more attentive listener than young Asa.   He also
read avidly and from the age of ten was much given to religious thought and reflection that grew more clear and precise as the years passed.   The result of his thinking and
reading always seemed the same to him, no matter what the
efforts were to avoid it.   How can there be any responsibility when there is no ability?   He looked upon sin in the same
light as an inherited disease; a person is equally unaccount-
able for either one.   He was not responsible for becoming a
Christian because it was utterly out of his power.   He had
no more consciousness of an obligation to become a Christian
than he had to become an angel.   His fate was already determined, he assumed, and he had no hope of being among
those chosen.[4]

Asa went to the district school and, proving a good
student through the years, was invited when he was seventeen to teach the winter school in what he said was a most
desirable district.   It was four miles from his father's farm
and was more than likely in the town of Warsaw.   While
thus employed he found himself in the midst of a powerful
revival of religion.   One of his good friends was converted
and, much to Asa's astonishment, was transformed into a
new person.   During this same period he learned that his
mother was praying for the salvation of his soul, as were
his friends.   The young school teacher wondered if there
was any point in listening to the old story about the utter
depravity of man and the doctrine of the Elect again.   He

had his doubts but sought instruction from the religious experience of the elders of the village.   The results were dis-
couraging: "Wait for God to give his sign," and so on.   After all, what sense do evangelism and revivalism make?
What sense does it make to listen for a call to come to God
when it has been decided ahead of time by God who shall be
with Him and who not?[5]

    Nevertheless, impressed by this experience of his
friend, Asa decided to try again and listened to the revivalist preacher.   What the preacher had to say, what affected
the young man so deeply, has not been recorded, but whatever it was the effect was profound.   Asa Mahan had his
first in a series of deeply religious experiences.   He recalled: "I apprehended, with absolute distinctness, God as
having ever loved me with a more than parental love, and
as having ever been ready to receive me, pardon me, love
me, and care for me, as a child, [if] I confessed my sin
to Him, implored His pardoning mercy, and sought His fa-
vour."[6]   He acted according to this refreshingly different
religious impulse and knelt in prayer.   He emphatically acknowledged that he was totally unworthy of God's grace and
simply promised to accept God's will as his own.   He plead-
ed to be spared the deadness and hopelessness of his past
religious understanding and asked for the ability to appreciate and respect God's love and glory.   In Out of Darkness
into Light, written many years later in England, Mahan
wrote of the result of his prayer.   "I had no sooner pro-
nounced these words, than I was consciously encircled in the
'everlasting arms.'   I was so overshadowed with a sense of
the manifested love of a forgiving God and Saviour, that my
whole mental being seemed to be dissolved, and pervaded
with an ineffable quietude and assurance.   I arose from my
knees without a doubt that I was an adopted member of the
family of God ... [and] could and did say, 'My Father and
my God.'   Such was my entry into the inner life."[7]

    After the initial exhilaration of his new found faith,
Asa was subject to occasional backsliding, and he felt tempted to resume the "worldly" ways of life he had followed in
despair when he had thought he was not included in God's
kingdom.   Once when tempted he retreated to a nearby forest and spent the day praying and meditating.   Mahan later
wrote that "there, in deep 'fellowship with the Father and
His Son Jesus Christ,' I became 'crucified to the world and
the world to me.'   From that good hour I have never felt
the least temptation to return to the worldly life."[8]

As a result of his experience in the forest, Asa felt
himself a consciously committed servant of Christ, dedicated
to the "winning of souls," and felt himself under an "enduement of power" for that service. But how could he most
usefully serve? No doubt the ministry was the best means
for achieving this goal, but did he have the ability to pursue
this profession? In one place he wrote as if he were diffident and needed encouragement while in another place as if
he confidently decided to go to college and seminary. [9] In
any case, he did make the ministry his life work, beginning
his dedicated service even before going to Hamilton College
and Andover Seminary. When not teaching or farming, he
was busy at eighteen trying to convert his friends and ac-
quaintances in the Orangeville area. He recalled that one
of his friends was converted at this time and continued until his death to be "a central light in the leading church in
the city of Buffalo." That same year he was called to teach
school in what he called a very ungodly neighborhood, and
he waged his usual battle. To begin with, not a single person would aid him in holding religious meetings. However,
he persisted until he had organized two meetings a week, always having to do the preaching himself; and by the time he
left the district a church had been started. [10] He taught winter school until 1820 and his classroom often had the ambience of a revival meeting. His achievements were not in-
substantial for a young man whose formal preparation for
the ministry was yet to begin.

A Problem and an Answer

Unfortunately, as Asa realized after the first exalta-
tions passed, his intuitions and religious experiences did
not fit any part of the Old School Presbyterian views he
had been taught. What, after all, were the implications of
his conversion experience? Man is inherently sinful and is
saved only by the grace of God. However, man has a role
to play in the drama of salvation and should not sit around
waiting passively for signs from God indicating whether he
is part of the elect or is to be cast into outer darkness.
A person is endowed with free will; what he does and what
he chooses is "up to him." God offers salvation as a gracious gift to every sinful person. It is up to each individual
--undeserving, to be sure--to accept or reject the gracious
gift of salvation. Man's destiny hinges on his own free, un-
forced acceptance of Jesus Christ as his Savior and Redeem-
er.

Asa was aware that these views--which were implied by his religious experience--already had been formulated in opposition to Old School views and were designated
by such labels as New School, New Light, and Freewill
Trinitarian. Asa, however, lacked the theological and philosophical acumen to defend these views against seasoned Old
School controversialists. In any case, at that time he really did not want to abandon his mother's church with its strict
Calvinism because it had constituted his community all his
life. He certainly had no desire to be outside the fold when
his mother remained inside it. However, he was even less
willing to ignore the promptings of his religious experience.
He drifted along trying to avoid conflict as much as possible.
He came to despise the emphasis on "creeds" and "confessions" and longed for people instead to concentrate on doing
something in Christ's name. But in college and seminary
he was forced into defending one form of Calvinism or another in order to avoid the appearance of being either disinterested in important matters or incapable of effectively arguing
for a position. So Asa decided to defend Dr. Emmons' form
of Calvinism. Why, we do not know--perhaps it was the
view held by his mother or the one that allowed for the most
direct contact of God with the world. But his heart was not
in it since all forms of Old School Calvinism, as far as he
could ascertain, claimed that man plays a wholly passive
role in conversion. Even when he argued for the system
he had selected, he said, his mind shrank back appalled at
the difficulties and perplexities presented. [11]

In seminary he was astonished at the arguments used
by one of his professors to reconcile the concepts of necessity and responsibility. Said the professor, "We have proved
these two doctrines to be true, as matters of fact. That is,
these two facts do exist. That is, they exist together. That
is, they co-exist. That is, they co-sist. That is, they con-
sist, or are consistent." When the same argument was used
again the next year, Mahan reported, "Some of the class
came out of the recitation room with their eyes standing out
as large as tea-saucers." He wrote that "such abortive at-
tempts to reconcile the palpably incompatible rendered such
incompatibility more palpable to my mind."[12]

Toward the end of Mahan's seminary training the inherent difficulties he saw in all forms of Old School Calvinism were becoming intolerable to him and a new point of departure needed. Professor Fitch of Yale College published
two discourses about that time that proved quite helpful to

the struggling student.   Asa noted that "in these discourses,
the position was taken and verified by proofs ... that sin
proper, that for which the creature is subject to condemnation, consists exclusively in a voluntary transgression of
known duty."   "This doctrine," he continued, "did not deny,
but fully admitted, a fallen, or what is called a sinful nature in man, but affirmed that we are accountable, not for
the mere existence of this nature, but for our voluntary actions relative to its promptings."[13]   In considering the relation of the human will to sin Mahan was finally persuaded to
change fundamentally his life-long beliefs and to reject completely the doctrine of necessity and adopt that of liberty.
Mahan had reached a very far-sweeping conclusion, one
which required him fundamentally to reconstruct his entire
system of theology and, as he said, to "'read with new
eyes' the word of God."

     Among his reasons for his change of opinion Mahan
wrote that Calvinistic determinism not only flatly contradicts
the teaching of the leading thinkers of the primitive church
but also the reports of ordinary consciousness.[14]   But why
should one accept a theory over what one directly experienced?   Mahan argued that we are all directly aware that
we "could have done otherwise"--that is, we are aware of
the ability to do either of two things or, having done one,
the ability to have done the other.   We are aware not simply that if the circumstances had been different we might
have acted differently but rather that in the very same cir-
cumstance we might have acted other than we did.   Unfortunately Old School views make moral responsibility impossible
and turn God into an unjust tyrant.   If men have no power
whatever to will or act differently than in fact they do, then
the concepts of merit and demerit, and the consequent propriety of reward and punishment, become meaningless and
inapplicable.   And God is transformed into a tyrant when he
admonishes men to give up their sinful ways since He is demanding of them what it is impossible for them to do.   God
must be seen on Judgment Day as eternally damning certain souls and saving others when none of the lot supposedly
could have done other than they did and so merit no judgment at all.   Were not such ridiculous consequences a re-
duction to absurdity of Old School Calvinism?   Mahan thought
the answer was surely "yes"!   He had to work out his view
in detail (his critique of Edwards and other Calvinistic efforts to make determinism compatible with moral responsibility came later), but he felt he had his bearings and a
compass to plot his further course.

Hamilton and Andover

Asa entered Hamilton College in 1821, and the reason
for his choice is quite clear, though he never mentioned it
himself. Hamilton College was located in Clinton, New York,
which was situated just a bit southeast of Vernon, where Asa
had been born. The Mahans had friends in Oneida County
who could be helpful to him in earning his way through college. Throughout his college years he preached in Clinton,
Vernon, New Hartford, Paris, or wherever a pulpit was
empty, and he labored in various revivals of religion in
Oneida County as well. He found this practical work of the
ministry, and his useful work in the poor neighborhoods ad-
jacent to the college, satisfying and emotionally sustaining
in contrast to chewing on the dry husks of theological doctrine.

The college course at Hamilton, patterned after Eastern schools, was strictly classical, and the following authors
and topics, while not exhaustive, constituted the curricular
core: Livy, Horace, Tully, Tacitus, Roman Antiquities,
Homer, Graeca Minora, Graeca Majora, arithmetic, Euclid,
algebra, fluxions, Webber's Mathematics, logic, mental and
moral philosophy (Locke, Paley, Butler), natural philosophy
(chemistry and physics), surveying, English grammar, American geography, and history. Composition, declamation, and
forensics were supposedly elements of all courses.[15] The
theory behind the inflexible curriculum was that classical
languages and mathematics, and to some extent philosophy,
disciplined and organized the mind of the student who then,
allegedly, could quickly master less rigorous disciplines
such as history, geography, and modern languages and literature. As we shall see, Mahan came to challenge this traditional view of education and defended the ideas of Francis
Wayland of Brown and Charles William Eliot of Harvard,
whose views came to dominate college education later in
the nineteenth century.

At Hamilton, as elsewhere, student literary societies
were at least as important educationally as college recitations and lectures--perhaps more important in the long run
--for here it was that students learned, if anywhere, to
write clearly, argue rigorously, and speak effectively. The
composition and forensic elements of the formal courses
were notorious failures. Moreover, through the years, the
societies acquired significant libraries, which not only supplemented but often surpassed the college collection. So-

cieties built up their libraries in various ways; the Philopeuthian Society at Hamilton, in addition to initiation fees,
depended largely on selling corn grown on college property
and fining members generously for overdue books, for being
late to a meeting, leaving early, missing it altogether, and
so on.

Asa was a member of Philopeuthian, though he contributed little to its treasury by way of fines, accumulating
throughout his college career the sum of ninety-five and a
quarter cents.   The truth of the matter is that he had very
little money to begin with and he was not given to wasting
any of it.   His thriftiness is further borne out by the fact
that he never withdrew books from the college library, the
charge there being twelve cents a month for a folio volume,
eight cents for a quarto, six cents for an octavo or lesser
volume, and fines for late returns.   There is good reason
to suspect that Theodore Strong, professor of mathematics
and natural philosophy, shared with Asa the books he withdrew from the library.   The College Library Register shows
Strong withdrawing Theory of the Earth, and Asa's commencement oration was entitled "Theories of the Earth."
Strong also withdrew Thomas Brown's work, and Asa was
acquainted with the views of this Scottish philosopher.   Asa
was occasionally president pro tem of Philopeuthian and
presided at the meeting on May 5, 1824, when the members
resolved to request the northeast corner room on the second
floor of the new college building and also fined Gudley "for
the detention of books remitted."[16]   It was thought to be
crucial and important business and perhaps, after all, it
really was.

Mahan served first as vice president and then president of the Hamilton Theological Society.   The members
earnestly debated such questions as "What is Meant by the
Unpardonable Sin?"   "What is the Scripture Doctrine of Election and Reprobation," and "What are the Standing Officers
in the Church of Christ and What are their Respective Qualifications?"   The title of the topic on the Doctrine of Election and Reprobation had the charming elaboration, "Do they
imply that some will be saved do what they will, and others
lost do what they can?"   As we have seen, Asa did not feel
free to say precisely what he thought on this topic during
his college years--indeed, he probably still was not certain
precisely what he did think--and the records of the Theological Society fail to enlighten us on what in fact he did
say.[17]

Student life was far from ideal at Hamilton during Asa's years and those immediately following. First, the relationship between students and faculty was that of adversaries. Part of the job of the faculty was to keep the students under surveillance and to report failures to observe the many rules of the college. Since they were not trusted to begin with, the major pastime of many students was to see how much they could get away with and to what extent they could frustrate their teachers. Second, the relationship between the members of the Board of Trustees, on the one hand, and President Henry Davis and the faculty, on the other, became strained and deteriorated rapidly over the famous cannon episode. Several students aimed a cannon at the room of an unpopular tutor, and the cannon, improperly handled, exploded causing a significant amount of damage. The faculty traced the culprits through the newspaper wadding, but the trustees refused to support them in punishing the students since the latter came from "respectable" and, it should be added, influential families. In addition, there was a dispute between President Davis and the rest of the faculty, on the one hand, and John Monteith, professor of language, and various members of the Board of Trustees, on the other --the latter group being admirers of the evangelist Charles Grandison Finney, whose upstate New York revivals were proving highly successful. Monteith also criticized Theodore Strong as being too scholarly and demanding in his teaching at Hamilton, thus frightening away students. In fact, Strong was a popular teacher, and a number of students in the class of 1824, disgusted by all the controversy at Hamilton, withdrew and finished their course at Union College. The security of faculty members was so slight that Strong left Hamilton for Rutgers University in 1827.[18]

Asa Mahan was a serious student, not a trouble maker, and was highly regarded by the faculty, of this there can be no doubt. The Minutes of the Faculty show that he was honored each year by being elected to deliver an oration at commencement, and he was graduated in 1824, after three years residence, with honors. F. D. Maltbie, C. Hall, and A. Mahan were the top three students, and Asa was invited to read the Philosophical Oration at his own commencement. The oration on "Theories of the Earth," written under the direction of Theodore Strong, was twice as long as prescribed but no one suggested that it be shortened. It was delivered next to last, just before the valedictory, when the audience was weary, but was still received with much applause.[19] President Davis and the rest of the

faculty thought he had done a first rate piece of work. This
recognition was important to the young scholar if we accept
Mahan's own judgment of later years. He wrote that an un-
healthy desire for recognition, even fame, was the cardinal
sin of his life until his second blessing.

Theodore Strong was Mahan's mentor at Hamilton,
and Asa often visited his home across the street from the
campus--a house destined to become famous in later years
as the home of Elihu Root. Strong's sister-in-law was Mary
Hartwell Dix, daughter of John and Hulda (Warren) Dix of
Littleton, Massachusetts, a young lady "of fine personal appearance and of a good family." Asa saw Mary not infre-
quently during his visits to the Strong household and the
young couple enjoyed the fine spacious living room no less
than their elders. Whether Mary lived with the Strongs or
simply spent long holidays with them remains unclear, but
in any case Asa and Mary were attracted to each other and
shared a mutual regard for the Strongs. Mary already exhibited the quickness of perception and ready tact that was
appreciated and praised in later years and her very presence then as later was "felt to be a blessing." Being close
to Mary and the Strongs were bright spots in Asa's Hamilton years, and who can doubt that Mary Dix was to be counted among those present at the 1824 commencement who so
cordially received his address! [20]

When Asa graduated from Hamilton College his friends
in the churches of Oneida County marked the event in a memorable manner. They combined their funds and bought him
a new suit of clothes for a graduation present and enough
other summer and winter clothing to take care of his needs
for years to come. The young man had touched the hearts
of the people with whom he had labored in revivals and other work of the church, and his heart in turn was warmed
by their remembrance of a shared past.

After the commencement exercises Asa quietly awaited, he said, "the openings of Providence." Needless to
say, he wanted to continue his studies in seminary, but he
had not even a remote idea of where the money might come
from to make this course of action possible. He later recalled, "After the anniversary services were over, and while
the great congregation were in the act of dispersing, an en-
deared ministerial friend, the Rev. Mr. Coe, pastor of the
Presbyterian Church in New Hartford, sought me out in the
crowd, and asked me where I had determined to pursue my

theological studies. 'I desire to go to Andover,' was my
reply. 'I am very glad to hear you say that,' remarked
my venerable friend.'' Asa explained that he would go to
Andover if he could secure fifty dollars from some source
since, he explained, neither he nor his parents could manage the matter. '''I will lend you the sum, and take your
note as my only security,' was the kind response; and more
kindly words, as it seemed to me, were never spoken.....
This, to me, surprising benefaction placed me in a line of
providences which determined my whole future life.''21

Andover Theological Seminary in Massachusetts was
less than Asa had hoped it would be, indeed had expected
it to be. Here surely there would be new and exciting theological discussions. But it turned out otherwise. It was
the same old business about whether Edwards, Hopkins,
Bellamy, or Emmons was right. After all, is there very
much difference between six and half a dozen?--all their
views had a common commitment to determinism. As we
have seen, Asa was embarrassed by the naive way one of
his professors tried to square determinism and moral responsibility, and, in any case, he was already in the process of working out a view of human agency that rejected
the view that one acts from the strongest inclination and
could not do otherwise.

Andover was disappointing in still another way. The
language and habits of the students were not markedly different from the low standards set by Hamilton students. He
felt that the students and faculty in general lacked moral commitments or spiritual vitality, that they solved problems of
theology as they had done those of geometry when in college
''and with no more seriousness or reverence in one case
than in the other.'' There was at Andover, moreover, a
dreariness about the very possibility of combatting sin and
immorality. What Mahan mused, was the cause of this
spiritual dreariness among Christians? No doubt much of
it was due to Calvinistic beliefs. If man is utterly depraved
and incapable of acting any way other than sinfully, then man
is likely to perform according to requirements. Calvinists
made a kind of piety of their very sinfulness! But even New
School Calvinism was not without its dreary side. To be
sure, Nathaniel Taylor and other Yale-taught divines believed
that man has free will and is able to accept the gift of salvation graciously offered by God to undeserving man. But
what, after all, was to be done about combatting sin? How
could a person overcome sin as God required of him. Then

the old story in part was re-installed. Man is free to
strive to overcome sin but he is puny and helpless and, being inherently sinful, is doomed to failure. Mahan wondered
if the New School theology went far enough. The Bible in-
forms a reader that Jesus demanded and expected believers
in his name to triumph over sin, to act in the way of the
Master himself. And Mahan believed that God would not demand of man what man in principle was incapable of doing.
But there was much counter-evidence in the Bible testifying
apparently to the hopelessly sinful nature of man. It was
a problem with which Asa Mahan would grapple for a number of years. [22]

        The one exception to the dreariness of Andover was
the famous Biblical scholar Moses Stuart. Chapter VII of
Romans always had been one of the bulwarks of the Calvinistic sold-under-sin view; the startling and crucial thing that
Stuart did for Mahan was to put that chapter in a whole new
light. According to Mahan, "Our learned Professor, to the
surprise of not a few of his pupils, laid out all his learning
and talents in rendering it demonstrably evident that the specific object of the apostle in this chapter is to elucidate a
legal in distinction from a proper Christian experience....
In the former state, 'he was carnal, sold under sin;' in the
latter, he was the Lord's freeman, 'delivered from the bond-
age of corruption into the glorious liberty of the children of
God.'"[23] Mahan came close to asking this question: If
God saves man from eternal damnation on the condition that
he freely accept God's love and grace, why could He not aid
man to combat sin on the same condition that His aid is
freely and lovingly prayed for? His thought was undeveloped
on this point, but he had a fleeting glimpse of the mature
holiness doctrine to come. This achievement was still in
the distance but the young pilgrim had begun what he was
to call his journey from darkness into light.

                    South Carolina and Orangeville

        In May of his senior year at the seminary Asa was
licensed to preach by the Oneida presbytery. George W.
Gale, the minister responsible for C. G. Finney's conversion, attended the meeting at which the licensing took place
and wrote the evangelist, "He was licensed [but] not before
being questioned, however, about reports which it was said
he had been instrumental in circulating about men and things."
"He confessed the charges and agreed to contradict them."[24]

There is no elaboration and Gale matter of factly passes
along the information as if it would be of interest to Finney.
He prefaced his remark by saying that Finney knew Mahan
was under the care of the Oneida presbytery, which suggests that Finney and Mahan were acquainted before they
worked together, as we shall see, at the Rochester Revival
of 1831.   That Mahan found some of the Andover professors
lukewarm Christians, plus the fact that he always felt it a
duty not only to speak the truth but the whole truth, as he
saw it, easily accounts for his spreading unfavorable reports.   One can hear him repeating endlessly the story about
the professor who made the students saucer-eyed with his
proof of the compatibility of determinism and moral responsibility.   He may have agreed to retract his "reports"
but he clearly never changed his mind.   Indeed, in his Autobiography published in 1882 Mahan did not hesitate to make
serious charges about the lack of spirituality at Andover in
his day.

> Never was I in an atmosphere less morally and
> spiritually vitalising than that which encircled us
> during those three years.   The President of our
> College sent an ungodly son to the Seminary the
> same year I entered it.   He was sent, not as a
> theological student, of course, but professedly to
> enlarge and perfect his linguistic education.   The
> real intent of the father was the conversion of his
> son through the saving influence which was sup-
> posed to pervade the institution.   The young man
> left no less ungodly than he was when he came
> among us; no influence encircling him, while there,
> which tended to any higher result. [25]

It is impossible to understand the episode reported by Gale,
and numerous other ones in later years, without realizing
that for Mahan character was a public matter and not in-
frequently required public judgment.   The only requirement
in judging character, he believed, was that a person reach
the judgment honestly, after careful consideration, and not
passionately.   And Mahan felt that others had the same right,
even duty, to judge his character in the same fashion.   In
1848, writing on the topic "Brotherly Love," he said,

> Character, our own not excepted, is public proper-
> ty.   So we regard and treat the character of oth-
> ers.... We regard ourselves, as having justly
> forfeited the esteem of no man, for having formed

and on proper occasions, expressed honest, and
only honest convictions in respect to his character, whether such judgments be favorable or unfavorable to his reputation, or whether we may
or may not have erred in judgment. No one,
therefore, should cease to be loved by us, as a
brother, whatever his opinions in respect to our
character may be, who has judged and spoken of
us in conformity with the principle just stated.
Suppose he has erred in judgment. Thus to err
is not only human, but the common frailty of all
finite intelligences. We cannot justly require all
men to think correctly or favorably of us. We
can, however, require them to think honestly. [26]

It should be noted, finally, that Mahan did not condemn Andover in a wholesale fashion. Throughout his life he highly
esteemed Moses Stuart, the professor from whom he first
learned to question the Calvinistic interpretation of Romans,
Chapter VII.

After graduating from Andover in September 1827,
young Mahan was appointed an agent of the American Tract
Society for the Carolinas. He labored first in Charleston,
South Carolina, where he succeeded in raising money to
erect a building which included a warehouse for storing
tracts awaiting distribution, offices for the Society and other religious groups in the city, and a hall on the second
floor for anniversary and other public religious services.
He also raised money to print tracts to put in the warehouse,
or Depository, as it was more elegantly termed, for subsequent distribution. Later Mahan was sent into the interior
to further the work of the Tract Society, where he labored
with equal success until he and a friend who now assisted
him were sent to North Carolina, where there was an even
wider and more fruitful field to be cultivated. However,
they received a letter from a minister who informed them
that the Society had appointed him as agent for most of
North Carolina; he warned them off his territory, so to
speak. Mahan and his friend mutually agreed, after careful deliberation, to return at once to New York and there
resign their commissions. Mahan wrote that they found on
their arrival, to the regret of their employers, that the
minister who had written them had violated completely all
the instructions which he had received from the Tract Society. The two young missionaries nevertheless resigned
as planned. [27]

The fact of the matter was that Mahan was quite happy
to be in New York City, and that for two reasons. First,
it was close to New Brunswick, New Jersey, where Theodore Strong now taught at Rutgers University, and where
Mary Dix either resided with her sister's family or again
made lengthy visits. Asa and Mary had remained in close
touch after the Hamilton years, though how they managed it
remains unknown. No doubt they exchanged numerous letters, though none are known to have survived. Also the
distance from Andover to either Littleton, Massachusetts
or New Brunswick was not great and we can imagine that
Asa managed more than one visit to the Dixes or Strongs
during his seminary years. The young couple wanted to
marry but should not such a union await a settled pastorate?

Moreover, it was advantageous to be in New York
City precisely at the time Mahan was there. It was May
and the annual conventions of the various religious societies
were being held. He was well placed to look for that settled pastorate. At one of these meetings he met "the celebrated Josiah Bissell from the city of Rochester," who invited Mahan to return with him to become pastor of the
Fourth Presbyterian church that he was in the process of
organizing in Rochester. Mahan accepted the invitation and
he and Mary Dix were promptly married in New Brunswick
on May 8, 1828. [28]

Asa and Mary Mahan travelled westward with happy
hearts and high hopes for their challenging work on the
"frontier." Unfortunately they experienced an immediate
setback. The young couple labored only a short period in
this new field when Asa was struck down "suddenly and
mysteriously by inflammatory rheumatism." He was utterly disabled in both ankles, knees, and left wrist, and lay a
helpless sufferer for several weeks at Coan Springs, from
whence, in a somewhat bettered condition, but still debil-
itated, he managed with Mary's help to travel to his father's
farm in Orangeville.

The Mahans remained in Orangeville for three months
while Asa recuperated. But he could not be idle even as a
convalescent. He was shocked by what had happened during
his long absence. The church which he had joined as a
young convert, and of which he was still a member, was
in a dying state as a result of a "disastrous pastorate," and
the few remaining members were seriously thinking of selling their building to another denomination. Mahan was able

to talk but still unable to walk so he told his friends if they
would carry him to the nearby church in a chair he would
preach to them.   They carried him to the church and this
unusual fact itself drew crowds of people to hear him.

> At first, the people listened with seeming amaze-
> ment, my emaciated form and deathlike counten-
> ance, no doubt, adding force to my utterances.   In
> a short time wonder gave place to serious thought
> upon the interests of the soul's eternity.   At the
> close of about three months of such labours, when
> my health was restored, and I had accepted a call
> to the pastorate of the church at Pittsford, some
> seven miles east of Rochester, a new pastor, a
> man of God, was in the midst of the church at
> Orangeville, and labouring there in a most power-
> ful revival which brought into the church the mass
> of the community around.   In this revival, also,
> my aged father, for whose conversion I had spe-
> cifically prayed every time I entered my closet
> for more than a dozen years, became a man of
> prayer. 29

Though Samuel was a member of the church, no doubt to
please his wife, he had remained a nominal Christian until
this revival occurred.

The Pittsford Pastorate

"The Church at Pittsford," to which Mahan referred,
was historically important as the first church in the village
and by Mahan's day had a significantly large congregation.
The church began in 1809 as the Second Congregational
Church of Northfield (a much wider area than the village)
and came under Presbyterian care in 1814.   It was eventually renamed the First Presbyterian Church of Pittsford.
The village grew substantially between 1816 and 1826, mainly due to the opening of the Erie Canal, on the banks of
which the village stood.   The congregation, growing apace,
built an impressive new church in Greek Revival style.   It
was constructed of limestone quarried nearby and was topped
by an admirable spire.   It was not an unimpressive pastorate for a young man. 30   Very likely Josiah Bissell and Joel
Parker, who was the minister of the Third Presbyterian
Church in Rochester, were helpful in securing Mahan's call
to Pittsford.   Bissell's relation to Asa is already known;

Joel Parker was an old friend and classmate of Hamilton
College days.

Excitement and drama came to the Rochester-Pitts-
ford area in 1830 with the appearance of Charles Grandison
Finney, the noted evangelist. Finney had been successful
throughout upper New York State in previous years--one of
his most important converts being Theodore Weld--and Bissell and Parker were eager to have him come to Rochester.
They both knew Finney well and already in 1829 had invited
him to come and fight the rampant sins of the "canawlers"
and other elements in the city. He was unable to come until the following year at which time he created quite a sen-
sation. His Rochester revival of 1830-31 surpassed anything
seen before and became national news. The revival cut
across theological divisions and even helped to some extent
to heal the wounds of the Presbyterian community in Rochester. In a Presbytery meeting Dr. Penny of the First Church
had accused Bissell and Parker of the Third Church of trying to turn the congregation of Rev. James' Second Church
against him, secure his resignation, and get a New School
pastor--probably Asa Mahan--to replace him. Bissell and
Parker replied that their objections to James were totally
misconstrued. In his Memoirs Finney wrote that "very soon
after the work commenced, the difficulties between Mr. Bissell and Dr. Penny were healed; and all the distractions and
collisions that had existed there were adjusted; so that a
spirit of universal kindness and fellowship pervaded all the
churches." That may well have been the case but Rev.
James nonetheless soon left Rochester. In addition, not
everyone approved wholly of Finney's "new measures" in
revival meetings. Traditionalists particularly disliked his
practice of having men and women pray together publicly,
for it suggested lack of taste and implied equality between
the sexes. [31]

Whatever reservations existed soon were swept aside
in the onrush of Finney's most successful revival. Not only
were lukewarm Christians brought wholeheartedly into the
fold but professing non-believers like Samuel D. Porter, an
influential Rochester merchant, were also "caught in his
net," to use the metaphor Finney himself liked to use. Porter remained close to Finney through the years and became
a trustee of Oberlin College, in which capacity, as we shall
see, he and Asa Mahan, each with the best intentions, sadly
misunderstood each other.

At one of the early meetings in the First Church the

building was so crowded that the walls spread and a beam
fell through the plaster of the ceiling. There was some
panic as people rushed out but no one was seriously hurt.
Perhaps the avoidance of catastrophe was taken as a positive omen; in any case, the accident seems to have stimulated rather than quenched religious ardor. Between September 1830 and March 1831 Finney preached ninety-six
sermons and held a multitude of "special sessions." Pittsford and Mahan were drawn into the movement as it spilled
over the confines of Rochester. Finney came to preach at
Mahan's church and, according to one observer, "the old
church was crowded night after night, upstairs and down,
and conversions were numbered by the score." Sixty people
joined Mahan's congregation as a result of the revival. Finney was nearly exhausted by his strenuous efforts, but he
kept up the furious pace through January and February. "A
final great effort was made in late February and early March,
an effort in which the evangelist was assisted by nine other
ministers from various western New York communities.
Among these were the Rev. William Wisner ... and Asa
Mahan."[32] Little did Finney and Mahan realize that in four
years they would be associated again, and far more intimate-
ly and during a much longer period, at the newly established
Oberlin Collegiate Institute in Ohio--Mahan as President and
Finney as Professor of Theology.

It must not be supposed that Mahan's time during the
Pittsford years was wholly taken up with dramatic and exciting events--indeed that was far from the case. Most of
his time was spent in regular pastoral duties and in family
life. He preached more than once on Sundays and during
week days as well, to say nothing of calling on his parishioners, counselling them, administering the Lord's Supper,
baptizing children, and the hundred and one other duties at-
tendant upon a conscientious minister. On November 23,
1829, he had the pleasure of baptizing his own daughter,
Anna Jenison. She was Mary's and his first child and had
been born in Orangeville on February 23, 1829. The Mahans were fond of naming their children after friends, and
Anna's middle name was given in honor of Dr. Charles Jenison of Orangeville, neighbor and friend of early days and
subsequently husband of Asa's sister Betsy. On June 27,
1830, Reverend Squire baptized their son, Theodore Strong,
named lovingly after Mary's brother-in-law who was still at
Rutgers and destined to become vice president.[33]

Asa and Mary were deeply fond of their growing family, but tragedy struck more than once. Asa recalled,

> I can never forget the pure agony which I exper-
> ienced when God took from us, in succession, two
> infant children, each that "thing of beauty," of
> about four months of age.... Those two counten-
> ances, as I look upon them for the last time, have
> ever since remained before my mind with the same
> distinctness as if the vision had occurred buy one
> hour ago. Of what occurred on the way to and
> from those burying-places, I have never been able
> to recall a single instance. I have only a faint
> recollection of seeing two little coffins let down
> gently into "the lap of God."

His pain and sorrow were intense and "with that sorrow no
divine consolations seemed to be intermingled." The consolation came only years later. "Some fifteen or sixteen
years after the death of our infant son, 'I had a vision in
my sleep.'" Mahan dreamt that he had died and as he
gratefully and slowly walked toward the throne of God "there
appeared directly before me a youth who approached very
near, and, with intense inquiry, looked me in the face....
'Suddenly his whole countenance lighted up with a smile of
joyful recognition: 'it is my father come at last.'" After
that vision "heaven has appeared more like home to me than
it could otherwise have done."[34]

Mahan's pastorate at Pittsford extended from August
1829 to March 1831. The vote on August 20 to call Mahan
as pastor was overwhelmingly yes, only two voters dissenting. And yet he left after one and a half years with more
than two against him. What had happened? In the first
place, it must be kept in mind that the Pittsford congregation, like many in those trying days, was a bit on the mer-
curial side and pastors came and went at a rapid rate. Indeed, Asa Mahan's tenure in office was longer than that of
many others. According to Smith Ordway, "Rev. Solomon
Allen was pastor of the church for two years. In 1811, Rev.
Silas Hubbard is spoken of, who was here a short time; and
till 1825, we have mention made of Rev. Aaron C. Collins,
Rev. Joseph F. Bliss, Rev. Chauncey Cook, Rev. John Taylor, Rev. Ralph Cushman, and Rev. William F. Curry."
Robert Wadhams continued the narrative, "Rev. William F.
Curry ... was ordained and installed July 14, 1825 [and] was
dismissed July 4, 1826. In 1827 Rev. Homer Adams came
and preached for two years. He was succeeded by Rev. Asa
Mahan who was installed Nov. 11, 1829, and dismissed March
4, 1831. Rev. Alfred E. Campbell followed for one year.
His successor Rev. Elijah Buck remained nine months...."[35]

It should be kept in mind that "dismissed" did not mean
"discharged" but simply that a person was given a letter
upon leaving saying that he was a member in good standing
of a given church. However, the friction had developed between Mahan and certain members of his congregation as a
result of his speaking his mind straightforwardly in the pulpit was clearly the case. "Dismissed," however, is not to
be taken as a measure of its severity.

It was not only the Pittsford Church that was in turmoil during these years. It was the age of the great controversy between Old and New School Presbyterianism and
many churches experienced a series of upheavals. On Fri-
day, February 4, 1831, the Pittsford congregation moved
and seconded the resolution that the church should become
"Strictly Presbyterian" in government. While the resolution
was a matter of church governance it was a certain sign of
theological alignment also. Mahan's New School views apparently were in eclipse, at least momentarily, and there
could be no better evidence of the fact that Finney's revival
was not correlated in people's minds with New School atti-
tudes. Ironically, the resolution was moved and seconded,
but never passed or even voted upon according to church
records. Indeed, when the church celebrated its Centennial
in 1909 it was not only New School (an academic matter by
then) but was also part of the holiness movement which Mahan promulgated so vigorously not long after his departure
from Pittsford. In his Centennial Sermon Rev. Ordway
Smith, pastor of the church, said, "The efficiency of any
church depends upon the indwelling of the Spirit of God in
the heart and life of its members.... Human effort alone,
avails little, but when coupled with the mighty power of God,
it is almost limitless." The function of a minister is "to
be the means of turning many souls from darkness into
light."[36] Who can doubt that Ordway Smith was well acquainted with the holiness books of Asa Mahan?

To be sure, there were additional reasons for Mahan's departure. He detested ministers who preached about
the sins of Sodom and Gomorrah and were singularly quiet
about the sins of their own country and their own parishes.
From first to last in his ministry Mahan reserved the right
to speak out on moral issues like temperance and slavery
even when he stepped on the toes of certain parishioners.
This propensity caused some of the congregation to look upon him as a troublemaker in contrast to his later Sixth Presbyterian congregation in Cincinnati, which largely stood by

him loyally and affectionately when the city as a whole condemned him as an abolitionist.   To defend strongly his own
moral and religious commitments while holding an official
position in a society or institution was to be a constant
source of trouble for Asa Mahan throughout a good portion
of his life.

It is clear that Mahan already in the latter part of
1830 and early in 1831 was seeking duties elsewhere.   The
Third Presbyterian Church of Rochester was without a pas-
tor--Parker had left Rochester for new work in New York
City--and Bissell was eager for Mahan to accept that position.   In early 1831 the Third Church extended a call to Mahan and for several months he seriously considered accepting the call.   However, some members of the congregation
of the Third Church, knowing of the difficulties at Pittsford,
did not favor the appointment even though Bissell and the
majority favored it.   Bissell wrote Finney on February 27,
1831,

> To suppose that we can settle a minister and have
> everybody satisfied is vain. ... I have however
> since the call of Mr. Mahan heard not one person
> speak of rumors of the dissatisfaction. ... The
> Society has called him and he has initially accept-
> ed.   I rejoice and thank God for it and I assume
> the responsibility of asserting that of all others he
> is our man. ... I rejoice that everybody is not
> perfectly gratified.   I wish no one was.   We would
> like mightily well to say now we have a minister
> who is just. ... I have made up my mind that no
> friend of the 3rd Church will if he duly considers
> the matter hear or know anything about 'doubts and
> fears.' ... Asa Mahan is our Minister.   Amen.

Apparently Finney had written inquiring about the matter, for
the redoubtable Mr. Bissell concluded,

> Now Br. F you just tell any man, woman, or
> child that begins to gab on the subject--be still
> and turn your deaf ear and your eyes of reproof
> and put a quietus on such stuff.   Rumors of his
> damaging Pittsford Ch. [are] false infinitely [so]
> there is no reason under the sun why Mr. Mahan
> is not of all others the anointed of the Lord for
> this Church. 37

Mahan, however, had other possibilities and really preferred to return to the East, preferably to New York City, for he thought that such a location offered the greatest opportunity for working fruitfully in the service of God. It was a momentous decision because it, and a strange chain of events, eventually landed Mahan in Cincinnati, where he was to play a stellar role in a drama of great import.

Mahan's labors in the Rochester revival brought him three calls to settle as pastor in addition to that of the Third Church: in New York City; Hartford, Connecticut; and Troy, New York. He and his family went to Clinton and stayed with friends while he thought matters over and visited Troy. Though he was fond of Dr. Beaman and thought highly of the congregation at Troy, he reluctantly decided against accepting this call. He decided against Hartford also, for he really wanted to go to New York City. [38] After all, not only was that the most useful and important place to be, but he would also be reunited with his good friend Joel Parker.

Although Mahan wanted to go to a church in New York, and the congregation there wanted him, he did not go. The events that interfered with his going and sent him to Cincinnati instead are so unlikely that, from different perspectives, they seem to be either a comedy of errors or the mysterious workings of Providence. Needless to say they were for Asa, and for others as well, the handwork of God.

Mahan journeyed to New York City between two Sabbaths at Troy only to discover that the committee from the church that wanted him had just left for Clinton to ask him officially to accept their call. Their boat and his had passed each other on the Hudson going in opposite directions! Parker assured him that the committee members would write him at Troy. They, however, on their own initiative, wrote him in care of Mr. Kirk in Albany, knowing that Mahan would stop to see him. And so he did; but Kirk, who had received the letter, was absent from his home when Mahan came by to see him. Since he had heard nothing, he wrote Parker inquiring how things stood. Fortunately for Mahan, he received a call from a congregation in Cincinnati and so had something to count on if anything went wrong with the New York offer. Ironically, Parker had left the city just before his friend's letter arrived. By the time he returned and found the letter awaiting him, there was less than forty-eight hours left before Mahan was to leave Clinton for Cincinnati, where he had decided to go since he had heard nothing from

New York.   Parker immediately dispatched the committee
members to Clinton.   They arrived at 4 p. m. on the very
day that Mahan had left at 9 a. m.   Before leaving Clinton,
Mahan had told his wife that if any news came from New
York he could be contacted in Pittsford, where he would
visit friends before going to Buffalo and on to Cincinnati.
The committee members at Clinton immediately wrote Mahan at Pittsford and the letter arrived before Mahan left for
Buffalo.   However the store which housed the post office
was closed and Mahan, knocking loudly at the door, was unable to rouse the clerk asleep within.   Mahan turned from
the door and began his journey to Buffalo and on to Cincinnati. [39]

> Years later Mahan observed,
>
>> Thus, contrary to my own wishes and efforts, and
>> to the most earnest desires and efforts of the
>> Church in New York, was I directed from that
>> city, and located [in Cincinnati], not myself, but
>> God, directing my footsteps thither, and thus de-
>> termining my life-future.   Had I settled in New
>> York, there is not the remotest probability that
>> myself or Brother Finney would ever have been
>> connected with Oberlin.   Settling in Cincinnati not
>> only gave being and permanence to the New Vine
>> Street Congregational Church, but in consequence
>> of my connection with the anti-slavery cause, with
>> Lane Seminary, and with the students seceding
>> from the same, insured our going to Oberlin in
>> the most favorable circumstances possible. [40]

As Asa Mahan liked to say, here was another case where
the mills of God grind slowly, but they grind exceedingly
small.

Chapter 2

CINCINNATI

Parish Work

By 1831 Cincinnati had grown to be a city of twenty-eight thousand people and was solidly established as the business center of the burgeoning West. Although it had a decent cultural life, the Presbyterians felt that the religious life of their city left something to be desired. Only six thousand people worshipped in "respectable churches," six thousand more in churches "where damnable error is preached," which left more than half of the population either completely unchurched or active in free-thinking societies. Moreover, the town was looked upon as morally corrupt and derelict, as well as religiously moribund. This view was held not only by Cincinnati Presbyterians but by many clergymen in the East as well. Going to Cincinnati as a minister must have been looked upon somewhat like a missionary assignment.[1]

Mahan's church was the Sixth Presbyterian of Cincinnati, which became the Sixth Street Congregational Church in 1846 and the Vine Street Congregational Church in 1848. The origins of this congregation throw considerable light on the drama of Mahan's four years in the river city. For while his regular pastoral and evangelical duties formed the warp of his life, highly exciting and even explosive events were linked together to form its weft.

The congregation of the Sixth Presbyterian had broken away from the First Presbyterian, the long-time minister of

26

which was Joshua L. Wilson.   Wilson was an Old School
Calvinist and an ardent supporter of the doctrine of the Depravity of Man and the doctrine of the Elect.   If one did
not agree that the elect and the damned were already determined, that in itself was a sign that one belonged to the
damned.   Numerous members of his congregation came to
hold New School views: salvation was a gracious gift of
God which unworthy man was free to accept or reject.   Several New School congregations splintered off from Wilson's
church, each with a special emphasis in addition to free-will
religious views.

One special emphasis of the Sixth Presbyterian congregation was temperance.   According to the Cincinnati Journal, a New School publication, "the Sixth Church at the time
of its organization, resolved itself into a temperance society
and made total abstinence the condition of membership."
The Records of the Church and Society indicate that on April
9, 1831, such a resolution was passed, though the condition
was not incorporated into the charter or by-laws. [2]   The
later Manual of the church states that "the cause which originated this church movement was pulpit defense of 'American Slavery,' drawn from the Bible, and denunciation of
those who agitated the subject of emancipation."   There is
no reference to the anti-slavery origins of the Sixth Presbyterian in the early church Records or in the Minutes of
the Board of Trustees.   So it might seem that the writers
of the Manual unwittingly translated later developments into
origins.   Several commentators have claimed such a translation on the ground that early 1831 was too early for antislavery origins of a church.   Such a claim, however, rests
on the assumption that anti-slavery agitation began in earnest
only with William Lloyd Garrison, an assumption which later
pastors and historians of the Vine Street Congregational
Church strenuously denied.   C. B. Boynton, who became
pastor in 1846, traces in detail the activities of Christian
anti-slavery societies, and the activities of individual abolitionists like John Rankin, which were on stage before the
dramatic entrance of Garrison. According to Boynton, the
founders of the Sixth Presbyterian left the First Presbyterian, then under the charge of Joshua L. Wilson, "because
of the pro-slavery teachings of their pastor."   The founders
of the new church so informed him, so an original antislavery commitment was not simply hearsay. [3]   The upshot
of the discussion seems to be that temperance was an explicit reason for founding the new church, and anti-slavery
commitment an implicit and informal one, a commitment

that was sharpened and brought to the fore by the activities
of its most prominent ministers in the early days, Asa Mahan and Jonathan Blanchard.

The nucleus of the Sixth Church congregation, and
those responsible for the call to Mahan, included Amos and
Mary Blanchard, Franklin and Catherine Vail, William Holyoke, John Melindy, and William S. Merrell, one of Mahan's
classmates at Hamilton College. Blanchard, a licensed minister from Vermont, and Wilson had already publicly clashed
before Mahan's arrival. Blanchard had been licensed by the
Presbytery of Cincinnati while Wilson was out of town, and
the latter, upon his return, charged Blanchard with heresy
and called for the revocation of his ordination. Blanchard,
in turn, accused Wilson of slander. The case was pending
before the presbytery when Mahan arrived. He immediately
came to his parishioner's defense both by challenging the
way the presbytery was handling the case and by signing a
letter, published in the Cincinnati Journal, pledging support
for Blanchard. 4

Wilson turned his attack from Blanchard to Mahan.
At a meeting in First Presbyterian on November 8, 1831,
the trustees of Lane Theological Seminary elected Mahan a
member of the Board. His election was the turning point
in the shift from Old to New School control of the board.
Wilson quickly resigned as a trustee of Lane Seminary and
gave Mahan's election as one of his reasons. As far as he
was concerned, the trustees simply wanted "to render the
Lane Theological Seminary entirely subservient to the New
School Theology." Wilson's attack, however, had only begun. In sermons, in communications to the synod, and in
editorials in the Cincinnati Standard, his Old School publication, Wilson blasted Mahan in general and specifically accused him of saying to friends that he, Mahan, had never
adopted the Confession of Faith of the Presbyterian Church
and never would. Mahan pointed out that he had after all
been ordained by the Oneida Presbytery. But what good was
that?--according to Wilson, the whole Oneida Presbytery
was heretical! A committee from the Cincinnati Presbytery
was appointed to investigate the allegations. Meanwhile,
William Holyoke and a colleague, representing the Sixth
Church, accused Wilson before the presbytery of "unchristian
conduct" in slandering Mahan in the press. Eventually the
charge and counter-charges were appealed to the synod,
where a settlement was made, though Mahan soon made his
own settlement by going to Oberlin in 1835, becoming a Con-

gregationalist, and helping to found the General Association
of the Western Reserve and thus seceding from the Plan of
Union between the Presbyterian and Congregational Churches. [5]

The end of the Plan of Union was in sight everywhere.
Wilson turned his attack from Mahan to Lyman Beecher and
formally charged the president of Lane Seminary with heresy,
slander, and hypocrisy; the hypocrisy, according to Wilson,
consisted in his pretension that the New School doctrine
squared with the Scriptures and the Westminster Confession.
Beecher was acquitted by the local presbytery and the synod
as well. Wilson appealed to the General Assembly but after
three years of litigation was silenced by the advice of his
peers. This litigation had "a disastrous effect on Presbyterianism in the West" and was an essential element in the
complete collapse of the Plan of Union in 1837. [6]

It must not be supposed that the bulk of Mahan's energy went into the Wilson affair. His biggest job was to en-
large his own congregation which at the time of his arrival
consisted of only twenty people who were worshipping in a
room on an upper floor of an abandoned college building, a
room "as forbidding as could be" and only too recently in-
habited by spiders and bats. When it was renovated the
room had a seating capacity of over two hundred. Under
Mahan's forceful preaching the congregation outgrew this
room and moved to a larger one on the main floor of the
college building which remained the meeting hall of the church
for the duration of Mahan's pastorate. [7]

The Records of the Sixth Presbyterian show a steady
growth in membership throughout Mahan's four years in Cincinnati. The new members came into fellowship in clusters
of five, ten, fifteen, and more, some by letter and some by
new profession of faith. The majority of Lane Seminarians
attended Mahan's church, many of them singing in the choir
and teaching Sabbath School. Some of them officially joined
the church even though they were not permanent Cincinnati
residents, a group including, among others, Henry B. Stanton, Robert L. Stanton, Amos Dresser, Lewis Bridgeman,
Huntington Lyman, and Elizabeth Allen, a young lady associated with the seminarians in teaching at a school for blacks
in 1834. Theodore Weld also attended whenever he was not
attending a black church. The seminarians were drawn to
Mahan from the beginning because he was outspoken on moral
issues--including the abolition of slavery--from the pulpit,
this time, in contrast to Pittsford, with the loyal support of

a large proportion of his congregation, and not simply after
he, as a trustee, championed their cause when the big explosion came at Lane. The congregation also was occasionally increased by defections from Wilson's First and Beecher's Second Church. It is not unlikely that a few passed in
the opposite direction, though, overall, Mahan was strongly
supported by his congregation in his antislavery activity.
The mainstays of his support, both morally and financially,
were William Holyoke and John Melindy, prominent businessmen of Cincinnati. The congregation continued to grow and
as late in his pastorate as May 1834 Mahan held a successful revival meeting, adding thirty-eight members to the
church. [8] His congregation was numbered in the middle hundreds when he left Cincinnati in 1835.

Mahan attended to the physical as well as the spiritual
needs of his flock. During the four years of his pastorate
Cincinnati was twice hit with a cholera epidemic. As the
pestilence approached, the churches of the city held a day
of fasting and prayer. In addition, Mahan carefully studied
medical accounts of the disease and learned the symptoms
and the best ways of counteracting them. He instructed his
assembled congregation on these matters and also visited,
conversed, and prayed in the home of every family of his
church "giving them such instructions and admonitions as
each case seemed to require." He urged upon every individual the promptest action the moment a symptom appeared.
The result was that only one member of his congregation
died, that one having ignored all the warnings and instructions.

Other congregations were not so fortunate. During
the first period of cholera one of the other Presbyterian
churches was without a pastor. Since there was little illness among his own people Mahan tended their sick and officiated at their funerals until, worn out by all responsibilities, he was himself stricken down by the pestilence. Appreciating his kindness, the members of this congregation
later took special pains to show their respect for the Mahans. "Whenever [Mrs. Mahan] entered that church, as
soon as she was seen in the 'broad aisle,' at least half a
dozen doors would be thrown open to welcome her."[9]

In addition to all his pastoral work Mahan also participated in revivals in nearby communities and was active
in a lengthy meeting in New Albany, Indiana, some distance
downstream from Cincinnati on the Ohio River. He was

eager for a large-scale revival, so he and other ministers
and elders of the Presbyterian Churches, along with Theodore Weld, wrote Finney in February 1832 urging him to
bring his revival campaign into the West, where the future
of the young country was being fashioned. Their joint feeling was "that there is no field on earth where there is a
more urgent call for your labours and in which there is a
greater prospect of your extensive usefulness than in this
great valley." Mahan and Weld were the prime movers in
this effort to bring Finney west, though there had been a
previous effort. In letters accompanying the general plea
Mahan wrote Finney that his "kind letter on many accounts
was as cold water to a thirsty soul" and told him about the
growth of the Sixth Presbyterian. Weld wrote, "You can
never move this great valley by working the lever in Boston,
New York, or Philadelphia." (As a token of his fastidious
spirit and an indicator of his inability to belong to any group
in later years, Weld signed the general plea at the bottom
of the sheet half way between the left column, where the
ministers had signed, and the right column, where the elders
had signed.) Finney decided not to go west but he apparently considered the possibility seriously, since he wrote Mahan inquiring about the cost of living in Cincinnati, to which
the latter replied, "It will cost about $7 or 800 dollars [a
year] to support your family here."[10]

In addition to revival efforts Mahan continued to work
in tract societies, temperance groups, Sabbath Schools, and
in official governing bodies of the church. From April to
September 1834 he acted as Moderator for the Cincinnati
Presbytery. In addition to this work he had enough energy
remaining to found a ministerial society for New School pastors which met regularly each month for "religious and literary improvement," the meeting place often being Mahan's
house on Fifth Street between Main and Sycamore. Throughout his whole stay in Cincinnati he was a trustee of Lane
Theological Seminary and, during a critical period, was a
member of the Executive Committee of the Board.[11] As we
shall see, this activity in behalf of Lane Seminary was to
have a profound influence on the course of his later life and
labors.

The Inner Life

Asa experienced an "aching void" in his heart all
through these years. His early experiences of the vivid

presence of God had already begun to wear off during his
college and seminary years. Even though he had rejected
Calvinistic views of salvation, and felt good about this progress, he still held what he called the legalistic view of
combatting sin and felt discouraged by the results it produced. On the legalistic view it was up to man himself to
overcome his sinful inclinations and nature but being spiritually puny and having a carnal nature he was doomed to
fail and to continue to disobey God's commandments. To be
sure, he had been helped in seminary by Moses Stuart's
analysis of Romans 7--it was a description of the legalistic
view, not an endorsement of it. God required, indeed demanded, that man obey his commandments and abandon his
evil ways. But how was this possible? Some "legalists"
spoke of asking for God's promised help through Christ and
the Holy Ghost, the result being a cooperative effort between
man and the Holy Ghost in combatting sin. This interpretation was certainly an improvement but again man seemed unable to pull his share of the load and submitting to sinful inclination seemed the inevitable outcome. [12]

        Mahan knew that he himself sinned in various ways--
sometimes losing his temper, for example--but he felt that
his besetting sin was that of undue ambition and pride. He
fought against it, he said, but his legalistic views about how
to combat sin and strive after a holy life never led him to
victory. In later life he characterized this deficiency in exaggerated terms perhaps, though the deficiency was no doubt
real.

            From childhood upwards one propensity existed
            and operated in my mind with a strength and su-
            premacy of control unsurpassed, as it seems to
            me, in the case of any other individual. I refer
            to the principle of ambition. . . . This principle
            was developed into a kind of madness when read-
            ing, while I was quite young, Pope's translation
            of Homer's "Iliad." . . . Oh, how I cursed my day
            that I had not been permitted to live at that time,
            and to have a name among those heroes. . . . [Even
            in my later life] there was a sphere for the play
            of the principle, to gain a name as a preacher and
            a theologian, and here that motive acted with great
            strength. . . . Whenever I had made an intense ef-
            fort of any kind, how strong was the desire to be
            praised for it! One desire and purpose seemed
            to be supreme in my mind--to be pure in heart

and life before God and men; but this did not ex-
clude this evil ambition. I saw the sin, confessed
it, and resolved upon its crucifixion. But to know
sin, to abhor it, to repent of it, and turn away
from it, do not kill it...."[13]

Moreover, he worried a good deal about both public
and private matters. Would any headway ever be made
against slavery and intemperance? How could he sustain
his family in case of further illness like his disability in
Rochester that sent Mary and him to his father's farm in
Orangeville? Yet if he had such a great belief in the wisdom of God and believed in Providence why should he worry
so about the present and future? Further, he found no deep-
down consolation in his religious beliefs. He was still as
unreconciled to the deaths of his infant children as he was
on the day they died. Yet had they not been lowered into
the "lap of God" and should he not be happy that they were
with Him? No doubt he should feel this way but he grieved
for them as much as ever and wanted them back.[14]

There was, he felt, some crucial religious dimension
missing not only in his life but in the lives of the vast majority of Christians. He read Fénelon, Madame Guyon, John
Wesley, John Fletcher, and other authors and felt that he
was getting close to a crucial insight but hadn't quite got
the matter right. The Methodists of Cincinnati apparently
thought that whether he knew it or not he had already been
granted "the second blessing," the in-dwelling of Christ in
his heart, for it had long been clear to them and to many
others in Cincinnati that Asa Mahan somehow seemed to
preach "with a power beyond his own." They held an annual camp meeting thirty miles from the river city and in
1834 asked their Presbyterian brother to preach to them.
It was a memorable experience for Mahan:

As I took my stand, on my arrival, in the presence of
the vast crowd before me, a consciousness of divine
power came over me of which I had never had an experience before. During the progress of the discourse
the hearts of the crowd were moved by the power
of the truth and of the spirit, "as the trees of
wood are moved by the wind." At the close of
the discourse, sinners of all classes, and in as-
tonishing numbers, crowded to the places of inquiry. The whole following night was spent by
ministers, without sleep at all, in directing in-

quirers to Christ, and a revival of religion occurred which is spoken of by people in the city
and all that region to this day. When I witnessed
these results, this sentiment forced itself upon
my mind: "He always wins who sides with God,"
and always wins such victories as his heart most
desires. During one of the intervals of worship,
I retired into the forest for personal meditation
and prayer. While there, with a sense of painful loneliness and isolation which it is impossible
to describe, I lifted my eyes and heart above, and
said in words to my Father in heaven, that "I was
willing, if need be, to be alone and to be despised
in the world; but there was one thing that I did
desire, and would venture to ask: that I might be conscious that my heart was pure in his sight, that I
might see God, and live and walk in the manifested
light of His countenance. If God would grant me this
one infinite good," I added, "I would accept any
burdens or afflictions that He might lay upon me."
That was the distinctly uttered vow which I took
with me from that forest. I have passed through
heated furnaces and deep waters since that time,
but have never taken back or regretted that vow.
The brightness of the final "rising of the Sun of
Righteousness" did not come at that moment. The
era was very near, however, when "God did become my everlasting light, and the days of my
mourning were ended."[15]

Another part of Asa's heart, far from being an aching
void, was abundantly filled with love. His devotion to Mary
and the children was deep and abiding. We have already
seen the agony and grief over the deaths of two children that
would not abate. His love for the ones that lived was no
less intense. Anna was now five and Lucy Dix Mahan, born
in Clinton, New York in 1831 where her parents had stayed
briefly between Pittsford and Cincinnati, was three years
old. There was a special bond between Lucy and her father
that had its beginning in an incident in Cincinnati in 1834.
Mahan wrote that he did not know what troubled the three-
year-old, though surely she had good reason to be upset at
any time since the family was harassed by townsmen because
of its anti-slavery views.

As I came down from my study and entered our
parlour one day, I found our second child, a little

daughter about three years of age, alone there, the
mother, with the elder daughter, having gone out
and left this one in the care of the kitchen-maid.
I found this child, from some cause--I never knew
what--in a state of mental agony such as I had
never witnessed before. Her grief had reached
a stage wholly past weeping, and which rendered
her utterly unable to speak a single word. As
she turned her face to me, there was the look of
death in her eyes. Of course I was deeply alarmed.
I did not attempt to allay her grief by words.
Grief asks our sympathy, not words. I said to
her at once, "My dear precious daughter, come
to your father and sit here upon his knee, laying
your head upon his bosom close to his heart." As
she came to me, I took her tenderly up, placed
her upon my knee, and pressed her head very gently to my heart. At every sight I apprehended that
the thread of life would break. I spoke not a word;
but at each paroxysm I pressed her more closely
to my heart. I soon perceived that those sighs became gradually less and less severe. At length
they wholly ceased. A little while after, she looked
up with a happy smile, and asked me if I recollect-
ed a certain event which had given her great pleasure. I entered at once into her new-born joy, en-
larging very affectionately and smilingly upon that
pleasing event. In a short time we were sweetly
conversing together there, the happiest child and
the happiest father I ever knew.... When she was
on a visit to our house, at the time when she was
quite forty years of age, she being herself a parent
then, I related to her the incident of her childhood
given above, a fact which she had of course forgotten. Then she understood the cause of the mysterious bond which had so linked her being with
mine....[16]

The Lane Rebels

Mahan's connection with Lane Seminary during the
Cincinnati years determined the course of his life--and also
that of several educational institutions--for years to come.
The part he played both as a trustee of Lane Seminary and
as a member of its Executive Board during a crisis was
crucially important. In these roles he participated in a dramatic chain of events that resulted in the Lane students, un-

der the leadership of the dynamic Theodore Weld, rebelling
against the trustees of the seminary, Mahan's being appointed president of Oberlin with Finney as professor of theology,
and many of the seminarians becoming the first theological
class at Oberlin. A picture of the beginnings of Lane Seminary done in broad strokes will be helpful in making clear
the chain of events that eventually led to the temporary lev-
elling of that institution and the elevation of another.

There was a need, the frontier clergymen thought,
for ministers to be trained in the West for service in that
part of the country. To be sure, there was the Western
Theological Seminary near Pittsburgh but that was not far
enough west. Cincinnati was the strategic location for training practically-minded ministers who could cope with the
rugged ways of the Ohio and Mississippi River territories.
Ebenezer Lane and his brother, originally from Maine, were
successful commission merchants in New Orleans, and they
donated $4,000 to found in Cincinnati a "work-study" insti-
tution "to prepare indigent young men for the ministry."
Elnathan Kemper provided land in Walnut Hills as a site for
the seminary, and the charter of Lane Seminary was granted
by the state on February 11, 1829, and the building program
started. The trustees appointed The Reverend George Beck-
with professor in April, he accepted in August, had three or
four students during the winter, and resigned in the summer
of 1830. Lane was not off to a good start; during the winter of 1830-31 it had no teachers and only two students to
occupy the whole of the seminary building. The problem
was that the board of trustees, of which Joshua Wilson was
president, had offered the presidency of the institution to
Lyman Beecher in October of 1830, partly because he seemed
like a good man and partly because Arthur and Lewis Tappan,
New York City merchants and abolitionists, agreed to give
the income from twenty thousand dollars to support the seminary if Beecher accepted. Beecher, however, was reluctant
to leave his Boston Congregational Church, and so Lane remained moribund. [17]

The Lane trustees continued to want Beecher, but Wilson had become suspicious. After all, Beecher was a Congregationalist and in 1831 had even reached an understanding
with one of the worst New School advocates, the evangelist
Finney. Wilson wanted nothing more to do with Beecher and
took the occasion of Mahan's appointment as a trustee in
1831 to blast both Beecher and Mahan and to resign from the
board. The trustees, now definitely New School in their com-

mitments, again invited Beecher to be president, and in
June 1832 he accepted the invitation.   Arthur Tappan agreed
to pay the whole of Beecher's salary. [18]

Students now poured into Lane from all parts of New
England, New York, and the West, and new professors were
added in quick succession.   The students at Lane were more
mature than those at other colleges and seminaries.   Many
of them had given up other jobs to enter the ministry and
many of the men were in their late twenties and even early
thirties.   Theodore Weld was by far the most significant of
the students; he had attended the Oneida Institute and had
been a highly successful lecturer and fund raiser for spreading the gospel of labor-learning (or "manual-labor") schools
like the Oneida Institute.   Under Weld, who was a genuinely
gifted orator, the students took the initiative in the affairs
of the seminary "and practiced piety mixed with practicality
in the Oneida manner."   The most important faculty appointments, in view of later developments, were those of Thomas
J. Biggs and John Morgan, the former condemning and the
latter defending the students when the big explosion came. [19]

The fuse for the explosion of 1834 was the slavery
issue.   Arthur and Lewis Tappan were dedicated abolitionists, as were Weld, Mahan, and Morgan.   In the summer
of 1833, when Lane was finally flourishing, the Reverend
Amos A. Phelps of Boston circulated among the clergymen
in the North a "Declaration of Sentiment" in favor of immediate emancipation.   Of the sixteen signatures from Ohio
three of them were Mahan's, Morgan's, and Weld's.   Weld,
who had cooperated with the Tappans in 1831 in helping to
lay the groundwork for the American Anti-Slavery Society,
had been appointed one of the first group of four agents of
the society.   At first the Lane students did not share Weld's
abolitionist viewpoint.   They were all strongly antislavery
but favored the colonization scheme.   From June 1833 to
February 1834 Weld talked earnestly with students individu-
ally and in small groups in preparation for a public discussion of abolition and colonization views among the seminarians and faculty members. [20]

The students invited the faculty to a meeting planned
for February 4, 1834, but the faculty asked them to postpone the antislavery discussion.   They said the time would
come when it would be in order to discuss such a topic but
neglected to give any indication of when that time might be.
The students met on February 4 as planned, and Weld and

his closest associates finished what they had started by individual talk.   Indeed, Weld did not hold the meeting until
he was reasonably certain that his views would carry the
day.   Through the individual talks and the debate, the students were all converted to the abolition viewpoint.   The
seminarians immediately started to apply practically the
antislavery principles they had adopted.   Several of them
went out lecturing against slavery, others wrote for the
Rights of Man and other periodicals, while still others established a lyceum especially for blacks in which lectures
were given on grammar, geography, arithmetic, and natural
philosophy.   Moreover, "a circulating library, evening school,
three Sabbath Schools, Bible classes for adults and two day
schools for boys were begun.   Later a 'select female school'
was established, and other special classes for girls were organized and were taught by four volunteers ... whose expenses were paid by Lewis Tappan."   A group of blacks,
having expressed a desire to see the institution, were invited to inspect the seminary buildings. [21]

        The majority of the Lane trustees became alarmed
at the views and activities of the seminarians, and not wholly without reason though no doubt they badly overreacted.
They did not agree with the students, to be sure, but their
main worry concerned the reaction of the townspeople.   There
were rumbles of more than displeasure.   In May 1834 the
editor of the Western Monthly Magazine sharply criticized
the meddling in serious matters by "minors, who are at
school."   To this condescending rebuke Weld published a
a blistering reply in the Cincinnati Journal.   However, even
the editors of the New School Journal criticized the students
for having "a higher estimate of their own powers, than do
others around them."[22]   Some townspeople even talked of
destroying the seminary buildings, though no mobs formed.
The faculty members took different stands on the issue.
Thomas J. Biggs, Professor of Church History, strongly
opposed the students while John Morgan, professor in the
"literary department" supported them.   President Beecher
and Professor Calvin E. Stowe, his son-in-law, thought the
activities of the students imprudent but hoped to avoid any
clash between the aroused townsmen and determined students.
In June of 1834 Beecher wrote, "if we and our friends do
not amplify the evil by too much alarm, impatience, and attempt at regulation, the evil will subside and pass away."[23]
Then he left for the East to raise funds for the seminary,
and during his absence trouble began in earnest.

        Acting on their own inclinations and under the spur of

Biggs, who had been unpopular with the students even before
the trouble started, the trustees appointed a committee to
investigate the activities of the seminarians. In August the
committee report recommended dissolving the Anti-Slavery
Society and prohibiting not only public but even private discussion of the slavery issue among the seminarians. Moreover, it recommended that the executive committee of the
board of trustees have the "power to dismiss any student
from the Seminary, when they shall think it necessary to
do so [Weld was the primary target here]; and to make any
rules and regulations ... which they may deem expedient."[24]
They also recommended that Morgan be dismissed from his
professorship at Lane. The executive committee of the
board immediately fired Morgan and adopted the other recommendations of the investigating committee. Mahan, a
member of the executive committee, was aghast at these de-
nials of basic human rights and insisted that the executive
committee lacked power to adopt the recommendations; only
the full board of trustees could pass on such matters. The
other members finally agreed but begrudgingly since the
board did not meet until October. Mahan had gained time
and immediately wrote Beecher that he should return to
Cincinnati immediately since "the Seminary would be dis-
mantled should any such code as was being proposed be
adopted." Being in the confidence of the students Mahan
knew that they would leave Lane if the Rules and Orders
passed, something which the other trustees probably did not
know, and this fact is essentially what Mahan was conveying
to Beecher. Beecher never answered his letter, and Mahan
could never understand why Lane's president, knowing the
seriousness of the situation stayed away. Nathaniel Wright,
head of the board, and Biggs also corresponded with Beecher
that fateful summer, so there can be no doubt that the president of Lane knew how serious the situation was.[25]

     In early October the board met to discuss and vote
upon the recommendations of the executive committee. It
was an ordeal that tested the depth of Mahan's commitment
to his principles, since his defense of the seminarians had
to be made against a deep and pervasive opposition. At the
end of the discussion fourteen trustees voted for the code
and three against it, the dissenters, in addition to Mahan,
being two elders of the Sixth Presbyterian, William Holyoke
and John Melindy. However the struggle was by no means
finished. Mahan strongly felt that the publication of the code,
outrageous as it was, would be useful in stirring up antislavery sentiment, not in Cincinnati to be sure, but further north.
When it was moved to publish the code Nathaniel Wright ob-

jected to publishing "Order 2," which he had written and
which gave the executive committee the power to dismiss
any student from the seminary, on the grounds that it was
not a public matter but concerned only the operations of the
seminary. Despite his objection, the trustees voted to approve the publication of all its resolutions. Before adjourn-
ment, however, Wright moved to reconsider publishing Order 2, and James Gallaher, who had become suspicious of
Mahan's support for publication, supported Wright this time.
Gallaher wondered why Mahan supported publishing the code
when he had argued and voted against it. Did he see something the others did not? He was no doubt puzzled even
more when Mahan then also changed his vote to support
Wright. But the board nevertheless then voted to publish
Order 2, the precise outcome which Mahan had intended to
produce. To further insure this outcome he had whispered
to Melindy to say to the board that he wondered if they
dared publish it. Relying on the irascible nature of one of
the trustees, Mahan was rewarded. Running true to form,
this trustee exclaimed that nothing could or would stop them
from doing so! Even so, the executive committee was not
wholly happy with its new power to expel students and postponed action on the motion to dismiss Weld and William T.
Allan. It may well be, as one commentator suggests, that
Mahan, Holyoke, and Melindy had been able to convince the
committee members to await Beecher's return. [26]

As a result of his role in the trustee meetings Mahan
was regarded more highly than ever by the seminarians, but
he and his family suffered numerous indignities not only from
unknown townspeople but even from friends in the New School
fellowship. In cowardly fashion a gang of children, shouting
"their father's an abolitionist," stoned Anna and Lucy as they
played in front of their home, and Lucy was injured when
she fell in running for shelter. And, Asa wrote, "for months,
when we lay down at night, we did so apprehending that our
dwelling might be mobbed before morning." The congregation of Beecher's Second Presbyterian, which was the church
Mahan had served, along with his own, during the cholera
outbreak before Beecher's arrival, would have nothing to do
with him any longer. When Mrs. Mahan revisited this
church no pew doors were opened to her and old friends in
the congregation refused even to speak to her because of
her husband's views on slavery and his defense of the Lane
seminarians. Mary Dix Mahan was every bit as stalwart as
Asa. That undaunted woman returned from Beecher's church
"and exhorted her husband to stand fast by his principles."[27]

The one cheering note in the whole situation was that Mahan's own congregation staunchly supported his antislavery views and his defense of the Lane students. Not only Holyoke and Melindy stood behind him but the less influential members of the congregation as well. The congregation met in Old College in November 1834 "for a social and friendly conference" concerning "the best interests of the church." After considerable discussion the following resolutions were adopted by a majority of the meeting: "Resolved, that is it inexpedient to erect a house of Worship at the present time [and] Resolved, that as members of this Society, we are satisfied with the ministerial labors of our pastor and will cordially cooperate with him." Since the minutes of the board of trustees of the church are filled with reports of efforts to secure a permanent home owned by the congregation, it was no doubt the abandonment, temporarily, of this goal that occasioned the considerable discussion. Only one affluent member of the church, George W. Neff, frequently the president of the board, resigned as a result of the abandonment of the effort to secure permanent quarters and of the vote of confidence in Mahan. [28] It might seem surprising that the two resolutions were yoked together so closely. On reflection, however, their close connection is obvious. Mahan had aroused the animosity of the Cincinnati community outside of the Sixth Presbyterian boundary, and without community support the effort to find permanent quarters was, temporarily at least, doomed. Except for Holyoke and Melindy the resources of this church were not large. The greatest tribute that his congregation could have paid Mahan was to choose him rather than a church edifice.

It would be a mistake to think that Mahan was a fanatic in his antislavery effort and defense of the Lane seminarians. Quite to the contrary, he was pressed into service against his inclinations by the demands of what he took to be the moral law. He did not make a hobby of preaching antislavery views or pressing his views on his parishioners. He preached one sermon on the moral demand for the immediate end of slavery and he signed Phelps' resolution, letting the matter rest there until the deteriorating situation at Lane required further action. Even these two acts prompted by conscience, however, were the cause of much unfavorable comment in Cincinnati. Even in the troubles at Lane he did not happily enter the fray; he wrote later that "when the Board met, I was, against my choice, compelled to take a stand more publicly and openly than I had ever done before." [29] He well knew that Family Mahan would suffer but was strength-

ened in the knowledge that he and Mary stood together. That
neither he nor Mary was fanatical or wild is further evident
in the fact that they, along with Maria Fletcher, who lived
with the Mahans and taught at the Select School for blacks,
were criticized by a fringe element associated with the Lane
students. Emeline Bishop and Phebe Mathews also taught at
the Select School and considered social relations with the
blacks the true mark of an emancipated mind, let the consequences be what they may. They were almost childish in
their innocence and were highly critical of the Mahans, Maria Fletcher, and others who thought that helping the blacks
the important thing and who had no conceit that the blacks
yearned for personal ties with white people. Both Augustus
Wattles and Theodore Weld had upon occasion rebuked the
excesses and romantic postures of Phebe Mathews. [30]

     Mahan, as we have seen, could not understand why
Beecher did not immediately return and keep the trustees
from wrecking Lane. The answer is that Beecher, contrary to the image projected in his Autobiography, was essentially in agreement with the majority of the trustees who
feared that irreparable harm would come to the seminary if
the students persisted in their ways; and, moreover, he
agreed with them in being irked by Weld, though he undoubtedly respected the genius of the man. Moreover, his views
on slavery were not as advanced as they later became, and
these later views seem to have been projected backwards to
the time of the Lane controversy. For example, according
to Lewis Tappan, rich New York merchant and ardent abolitionist, while Beecher at this time believed in immediate
emancipation he thought that blacks should be segregated in
one area of the United States. One must be careful, however, in accepting what Tappan said since he had a habit of
thinking the worst of people, a fault which his close friend
Weld had to point out to him more than once. [31]

     Beecher visited Tappan in his New York store in Sep-
tember, precisely at the time when he should have gone directly to Cincinnati. He told Tappan that the students had
done provocative things, one going to board with a colored
family, others "handing out" colored ladies from a barouche
of friends who had come to visit the seminary, and so on.
Tappan objected since, as he said, if Weld were not discreet,
where should one look for discretion? [32] As is so often the
case in disagreements there was partial truth on both sides.
Indeed, Weld and most of the students were sober, substantial people, though there was a fringe of students and their

friends like Emeline Bishop and Phebe Mathews who took de-
light precisely in alienating the community.

From his visit to Lewis Tappan's store, and from the
fact that on October 13 Beecher signed a statement which declared that there was "nothing in the regulations which is
not common law in all well-regulated institutions," it is
clear that Beecher essentially agreed with the majority of
the trustees; he only regretted the clumsy way they went
about things. That he agreed with the trustees is further
indicated in a lecture delivered at Miami University in September on his way back to Cincinnati--a return still further
delayed by other side trips in Ohio--which contained "sar-
casms at the expense of the rebellious students which might
have been copied from James Hall's Western Monthly Magazine, and restates in specific terms the Lane trustees' opposition to student discussion of controversial public issues."[33]

Beecher worked hard to save the seminary after he
returned to Cincinnati. He persuaded the executive committee to rescind their resolution to dismiss Weld and to
ban private discussions. However the executive committee
of the board still had the power to dismiss students without
hearings, a provision which Beecher succeeded in getting rid
of too late. There was no effort to reinstate Morgan. In
view of all the events that had occurred since the previous
June, the seminarians in October sent a committee to the
faculty requesting that the code be explained. When the
students asked if they could discuss the nature of the code
the answer was "no." At that point, Mahan later wrote,
the students had to choose between submission or leaving
the seminary. The students rejected the code and all but
a dozen rose and left the meeting and the seminary.[34]

A few of the Lane Rebels scattered to other institutions, including Auburn, Yale, Western, and Miami, but the
bulk of them stayed together and formed a seminary-in-exile
in nearby Cumminsville, where a sympathizer turned over
his spacious house to take care of their immediate need of
new quarters. Arthur Tappan sent five thousand dollars to
help with their cost of living. As Mahan wrote in his Autobiography, suddenly there were two institutions in the vicin-
ity of Cincinnati, one full of students and inadequate facil-
ities and the other with large buildings but few students.
Beginning the first of November the Lane Rebels of Cumminsville studied their favorite subjects, listened to a few

lectures on physiology from Dr. Gamaliel Bailey, and com-
muted to the river city to continue their Sabbath Schools,
lyceum, and other work in behalf of the black population--
work which was increasingly successful. But the seminary-
in-exile could not go on forever. The students would have
to finish their theological training elsewhere. They talked
over their future with Asa Mahan. Should they go to Andover, Yale, Auburn? It was difficult to be enthusiastic
about any of them.[35] As it turned out, they would go to
Oberlin, a "peculiar" new institution quite different from
any other seminary in the country, and Asa Mahan would
go with them as president of that institution. But "going
to Oberlin" proved, like so many things in Asa's life, a
complicated affair.

Going to Oberlin

        The Oberlin Collegiate Institute had been founded in
1833 by John J. Shipherd and other settlers holding New
School sentiments. It was located on the Western Reserve
about thirty miles southwest of Cleveland and only a few
miles from Elyria. Oberlin had been a shoe-string operation to begin with but by the fall of 1834 it was in desper-
ate need of money, students, teachers, and a president. In
October Henry Brown resigned as president of the board of
trustees, and John Keep, a Cleveland minister, was appointed to replace him. Keep's son Theodore, wanting to follow
his father's occupation, had left in early October to enroll
in Lane Seminary.[36]

        Shipherd, who was Oberlin's founder along with Philo
Stewart, and general financial agent, decided the only way
to meet the many needs of the college was to go East and
persuade Arthur and Lewis Tappan, or other socially minded
businessmen in New York City, to support his fledgling institution. He was not eager to start the journey since it
interfered with family obligations. On November 23, 1834,
he wrote his brother Fayette that he would go to Cincinnati
and "how much further I know not," which, contrary to the
accepted opinion, shows that he intended to see what might
be salvaged of Lane for Oberlin before leaving Oberlin. "I
am tempted to sacrifice the interests of the Institution and
go directly to you, hoping once more to meet dear sister
but fear ... I should thus sacrifice the cause of Christ to
self and friends which neither you nor loved sister would
approve."[37] By November 27 he had travelled as far south

as Mansfield, Ohio, where he wrote Nathan Fletcher, agent
of the Oberlin Collegiate Institute, that a horse he had
bought from Brother Kinney was "sullen." In fact "his
whole team is not what I thought it was [and] will not answer the Institute's purpose at all." Brother Kinney would
have to take it back. In spite of transportation problems
he arrived in Columbus, where he met Theodore Keep, son
of the president of the Institute's board of trustees, John
Keep. The young man, who had intended to enroll at Lane,
told him in detail what had happened there and urged him
to go to Cincinnati to see what Oberlin might salvage from
the shambles. His inclination thus reinforced, Shipherd
nevertheless prayed for guidance and concluded that the Lord
also wanted him to go to Cincinnati instead of proceeding directly to the East on the "National Road." Being firmly convinced now, he went directly to Cincinnati and sought out
the house of Asa Mahan. He knew the pastor of the Sixth
Presbyterian had played a crucial role in supporting the Lane
Rebels, as the seminarians came to be called, and so was
the most promising person to see, but he also had a personal reason for going to him immediately. Maria Fletcher,
who lived at the home of the Mahans and taught at the "Select female school for colored ladies," was the daughter of
Nathan Fletcher of Oberlin. [38]

Mahan introduced Shipherd to the rebels and the agent,
eager and eloquent, convinced the seminarians-in-exile that
going to Oberlin was a good idea. They agreed to come,
however, and to bring Arthur Tappan's money, only if Mahan were appointed president of Oberlin, John Morgan added
to the faculty, Negroes admitted to the student body, and if
the trustees would agree not to interfere in academic affairs.
In addition, they recommended that Theodore Weld be appointed Professor of Theology. The Lane rebels were never
reticent about making known what they wanted. As early as
1831-32, before Beecher had become President of Lane, they
strenuously urged Mahan to help block certain faculty appointments and support others. [39]

Shipherd's enthusiasm was unbounded, and understandably so since here were money, students, and a president,
all of which the Oberlin Collegiate Institute desperately needed. He immediately mounted a campaign to bring this prize
home and wrote an impressive number of letters to marshall
support. On December 13 he wrote John Keep that he had
found the man for the president of their institution, namely
"Br. Asa Mahan ... a revival minister of the millennial

stamp." Fond of giving reasons, as his correspondence
shows, he confined himself this time to only nine reasons
why Brother Asa was their man (he later gave sixteen reasons why Negroes should be admitted to Oberlin), including
among them that the students would come if Mahan did, that
Finney thought Mahan had the best mind in western New York
while he was there, that Mahan had a talent for presiding
over deliberative bodies, that he was a hard worker, that
he was "a man of inflexible Christian principle who follows
the straight line of rectitude while even great and good men
[vacillate]," and that he had "a well educated and excellent
wife who is indeed a help meet and two well managed little
daughters." Shipherd asked Keep to have the board meet
as soon as possible to ratify "Br. Mahan as the man of my
choice." Two days later he wrote Keep again saying "I am
obliged to add ... that Br. T. D. Weld said that 'Br. Mahan has the best mind west of the mountains'; and there cannot be a doubt about the propriety of electing him as President." Shipherd was not one to take things for granted. On
the same day he wrote Eliphalet Redington and Addison Tracy
in Amherst, Ohio, just north of Oberlin, asking one or both
of them to concur with him in requesting Keep to call an
extra meeting of the board without delay. (At least two requests were needed to call a special meeting of the board.)
"I believe God has here put my hand on the end of a chain,
linking men and money to our dear Seminary in such a manner as will fill our hearts with gratitude...." Still on the
same day he wrote Nathan Fletcher, "Do not suffer the election to fail; for everything, money and all, depend upon their
election."[46] Fletcher, loyal to Shipherd and a committed
abolitionist, became the main proponent of his friend's views
among the trustees.

Having made clear to the Oberlin trustees that financial support depended upon all the conditions being accepted,
including the admission of Negroes to the Institute, Shipherd
urged them to act promptly in accepting the conditions. Assuming that the trustees would be as delighted as he in Oberlin's good fortune, he asked Mahan to accompany him in a
search for Weld, who was giving antislavery lectures some-
where in southern Ohio but whose precise location was unknown. Securing a month's leave of absence from the Sixth
Presbyterian, Mahan accompanied Shipherd up the Ohio River
to Ripley, where John Rankin, also spreading the gospel of
immediate emancipation, directed them to Weld. When he
was told that his peers wanted him appointed professor of
theology Weld declined on the grounds that his education was

insufficient for such a job.   He recommended Charles G.
Finney, so Mahan and Shipherd continued their journey to
New York City to get commitments both from the Tappans
and Finney. [41]

Meanwhile, in Oberlin the trustees and many of the
students did not take kindly to Shipherd's proposal, much
to his surprise when he heard the news.   They were happy
to have Mahan as president and the support of the Tappans,
but they were upset about the condition of admitting black
students to Oberlin.   In late December a petition was circulated among the students on the question of admitting Negroes.   Twenty-six students signed in favor of the proposal
and thirty-two against it.   Of those signing the petition a
majority of men favored it while a majority of women disapproved.   P. P. Stewart, co-founder of the Oberlin Colony
was incensed and "at once proclaimed Bro. Shipherd mad!!,
crazy, etc."   The board of trustees met in Elyria on January 1, 1835, to decide the issue.   The meeting was held
in Elyria since the Oberlin community was in considerable
turmoil.   The meeting of the board was far from calm itself, one member characterizing it as full of "rancour and
malevolence."   Mahan and Morgan were unanimously elected,
but the motion to admit black students was tabled.   The
minutes of the meeting contain the following entry: "Resolved, That the Board do not feel prepared till they have
other and more definite information on the subject to give
a pledge respecting the course they will pursue in regard
to the education of the people of Color: wishing that this
institution should be on the same ground in respect to the
admission of students with other similar institutions of our
land."[42]

Mahan and Shipherd were successful in New York
City in January 1835 in convincing the Tappans to support
Oberlin and Finney to become Professor of Theology there.
Letters from the Lane Rebels, including H. B. Stanton and
George Whipple, to Finney and the Tappans supported Shipherd's eloquence in behalf of his beloved institute.   The Tappans were generous indeed in their support of the rebels and
Oberlin.   Arthur Tappan donated ten thousand dollars to the
college, while Lewis Tappan and other businessmen agreed
to pay eight professors six hundred dollars annually.   Finney
accepted the theology professorship on the condition that he
be allowed to spend several months each winter preaching at
the Broadway Tabernacle, which had been built in Manhattan
expressly for his use, and that the Oberlin trustees "commit

the internal management of the institute entirely to the Faculty, inclusive of the reception of students." The surprising
size of the Tappans' support of Oberlin resulted from Finney's acceptance of the professorship of theology. They had
long been staunch Finney supporters and considered him ex-
actly the right man for the job. The extent of the Tappans'
benefaction in fact was so great that some of the Lane Rebels began to worry, which was not unusual for them. On
January 22, 1835, Huntington Lyman and Henry B. Stanton
wrote Weld that "now the danger seems to us to be this,
that having become suddenly rich and riding upon the high
tide of success, they [the Tappans, Mahan, and Finney] will
transmute every pleasant looking abolitionist into an Oberlin
professor." "An institution which meets with such favor
and which has secured such names as Mahan and Finney can
command the best talent of the country. Do write without
delay, and use your influence to have them observe great
caution in their selections. Direct them to those who would
be the best advisers."[43]

        Shipherd's dream turned into a nightmare when the
news arrived that the Oberlin trustees at their January first
meeting had tabled the resolution to admit blacks to Oberlin.
Mahan and the Lane Rebels were also dismayed. The great
prospects for Oberlin were completely in jeopardy. Shipherd immediately wrote the trustees and sent a Pastoral Letter to the members of the Oberlin Church expressing his
deep disappointment at the trustees' decision--"surprising
and grievous to my soul"--and pointed out that Negroes already had been admitted to full privileges at other institutions including Princeton, Lane, and Western Reserve College. There would be no trouble at Oberlin if black students
were admitted, he thought, but in any case considerations of
"worldly expediency" should never interfere with doing what
is "eternally right." Moreover, the crucial matter was not
the admission of blacks but that the trustees not interfere
with the internal, academic matters of the college. The
difficulties at Lane, he wrote, did not grow out of the admission of Negroes "but out of the trustees' interference with
the Students' right of free discussion, and those matters
which belong to the Faculty to manage." He threatened to
resign as agent if the Oberlin trustees would not guarantee
"that the Faculty shall control the internal affairs of the institute and decide upon the reception of students." Here,
it appeared, was a carefully thought out strategy. The trustees did not have to agree to admit blacks. If they agreed,
however, to let the faculty decide admission policy and if

they appointed Mahan, Finney, and Morgan, then the faculty
policy would be to admit blacks. [44]   What was the decision
of the board to be?   Oberlin's future and Mahan's hung in
the balance.

The trustees met again on February 9, 1835, this
time in Oberlin and in Shipherd's house.   According to John
Keep, this meeting was no less explosive than the previous
one in Elyria had been--it was "riotous, turbulent and filled
with detraction [and] slander."   There were nine trustees
and the outcome was very much in doubt, the two factions
seemingly equal in strength.   Nathan Fletcher led the pro-
Shipherd faction, while P. P. Stewart, co-founder of Oberlin,
led the anti-Shipherd faction.   Three trustees sided with
Fletcher and three with Stewart.   As president of the board,
John Keep cast the deciding ballot.   He was a friend of
Weld, an admirer of Finney, and an abolitionist.   He voted
with Fletcher and the issue was resolved; Shipherd had won
the day and Mahan was now free to accept the presidency
which had been unanimously extended to him as a result of
the January first meeting.   The decision was dramatic, but
the resolution passed by the trustees was not.   According
to the minutes of the meeting, the trustees "Resolved That
the question in respect to the admission of students into this
Seminary be in all cases left to the decision of the Faculty
and to them be committed also the internal management of
its concerns, provided always that they be holden amenable
to the Board and not liable to censure or interruption from
the Board so long as their measure shall not infringe upon
the laws or general principles of the Institution. "[45]   Not
only was it undramatic but some critics thought it hedged on
basic issues.   In any case, it ensured the admission of Negroes and hence was acceptable to Mahan, Finney, Weld, the
Tappans, and the bulk of the Lane Rebels.   The outcome,
needless to say, was not kindly received by all of Oberlin's
friends.   Shipherd felt obliged to defend himself against
charges of "selling out," and wrote to E. P. Sturges, in
April, "Some talk as if the Tappans of New York had bought
us; but our principles are the same [as] they were before
they were invited to subscribe."   However, "I have not
changed at all since I left home or before to get their money
or any other."[46]

That Mahan was eager for the Oberlin chapter of his
life to begin, there can be no doubt.   There he would be
able to spread the word of God more widely than ever before and to teach mental and moral philosophy as well, a

role he had looked forward to increasingly much through the
years as he continued his careful study of his favorite subject. His eagerness to begin work at Oberlin comes through
nowhere more clearly than in his letter to Nathan Fletcher
of March 1835, written while he was still in New York City.

> The residence of your daughter in my family has
> endeared to us all that are dear to her.... I
> know you as [an] endeared brother in Christ. But
> I have not time nor a disposition for compliments
> now. We are doing a great work and cannot de-
> scend to such [objects?] ... As soon as possible
> after my arrival in Cincinnati I intend to start for
> Oberlin. I hope some log house will be prepared
> for reception. There we shall rejoice to stay till
> further accommodations are provided. Myself and
> all associated with me come upon the field not to
> live in splendor but to work for God and a dying
> world.... Brother Finney is a man of God filled
> of the Holy Ghost and of faith. [47]

By the time Mahan returned to Cincinnati it was well
known there that he and his family were leaving for Oberlin.
While this piece of information scarcely came as unhappy
news to the redoubtable Joshua Wilson, it was a different
matter as far as the congregation at Sixth Presbyterian was
concerned. He had loyal friends there who not only retained
but even extended the liberal impulse that Mahan had initially given it. Jonathan Blanchard was soon to carry on as
pastor the abolition tradition which the founders and the first
pastor of the Sixth Church had inaugurated. [48]

Asa helped Mary pack their belongings and then left
for Oberlin ahead of the family in order to assume his new
duties as soon as possible. Mary and the children were accompanied to Oberlin by Maria Fletcher and Sarah Rudd, or
Sally Rudd, as she was generally called, who had been a
member of the congregation at Sixth Church. She would be
instrumental in persuading her niece, Caroline Mary Rudd,
to enroll at Oberlin, which, as we shall see, had momentous consequences.

Although he was leaving Cincinnati, Mahan in fact
was accompanied by a part of it that was deeply significant
and meaningful to him. From the beginning he had been a
friend and helper of the Lane seminarians, and many of
them had chosen his church as their center of worship. Now

he and they were starting on a dramatic new adventure together, a trek from the Ohio River to Lake Erie, from the
Ohio Valley to the Western Reserve. It was a momentous
journey and the new Oberlin was to leave an indelible mark
on the Western Reserve and far beyond. Asa Mahan was
destined to become the Number One "Irreconcilable Ober-
linian" in spirit as well as in fact.

Chapter 3

OBERLIN

Asa Mahan and his family lived and worked in Oberlin for fifteen useful, productive, gratifying, frustrating, sad and eventually tragic years. The one unifying factor was that they were exciting years, considered either in terms of external events or the life of the mind.

Entering the academic scene did not wholly change the tenor of Asa's life by any means. Though he no longer had regular pastoral duties, he shared the pulpit in Oberlin with Finney in the early years and was subsequently at different intervals associate pastor of the First Congregational Church. He regularly preached in communities near Oberlin, some of which had no regular pastor, and preached at numerous revivals at home and abroad. During the long winter vacation (Oberlin had no summer vacation) he usually preached at Congregational and Presbyterian churches in Boston, Providence, New York City, and elsewhere in the East. After the financial failure of Arthur Tappan's company and the Panic of 1837 Oberlin not only lost its rosy financial future but was reduced to near bankruptcy and Mahan for several years drew no salary and depended upon his winter preaching as his major source of income.[1]

Mahan, moreover, continued to speak and act against slavery but what had brought him nothing but trouble in Cincinnati brought him respect in Oberlin, where the whole community shared antislavery sentiments. Even the trustees, colonists, and faculty who had opposed Shipherd's request for the admission of blacks changed their minds and became

dedicated abolitionists. To be sure, the community was
despised and reviled by many outsiders (although Oberlin
always had its handful of adherents in every community who
acted as leaven in the rising antislavery sentiments in the
North), but in any case Mahan had the support of his peers
and was no longer standing up with a lonely few in the river
city.

Mahan began his antislavery work soon after arriving
in Oberlin. In July 1835, along with several students, he
travelled to Hudson, Ohio, for a meeting at which the dynamic Weld and he, among others, were scheduled to speak.
One of the students, Philip Doddridge Adams, recalled that
Weld "was one of the most powerful speakers I ever heard"
and "our Prest. was by no means backward on that occasion.... His remarks were to the point ... and [he] makes
no mean appearance on the stage."[2] Mahan's stage presence
must have been impressive for, as we shall see, his free-
wheeling style and pungent talk never failed to fascinate as
well as, in some cases, to convince.

As in the past, Mahan attacked slavery from the pulpit and in Christian periodicals. Perhaps his most majestic
denunciation of slavery appeared in the Oberlin Evangelist,
where he wrote,

No man can distinctly apprehend [it] without his
reason and conscience reprobating slavery as the
consummation of injustice and oppression, and as
the embodiment of the highest evils which man's
inhumanity has ever inflicted upon man. No man
can practice nor apologize for this abomination,
without being haunted, as by a spirit of darkness,
with his own conscience, and without that conscience being lit up with occasional flashes from
the pyre of the eternal judgment.[3]

Majestic as this denunciation is, it nevertheless fails
to reveal the depths of Mahan's hatred of slavery. Nothing
was more important in this man's life than his Christian
commitment and yet in his Moral Science, written during
his Oberlin years, he said that if anyone could convince him
that the Bible sanctioned slavery he would not embrace slavery but would abandon the Bible. No one could ever convince him that in fact the Bible did sanction slavery since
the texts, correctly interpreted, as well as the spirit of the
New Testament, he felt, testified the other way. Neverthe-

less, given the hypothetical situation, he would have rejected
the Scriptures as false because they would have been immoral. 4 No other stand could so clearly reveal the centrality of morality in this man's life and the centrality of
morality in his conception of religion. There was no teleological suspension of the moral in his religious commitment
nor was there the slightest identification or morality with
God's will. The right is independent even of God's will,
although God always chooses to do right for its own sake.

        In most aspects Mahan's way of life was entirely al-
tered at Oberlin. Family life became much more complicated; Asa and Mary had five more children as well as a
large extended family of student boarders and faculty and
hired-help roomers. But the most profound change concerned the quality of his inner life. While he of course
had had knowledge about sanctification, he had never experienced it until this long-sought-for goal was bestowed at
Oberlin. Moreover, Asa's main job was no longer preaching but being a college president and professor of mental
and moral philosophy, a more than full time job for anyone
endowed with less vigor, enthusiasm, and drive than this
robust western New Yorker. Also his speaking out against
slavery and other moral evils widened out into militant action both as an individual and as a member of organized reform groups including antislavery organizations and political
reform parties such as the Liberty and Free Soil parties.
He was later, after Oberlin, to become active in the Republican Party.

Family Life

        A son was born in 1836 to Asa and Mary Mahan.
Still unreconciled to the death of their first son in Pittsford they named their second son, as they had the first,
Theodore Strong. The name had now come to have a double
meaning for them, each revered. No doubt Theodore Strong,
still in New Brunswick, understood the double entendre more
than most. Mary Keep, named in honor of their beloved
John Keep, was born in 1837, and the irony of the honor
was locked away in one of the rooms of the future that no
eye could then penetrate. Three more daughters arrived on
the scene in due course: Sarah S. in 1840, Elizabeth M. in
1843, and Almira B. in 1846. Anna Jenison received her
A.B. from Oberlin in 1848, only a few years after the first
A.B. degrees were granted to women, while her sister Lucy

Dix was enrolled in the Preparatory Department during 1844-
45 and then in the Literary Department in 1845-47 and 1848-
50. As we have seen, there was a special bond between
Asa and Lucy Dix, and he felt very close to little Theodore
also, for reasons easily understood. Mary, too, was devoted to her son. There was, however, ample parental love
in the hearts of Asa and Mary for generous servings to all
their children. [5] Family Mahan may not have been a seam-
less whole but it was tightly knit.

The extended family seems incredibly large until one
understands the stringent living conditions in early Oberlin.
In the United States Census for 1840 no fewer than eighteen
people are listed under Mahan's name! In addition to Mary
and the children this number included students, professors,
and hired help who either lived and/or boarded at the president's house, to say nothing of Sarah Rudd, who acted as
general housekeeper for the hotel-in-miniature. It must not
be supposed, however, that the household was unique in serving the community; most households had roomers and boarders both to supplement their income and, because of the
paucity of houses and dormitories, to help share what they
had, in Christian spirit, with others. [6]

Sarah Rudd, a member of Mahan's congregation in
Cincinnati who had come to Oberlin with his family, acted
as general housekeeper and did such an admirable job of
keeping order that Mahan was able to write his sermons
and philosophical books in his study at home. It would be
less than fair, however, not to add that the president's powers of concentration were strongly developed. Sally, as she
was generally called, wrote her niece Caroline Mary Rudd
urging her to come to Oberlin, where she could work to pay
for her education. Her letter presents a vignette of life on
the corner of West College and Professor Streets:

> Perhaps you will wonder what you have to do.
> Your work would be the same as a daughter's
> would--we have a girl that does the washing and
> kitchen work. You would have the parlors and
> Mr. Mahans study to keep in order, and what little
> chamber work there will be to do, but our
> chambers will all be occupied with boarders
> that take care of their own rooms, except what
> we reserve for spare chambers. We expect
> Professors and wives to occupy 3 of them (they
> have no children by the way) Mrs. Mahans nur-

sery is below--and I have the sweetest little
bedroom below you ever saw, our house is
very pleasant and convenient--Mrs. Mahan would
want you to see to the children and probably
teach them and be ready (when not occupied
with your studys) to wait on company and be
[a] kind of minute man--She has three children
two little girls one seven and the other coming 5
and a little Oberlin boy ten months old.   I give
you these particulars, thinking your Father might
wish to know something about [what] your place
would be.   I shall be with you to release you any
time, for your study and recitations.   Mrs. Mahan
has a great many calls out, has much to do in the
Ladies department, not as a teacher but as a coun-
cilor.   They have a board of females to assist the
Principal, of which she is President, and the young
Ladies are constantly coming to her for council
and she wants her time free as possible.   As for
myself, I can hardly tell what place I do fill unless it is the supervisor of domestic concerns.... [7]

Caroline Mary accepted her Aunt Sally's invitation and enrolled at Oberlin in 1835.   Later she pursued the course of
study leading to the undergraduate degree and was one of
the three women in the class of 1841 to be awarded the
A. B. degree, the first degrees ever to be conferred on
women for taking the same college course as men.   Women
had been admitted to Oberlin from its beginning but had always taken a special course under the auspices of the Ladies
Department.

Complicating family life further, the president's house
was something of a commissary for students.   As part of
their remuneration for services the Institute had given farms
to both Mahan and Finney, and Mahan worked his industrious-
ly, as he did everything.   The produce was sometimes sold
at reduced rates to students, one of whom remembered with
gratitude the old black lady who was "at the head of the cul-
inary department of President Mahan's household."   "My
milk was purchased at President Mahan's, and it often occurred that the measure was bounteous and this dear old
mother would slip in a biscuit or a nice piece of bread and
butter."   In this way "self-supporting students, and in fact
most of the students were of that class, were thus encouraged and helped without any parading of benevolence...."[8]

Mahan's farm figured in one of the apocryphal stories

told about him in Oberlin as late as 1897. It is worth re-
cording since there is usually an element of fundamental
truth enthroned in such stories. First, the uncontested facts.
Mahan's farm was at the south end of town and his barn was
generally well filled with grain and hay after harvest time.
One summer Oberlin was hit with a particularly severe rain
storm accompanied by much thunder and lightning, one bolt
of which struck a building in the south part of town. By
the time fire fighters arrived the situation was so hopeless
that they returned to their homes. According to C. S. Hopkins,

> It is said that Pres. Mahan started out in the
> storm to see what was burning. Going down South
> Main street he met someone returning from the
> fire. He inquired what was burning. When he
> was told that it was his own barn that was being
> destroyed, he said, "Oh, is that all," and then
> returned to his home. [9]

It is fair to say that while Mahan never ignored windfalls,
he never sought them either. He enjoyed the material benefits when he had them but was not grieved when they disappeared. He saved his grief for matters of the heart. Yes,
they were in the lap of God, but....

The board at the president's house was plain and
wholesome, partly as a matter of dietary principle and partly of necessity since many commodities were unobtainable
on the frontier. Family Mahan flourished physically on what
might best be described as a modified Graham diet. "Grahamism" was the rage in early Oberlin due mainly to the
influence of Finney. Sylvester Graham promoted the use of
whole wheat flour and vegetables, prohibited eating meat,
drinking alcohol, coffee or tea, and even took a dim view
of condiments of any sort, including salt and pepper. Finney constantly rebuked Brewster and Thirza Pelton for serving tea and coffee at their inn, as well as providing salt and
pepper for guests. Thirza, however, held her own with
Finney, at least until 1850. [10] The Mahans used salt and
perhaps had meat occasionally but emphatically rejected all
stimulants. No alcohol, tea, or coffee for Family Mahan.
The members of the extended family heartily agreed (since
no doubt they would not have been boarders in the first place
had they not). Harry E. Woodcock, class of 1845, wrote
that "I was soon invited to make my home in the President's
family where I remained as at my mother's table." According to Woodcock,

On one occasion a gubernatorial candidate of the
Liberty party, having an appointment to address
the citizens Monday arrived Saturday to tarry with
the President.   Monday morning as we were seated
at the table, he said, with an expression of pen-
ance, "Madam, I have [a] miserable habit; I cannot speak today unless I have a cup of tea."   A
drawing of tea was obtained from an old lady who
was [a] neighbor and the would be governor was
his miserable self again and delivered his speech.
The President knew how to sympathize with him
as he had formerly been adicted [sic] to his cup
of coffee.   He had long since discarded it and
found that he enjoyed life better without it. [11]

Mahan, then, was neither a dietary fanatic as some people
in the community were nor was he one to force his prefer-
ences on others.   Plain and wholesome eating and drinking
seemed like commonsense truisms, but following common
sense, he realized, was not always easy and in any case
there seemed no point in making a fetish of such matters.
Drinking alcohol, however, he believed to be an unredeem-
able evil.

Diet was only a part of the concern for health in
early Oberlin.   There was a populist revolt against standard
or "regular" medical practice, strong in Oberlin at the time
but by no means limited to it.   It occurred throughout the
United States but was particularly strong in Ohio.   It was
not simply undirected malcontent of ignorant people; the educated and uneducated alike could see that calomel and blood-
letting, the standard stock in trade of physicians at the time,
were rarely adequate to most illnesses and harmful in others.
(Surgeons were held in much higher regard.)   Finney, for
example, believed, no doubt with good reason, that his treatment for cholera had not simply been ineffectual but harmful.
As late as 1858 Timothy B. Hudson, a member of the faculty, wrote an article for the Oberlin Students' Monthly entitled "Popular Distrust of Regular Physicians," a detailed
indictment of the medical profession.   It is little wonder that
homeopathy and other medical approaches gained favor in
Oberlin, though ultimately the regular practitioners remained
secure, partly because the criticism ebbed and partly because they incorporated the points that were sound in the
criticisms of regular practices and in such opposing medical
viewpoints as homeopathy.   Dr. Isaac Jennings carried re-
bellion to an extreme and eventually gave up prescribing

drugs altogether, except placebos. His influence was strong while Finney supported his view but eventually waned when Finney became less interested in the whole matter. Homer Johnson opened an office in Oberlin in 1846, and he had little respect for the unaided restorative powers of the human body. "In his methods he was the exact opposite of Dr. Jennings; he had the reputation of using drugs generously and in large doses." He was a successful practitioner of medicine in Oberlin for forty years. [12]

Asa Mahan, like Finney and Hudson, was critical of standard medical practices and was instead drawn to the homeopathic view of medicine, believing, as he did, that creating immunity to disease was far more effective than curing disease once incurred. Strangely enough, as we shall see, after leaving Oberlin he was president of the Cleveland Homeopathic Hospital for a short time. He was drawn to homeopathy also because homeopathic hospitals and medical schools were open to women while the standard institutions rigidly refused to admit them. All of the women physicians in Oberlin during the nineteenth century were trained in homeopathic institutions.

The regular physicians in Oberlin took a dim view of both Finney and Mahan. Homer Johnson in particular disliked Mahan and was active in trying to get rid of him as president of the Oberlin Collegiate Institute. No doubt part of his antagonism was based on the president's disdain for dispensing drugs and his preference for homeopathy. It is certain that Johnson held Mahan's views of holiness and sanctification in contempt and disliked Mahan as a person, all of which contributed to his efforts to unseat the president. [13] The records do not reveal what Mahan's feelings toward Johnson were, but there are no a priori grounds to suggest that they were cordial.

The Experience of Holiness

Asa Mahan carried to Oberlin "an aching void in his heart." He had never recovered the vivid feeling of the presence of God that had accompanied his entrance into the Christian life at age seventeen. The freshness of that experience had grown stale through college and seminary years. And even though he never lost the assurance of being saved by freely accepting the gracious gift of God, he became increasingly discouraged by his own efforts to combat sinful

inclinations. Like most Christians, he wrote, he expected to fail because everyone is "sold in sin." To be
sure, he had joyful intimations of things to come at the Methodist camp meeting near Cincinnati. It will be recalled that
as he preached on this occasion he felt that a "divine power
came over me of which I had never had an experience before." After preaching he retired to a forest and prayed
"that I might be conscious that my heart was pure in His
sight, that I might see God, and live and walk in the manifested light of His countenance." Asa felt he was moving
in the right direction, but the desired results were not forth-
coming.14 It was at Oberlin finally that the result he sought
was forthcoming.

Mahan's aching void was filled as a result of two distinctly different experiences. During his second summer at
Oberlin he and Finney took the tabernacle tent to Mansfield,
Ohio and preached to "great congregations of unregenerate
persons and [to] Christians." While the camp meeting was
in progress he picked up a copy of Clarke on the Promises,
which "providentially lay by me," and on the title page he
read this passage: "Whereby are given unto us exceeding
great and precious promises: that by these ye may be par-
takers of the divine nature, having escaped the corruption
that is in the world through lust." Mahan was thunderstruck.
"No words can describe the effect which the reading of that
passage had upon my mind. I seemed at once to be fanned
by 'the wings of the morning' whose everlasting light was
about to dawn upon my waiting spirit."15 He now believed
that all things pertaining to a holy and godly life are given
in the knowledge of Christ. But, as he later frequently
stressed, there are two crucially different ways of knowing
--knowing about something and being directly aware or acquainted with it. After reading this book he knew about holiness: he believed that God would grant a person release
from every specific sin whenever by faith he asked Him to
do it, for God does not promise things He is unwilling to
do; and he further believed that the purpose for which the
promises were given was, upon supplication, to transform
man's nature so there was no longer a predilection or disposition to transgress God's law and the moral law.

Although Mahan felt all these views to be true, he
knew he still lacked the transforming awareness of the presence of Christ. He had discursive knowledge about God but
was not directly acquainted with Him. Feeling that God was
for him "still far off in Heaven," he prayed after his return

to Oberlin, as he had done at the Methodist camp meeting,
to see God and feel his inner presence. He "entreated the
Father of mercies, for Christ's sake, to lead me out of
darkness into the light after which I was seeking." The next
day he entered the room of a faculty member who was living
in his home and discussed the nature of St. Paul's "undying
and all-constraining flame" of devotion. "While thus speaking upon the subject, I suddenly rose from my seat with the
joyful exclamation, 'I have found it!' and without uttering
another word, I returned to my study, and again falling upon
my knees, returned most fervent thanksgiving to God." Asa
was convinced that while talking about Paul he had seen God
and "felt an instantaneous enlargement, expansion, and in-
vigoration of all my receptive capacities." "The rock of the
heart was struck with the rod of love divine." However,
Mahan was struck with loathing several days later when he
thought of his enslavement to his temper, appetites, and
secret ambition. Near despair, he prayed earnestly that
he might be fully searched, cleansed, and led in the way
everlasting. He felt that his plea was heard. "After the
process of searching and self-revelation was completed, the
waters of life seemed to flow through every department of
my nature, rolling down as the river of life into the Dead
Sea of the propensities, and everywhere with the same healing and vitalising efficacy." Soon after this experience, upon retiring to his bedroom, he received what he described
as a personal manifestation of the presence of Christ. "I
did not 'fall at his feet as dead,' the manifestation being too
mildly loving for that. My breathing, however, stopped in
an instant, and it was some time before I could recover it
again." His joy, he wrote, was full, and he later described
this manifestation as his "first full baptism of the Spirit."[16]

Preaching from this new standpoint Mahan and Finney,
also an advocate of the holiness view, were immediately
asked by a student at a public meeting,

> What degree of sanctification do the Scriptures
> authorize us to trust Christ for? May we, or
> may we not, trust Him to save us from all sin,
> and to sanctify us wholly, and to do it in this
> present life? I would very earnestly appeal to
> our beloved instructors, President Mahan and Pro-
> fessor Finney, for a specific answer to this ques-
> tion.[17]

Mahan and Finney were initially taken aback. To reply

"yes" might suggest that a sanctified person was no longer capable of sinning, the terrible heresy of antinomianism present in John Humphrey Noyes' Perfectionism. Mahan replied that he would give the question prayerful and careful attention and would, the Lord permitting, furnish in due time a full and specific answer. With this question in mind Mahan and Finney spent the winter off-term in New York City preaching and searching the Scriptures for an answer. The writings of John Wesley and James B. Taylor on Christian Perfection were helpful at this time.

Mahan's "full and specific answer" was published in 1839 as the Scripture Doctrine of Christian Perfection, "a series of discourses designed to throw light on the way of holiness." This book proved to be immensely influential in the holiness movement.[18] It was first published by D. S. King in Boston and was reprinted by this firm and its successor, Waite and Peirce, ten times. In 1850 J. M. Fitch of Oberlin reprinted it for the eleventh time.

In his influential book Mahan distinguished between salvation from sin and the continuous battle against sin. Theologically speaking, the first is a matter of justification through faith; the latter a matter of perfection, holiness, or sanctification. Protestants in general hold the standard Reformation doctrine concerning the former: man is an inherently sinful creature and can never merit salvation; however God, out of grace, saves some. For free-will Trinitarians it is up to each individual to accept or reject God's gracious gift; those who do are saved, those who do not are damned. In short, man's role in salvation is limited to choosing freely one way or another; God's role is to actually provide salvation when it is chosen even though the agent is unworthy of it.

Christian perfection, or holiness, on the other hand, refers to man's capacity for following God's commandments. Is it possible--and if so, how?--to wage successful warfare against the ever present enemy, sinful dispositions and tendencies? Here the ranks of Protestantism are markedly split and two quite different answers--let us call one the legalistic and the other evangelistic--are given, which have significantly different results. The legalistic answer says that overcoming sin is quite different from salvation. A sanctified life is not a gracious gift of God to be sought by earnest prayerfulness but is something that man must heroically struggle to achieve for himself. However, given the sinful

nature of man, such efforts are bound to fail and such failures dishearten the Christian until he makes a sort of piety
out of inevitable wickedness. "Oh, dear, how sinful I am!
Thankfully I am saved by the grace of God in spite of my
inherent shortcomings!"[19]

The evangelistic alternative, Mahan averred, is the
only successful way to combat sin. According to this view,
sanctification is quite similar to salvation. It is just as
hopeless for man to think he can overcome sin by his own
effort as it is to think he can earn salvation through good
works. Victory over sin, like salvation, is a gracious gift
of God. The in-dwelling Christ, the Spirit of God in man's
heart, is the victor over sin, not man himself. The role
of man in receiving this second gracious gift of God is to
pray sincerely and earnestly for it: "If you will open the
door, the Son of God will enter in, and confer this blessed
inheritance upon you." "Ask and it shall be given you."[20]

However, Mahan emphasized, one must ever be alert
to avoid the opposite error of legalism, namely, antinomianism, the notion that once "the Son of God enters in" a person becomes incapable of sinful behavior--by definition, so
to speak, since it is now the Spirit of God acting. According to Mahan, the presence of the Spirit does not supplant
the agency of the human being; the Spirit is present only because a person freely, and without constraint, sincerely
sought its presence. And the continuing presence of the
Spirit is dependent upon the constantly renewed decision to
ask for and prayerfully seek that presence. The human being can always succumb to his previous sinful ways and thus
lose the Spirit's domination of his life. Our first parents
and the fallen angels were once completely pure, or entirely
sanctified, and still they were tempted and fell. A fully and
wisely instructed sanctified believer "is perfected in watchfulness, as well as in other Christian virtues, and, like the
prudent general, is never for a moment off his guard." Finally, the antinomian view of perfection is wrong, Mahan
claimed, since it is perfectly possible for a person to have
a will that is "perfect in holiness" and yet act imperfectly.
A will is perfect in holiness when a person loves God with
all his heart and his neighbor as himself. It does not follow from this fact, however, that a man's action is perfect
since man, even with the in-dwelling Spirit of Christ, unlike
God does not possess perfect wisdom and may wrongly in-
terpret his duty in complicated cases.[21]

Mahan's commitment to Christian Perfection, his

espousal of "the way of holiness," had profound consequences
both for him and his family. As we have seen, he had long
considered his chief sins to be pride, ambition, and loss of
temper. With his new religious convictions he prayed specifically for the removal of each of "these evil propensities"
and sincerely believed that they "were crucified" by the in-
dwelling Spirit of Christ. In a letter to his wife he wrote
that he was no longer aware "of any desire for a name among
men, or any wish to pursue any object, but the glory of
Christ." In Out of Darkness into Light he wrote that "in my
new life ... it became just as natural and easy to be quiet
and patient, as it had formerly been to be angry, under pro-
vocation."22

      Mahan also lost, he felt, many fears that had haunted
him through the years, including his horror of dying and re-
pugnance at the thought of being put in a coffin and lowered
into the ground. He also became reconciled to the loss of
loved ones and lost his tormenting grief over the deaths of
his infant children. He never ceased to think about them
but now joyfully looked forward to seeing them again. Now
he could dream that his infant son, grown to manhood, greet-
ed him in Heaven, "It is my father come at last."

      Now that he experienced a deeper "love, gratitude,
and adoration, toward God"--a feeling of bliss fixed upon
one "changeless center"--Asa Mahan wanted to communicate
these feelings to his children. He read and talked to them
about Jesus, especially of his love for children.

           As I began to read the wonderful account pertaining
           to this subject, our little son, just upwards of
           three years of age, came to me, and putting his
           elbows upon my knee, looked me intensely in the
           face. As I read on, and commented upon what I
           read, "Oh!" he exclaimed, while the most affec-
           tionate wonder sat upon his countenance. Such ex-
           clamations were repeated as every new feature of
           Christ's character lifted its divine form before that
           child's mind.... Often would he come into my
           study, and say to me, "Pa, won't you talk to me
           about the dear Jesus?" As I would speak to him
           upon the subject, "Oh!" he would exclaim. As I
           would tell him how happy it made me to think about
           Christ, "It makes me happy too" he would reply.23

      The Oberlin community in general was caught up by
the holiness viewpoint. In addition to Mahan and Finney,

faculty members John Morgan and Henry Cowles were influential advocates of the doctrine. By 1840 Cowles was describing the experience of holiness in Pentecostal terms, em-
phasizing the spiritual dimension of the Holy Spirit's work
and completely downplaying any miraculous dimension in the
enduement of power. Other faculty members, however, not
only failed to embrace the new outlook but were suspicious
and hostile toward it. John Cowles was openly contemptuous of it while James Dascomb and James H. Fairchild
opposed it more passively and diplomatically. Those who
opposed the doctrine held Mahan primarily responsible for
its propagation, no doubt because of the wide sale of Christian Perfection and the vigor with which Mahan spread the
view in his winter preaching tours. Moreover, these dis-
sident members of the faculty felt that Mahan as president
presented holiness as somehow the viewpoint of all Oberlin,
which it was not. However it cannot be denied that for
years it was the generally held view of the community. The
dissidents, and even other advocates of sanctification, also
felt that Mahan in pressing the view too ardently unneces-
sarily alienated Congregational and Presbyterian brethren
who found the view repugnant even though they were New
School and New Light in outlook. The dissidents also thought
that the holiness view led Mahan, unlike Finney, Morgan,
and Cowles to a holier than thou attitude, to an estimate of his
own religious and moral attainments that was too high and an
estimate of the attainments of others that was too low. The rest
of the faculty apparently came to share this view, as did some
of the townspeople though the majority of the students, colonists,
and friends of Oberlin in the East and elsewhere did not
share this opinion. They saw Mahan as constantly pressing
to keep himself and others from falling away from an ever
renewing sense of the presence of God and the absolute demands of duty. To keep the freshness of God's presence
and the claims of conscience before mankind, they understood, was exhausting, unpopular, and sometimes heart breaking. 24

        To promote and extend the holiness viewpoint the in-
stitute in 1838 founded the Oberlin Evangelist, which was
published continuously until December 1862. It was printed
every two weeks and was written for a general audience.
This periodical contained for the most part sermons on sanctification written by President Mahan and Professors Finney,
Henry Cowles, and others, as well as articles on every reform movement of the day. Mahan was by far the most pro-
lific contributor to the Evangelist, and he was urged by his

friends to publish a collection of his articles. In 1847 Harper and Brothers of New York City published twelve of his
articles on sanctification, and also a new piece, under the
title The True Believer. Harpers was still reprinting the
book in 1857. In the Preface Mahan wrote that he hoped the
book would be remembered here and there as having provided guidance to "the highway of holiness." "This [hope],"
he wrote, "is the only form of ambition now known to the
author."[25]

        Horace Taylor was the first editor of the Evangelist
and Henry Cowles succeeded him in 1844. The reason for
Taylor's replacement was a sad blow to the community.
Taylor seduced a young woman and tried to cover up the
results by an abortion. He also embezzled funds from the
college and the Evangelist. The community was shocked but
made no effort to hide or suppress the embarrassing case.
In the Oberlin Evangelist, December 20, 1843, Mahan, Henry Cowles, Thome, and Whipple wrote:

        We had been for a considerable time, painfully
        conscious that [Taylor] was not the spiritual man
        that we once thought him to be. One of our num-
        ber, Prest. Mahan, had often expressed the con-
        viction, that his influence was greatly injurious to
        the Evangelist, and that without a great change in
        his spiritual state, (a change which we earnestly
        hoped for,) he must be removed. Yet none of us
        suspected that what we saw arose from what now
        appears. When the first shock of surprise and
        horror was over, then the steel entered our souls.[26]

Taylor was arrested, tried, found guilty, and was sentenced
to a year in prison. He returned to the Oberlin community,
however, and, in the eyes of some people, worked hard to
oust Mahan as president.

        In religious circles the response to the new Oberlin
doctrine of holiness was mixed. The Methodists tended to
be friendly toward it; to them it did not seem very new but
sounded much the same as John Wesley's notion of "the second blessing." In the Preface to the second edition of her
Way of Holiness (1848) Phoebe Palmer prominently featured
Mahan's endorsement of her book. The Presbyterians and
Congregationalists, however, were quite a different matter.
Even New School Presbyterians and New Light Congregationalists looked upon this "new" doctrine as a sort of heresy.

A council of Congregational ministers in Boston, called to ordain a young minister, asked him if he would allow Mahan or Finney to preach in his pulpit. Upon receiving his affirmative answer the council debated five hours whether to continue the ordination! The Presbytery of Poughkeepsie dismissed two of its ministers because they embraced the Oberlin view. One minister was asked if Sacraments administered by an Oberlin clergyman were valid and he replied yes because there is a difference between a pastorate and its incumbent! [27]

In the Watchman of the Valley the editor condemned the divisions within Congregational and Presbyterian churches that the Oberlin doctrine caused. "In one case the seceding Church was organized by President Mahan; in another it was made up of those who preferred Oberlin sympathies." Mahan replied that the Presbyteries were responsible for forcing divisions. [28] The convention at Cleveland had adopted rules for the special purpose of excluding Oberlin. Hence, those who shared Oberlin's views had no other course than to go their own ways as independent Congregational churches.

It must not be supposed that Oberlin received only critical notice. There were pockets of Oberlin sympathizers everywhere. Mahan no doubt was cheered when he read the following words from an editorial in the Morning Star:

> We heartily wish our brethren at Oberlin abundant
> success. Though not of the same denomination as
> ourselves, and differing from us in some important
> points of doctrine, we feel that they are doing a
> good work. The Congregational and Presbyterian
> churches need such an influence among them, and
> though numbers of them have not appreciated its
> labors of love, and not a few have openly repudi-
> ated it, and bitterly persecuted its votaries, yet
> there is scarcely a church in the land that has not
> in some way been reached and benefited by it. [29]

The brethren educated at Oberlin, the editorial continued, have been full of zest and have gone forth to do good things. By their fruits shall ye know them.

College President

Being a college president was a new role for Mahan,

but he was by no means unprepared for it. Ever since leaving Hamilton he had been critical of the quality of student
life and of the rigid classical curriculum invariably prescribed. He long pondered the question of how both could
be improved and to this end he read widely in the literature
of higher education. Nor was he uninformed about the practical and political issues facing the number one administra-
tor of a liberal arts college. We will consider each of
these matters in order.

As a student at Hamilton Mahan had been appalled by
the lawless behavior of many of his peers. The cannon episode was extreme, of course, but in small things as well
as large the students often broke rules in a rebellious fashion, breaking them on principle, so to speak. Why was
this the case? Mahan considered the question during his
Pittsford and Cincinnati years and concluded that the fault
lay with the very structure of college government and discipline. The faculty expected students to be disobedient and
disrespectful--weren't all students?--so they acted with sus-
picion from the start, checking rooms during study hours,
attendance and behavior at chapel, and so on through the
more than one hundred college rules and regulations. The
students acted according to what was expected of them and
it became a kind of duty to frustrate their teachers.

Another cause of lawlessness, Mahan felt, was the
rigid caste system. Students were to rise when the faculty
entered the classroom or chapel, give them the inside of
the walk and lift their hats and bow in recognition. In addressing faculty members students were required to use full
titles while the students were addressed bluntly as "Jones,"
"Parker," or "Mahan." In chapel and other assembly occasions the faculty sat en masse in front, the seniors as a
block behind them, and so on to the freshman class in the
back of the hall. The overall effect of this caste distinction
was to eliminate any sense of belonging to a community and
to produce a "club loyalty" that was antagonistic to the college as a whole and which resulted in that lawlessness which
the faculty had expected all along. [30]

As president of Oberlin he was determined, Mahan
wrote, to treat students as responsible human beings both
because they were responsible and because so acting would
help avoid a re-enactment of the usual scene, views shared
by the rest of the Oberlin faculty. A code of conduct was
drawn up but not printed until it had been read in public

assembly and had received the approval of the students. According to James H. Fairchild, student and faculty member during Mahan's tenure and eventually third president of Oberlin, no strict personal surveillance was ever undertaken to enforce the rules and no monitorial system ever adopted. "The student has been thrown greatly on his own responsibility, with the understanding that the continued enjoyment of the privileges of the school must depend upon his satisfactory deportment."[31] No study hours were ever prescribed, though years later a limit was put on the amount of time that could be spent in ball playing and other sports that kept students away from study.

In addition there was no formal show of respect and veneration required of the students toward the faculty; the respect and veneration would be informal and mutual as in family life. E. J. Comings, class of 1838, gives us a glimpse into the informal ways of Oberlin:

> The first time I met Pres. Mahan was in June 1835. At the close of his class lecture he grasped my hand heartily, locked his arm into mine-- great, green Green Mountain Boy as I was--and proposed a walk. I listened to his fatherly counsels, and drank in the spirit of kindness with which they were given. Surely I said, this is not much like another college president whom I have known. The next time I saw him, he had a spade and wheelbarrow working like Patrick to build a sidewalk. This coming down to other men's level --this readiness for anything really needful--was one grand secret of the wonderful power of those men, Mahan, Morgan, and others. God bless them![32]

Finally, there was no separation of classes in seating at chapel or at assemblies of any kind. In all such gatherings "pupils and spectators were to be seated promiscuously, like people elsewhere on public occasions." The only segregated seating was between men and women. Most faculty members preferred it that way but they all agreed that such decorum was necessary to allay the fears of outsiders that co-education was an immoral thing to begin with. And yet in dining and social affairs men and women freely mixed. Apparently these did not count as official occasions.

The result of the informal ambience was, on the whole,

encouraging. At Oberlin--and later at Adrian College--there
was little of the mischief and disorder that characterized
most campuses, and there was no hazing of members in
lower classes. Visitors in Oberlin were usually well impressed. Asa's old friend Joel Parker found the students
feeding birds for relaxation; Jabez Burns, a Scottish clergyman, said he never witnessed more genuine, unaffected piety
than there; and the principal of the Ladies Seminary in Gene-
va, New York, found the behavior and conversation of the
Oberlin men and women better than at her own tables where
only women were present. [33]

That the absence of harshness and the presence of
trust was rewarded is not surprising. No doubt in part the
students acted in a trustworthy fashion because they were
treated in that manner. It must also be kept in mind, however, that a good deal of piety existed among the Oberlin
students from the beginning, and that even more piety was
imported with the mature and older Lane Rebels. Indeed,
checking on Lyman, Whipple, and Thome to see that they
attended chapel and tended to their studies would somehow
have seemed absurd. However, there can be little doubt
that the trust of the faculty and the reliability of the advanced students acted as a powerful example to the students
in the preparatory department.

In spite of what has been said it would be a grave
mistake to think that all was sunshine and light between
teachers and students. To begin with, there was the famous,
or infamous, case of Delazon Smith. Smith and several other students declared themselves to be atheists and were accordingly dismissed from the Oberlin Church, several of
them expelled from the college, and Smith expelled from the
literary societies of which he was a member. Leaving the
village for Cleveland after several months, he retaliated by
publishing a pamphlet, "Oberlin Unmasked," in which he
damned everything about the institution including its faculty,
food, morals, and religion. The pamphlet was greedily de-
voured by all who were opposed to co-education, abolitionism, and sanctification, and was reprinted to meet the large
demand. [34]

Even if one dismisses "Oberlin Unmasked" as self
serving and biased, the Faculty Records show that Oberlin
was not without disciplinary problems, some connected with
the co-educational feature of the Institute and others not.
On May 13, 1835, a student confessed to stealing various

articles, and the next day "it was voted that the President
be appointed to advise the said H___ K___ to leave the Institution as a better course--better for her and the other
members of the Institution." Even expulsion, it would seem,
was done gently. On June 27, 1836, "a petition was presented signed by several students praying that the partition
in the hall between the Ladies' and Gentlemen's departments
be made more secure." The Agent was requested to secure
it, but perhaps he was not sufficiently thorough since on
February 26 it "appeared that Mr. W___ had visited the
room of one of the young Ladies without permission, though
he was fully aware at the time that he was violating a fundamental law of the Institution." It was voted that in the
future all such violations should be punished with expulsion.
On October 23, 1837, it was resolved "that O___ H___ be
publicly expelled from this institution for the inexcusable vio-
lation of two marriage engagements ... and for lying in regard to the last of those engagements." In June of 1840 the
faculty voted that no woman student would be permitted to
room with any family "in which the rules of the Boarding
Hall respecting the intercourse of ladies and gentlemen are
not observed." In July, however, the real bomb exploded.
A student named Horace Norton had written vulgar and soliciting letters to a woman student, and when he appeared
at the rendezvous met, instead of the student, a group of
men including Timothy Hudson of the faculty. Hudson prayed
over Norton, and when he did not repent Hudson lashed him.
Norton of course was expelled, but the majority of the faculty did not condone what the "avengers" had done. Mahan
joined the minority (including Cowles, Fairchild, and Hudson)
in refusing to condemn Hudson. [35] Norton's parents sued
Hudson and the others at the scene and secured damages.

In 1843 there was a less dramatic episode but, in its
fundamental bearings on the reputation of the Institute, one
just as serious. Five women were present at the faculty
meeting on April 22 "to answer charges of having received
visits from young gentlemen at their rooms." By 1845 the
problems resulting from co-education seemed to require in-
vestigation, and Professors Amasa Walker and Henry Cowles
and also Mary Dix Mahan were appointed members of a committee charged with inquiring into the matter and making
recommendations. The committee concluded that men and
women were sometimes too much engrossed in each other's
company. "This tendency makes it necessary to adopt specific rules respecting calls, visits, late hours, study hours,
walking out in the evening, rides into the country, etc." A

correlative problem was that couples became engaged too
early and then frequently revoked their commitments. Apparently the aforementioned rules were the remedy for this
kind of situation also. The committee emphasized that the
results of co-education were very valuable but that closer
supervision was necessary. 36

    The faculty was justifiably concerned about student be-
havior and was not simply being prudish since, given the
climate of opinion at the time, any co-educational enterprise
was suspect to begin with, and hence any events, even wholly innocent ones, that could be construed adversely had to
be avoided. Happily the feeling against co-education at Oberlin softened when the public became acquainted with its product. Oberlin students had a wide exposure to the public and
their high quality and standard became generally recognized.
Even while they were students they scattered widely during
the three-month winter off-term and most of them taught
school or preached in widely scattered communities. After
graduation many students became teachers, ministers, missionaries, and health officials throughout the state, nation,
and world. And so it was that the critics of Oberlin had
the opportunity to see the products of the college, and they
liked what they saw--industrious, practical, moral, and pious
people. The institution which produced them demanded respect.

    Mahan already had doubts about the value of a rigid
classical education when he was a student at Hamilton, and
he was a definite opponent of it by the time he was elected
president of the Oberlin Collegiate Institute. Such an education, he felt, was pernicious, impractical, and superficial.
He was influenced in his thinking by the educational philosophy of Francis Wayland, president of Brown University,
though he made no more headway in curricular changes at
Oberlin than Wayland managed at Brown. He had more success at Adrian, and Wayland eventually succeeded in intro-
ducing some changes in the Brown curriculum. But it remained for Charles William Eliot, the first non-ministerial
president at Harvard College, to break the back of the classical curriculum--the first vertebrae cracking in 1869.

    President Mahan felt that much of classical literature,
particularly Roman authors, was morally pernicious and an-
tithetical to Christian values, the reading of which seemed
like an odd preparation for the ministry or any other occupation. Needless to say, he did not advocate the total elim-

ination of classical authors--such a view would have received no hearing at all--but advocated that less time be
spent on them and that there be substituted classics more
suitable for Christians. During his first week in Oberlin
Mahan was "interviewed" by a student who reported his an-
tipathy to the "heathen classics," after which a debate was
promptly arranged between the president and the professor
of classics, Seth Waldo, before the Oberlin Lyceum. From
a letter written soon after the debate by Henry Brown, a
student who had heard the debate, it seemed to have been
an uneven match: "The Pres. not only proved their pernicious influence and got the better of the Profes., but upset him and trod him under feet, and now in that respect
rules 'cock of the walk.'"[37] Some students as a lark built
a fire and tossed their worn out Virgils into it carefully
saving their good copies for the next day's recitations. The
incident was reported in the press as a serious burning of
the classics and did Oberlin much harm, much to Mahan's
mortification. His sense of humor did not help matters.
Seeing it for the prank it was, he remarked that never before had the classics given off more light. Waldo was
frightened, needlessly so, about the future of classics at
Oberlin and resigned. Mahan regretted the incident and
said so, the only time Fairchild remarked in later years
to D. L. Leonard that he could remember the president saying he regretted anything. [38]

        Mahan also strongly believed that a rigid classical
education was impractical and undemocratic. America was
growing and needed colleges to prepare its young people for
other occupations in addition to the ministry. Instead of
spending so much time on the classics, he would have students also study seriously the natural sciences, American
law, history, biography, literature, and modern languages. [39]
America needed well educated teachers, lawyers, economists,
politicians, and an educated citizenry in general; and a rigid
classical course was ill-adapted to achieve these goals.

        The proponents of a classical education, of course,
had a response, one that consisted in pointing out what they
took to be the whole point of a liberal education. Studying
Greek and Latin grammar, proving mathematical theorems,
and testing the validity of syllogisms strengthened and disciplined the mind so that a person could think well in all
areas and could acquire the rest of his knowledge without a
formal or detailed course of instruction in it. Mahan was
unimpressed by this argument. Was there any conclusive

evidence to show that there was a carry-over effect from
one study to another? Mahan was unconvinced and in any
case whatever "discipline" was involved in the study of Greek
and Latin literature could just as surely be gained by the
study of Hebrew and Greek Scriptures.[40] Moreover, experience showed that students did not easily pick up other
subjects as a result of having a disciplined mind. The best
way to study modern languages, history, politics, art, and
literature is to study them systematically and not expect to
learn them on the side.

    Mahan managed to introduce certain curricular re-
forms including either the introduction or increased support
of courses such as Hebrew, Cousin's psychology, anatomy
and physiology, political economy, public speaking, Cowper's
poetry, Milton's poetry, the science and art of sacred music, and lessons in the English Bible, courses not to be
found in the catalogues of most other colleges. John Morgan
was cool even to these modest changes, while John Cowles
violently objected to them insisting that "nothing could ever
be made of a course in English Poetry." Cowles was astonished that Milton possibly could be of use in so advanced a
class as the third year of college. He was also against co-
education, holiness, and dietary reforms. He and Mahan
clashed, and the latter wrote to Finney asking him to try
his hand at bringing Cowles to reason. In June 1839 Finney
wrote Cowles and criticized him for having "disappointed
and pained some of your best friends." The trustees fired
Cowles in October, and he retaliated by publishing sixteen
letters bitterly attacking Oberlin.[41]

    In the long run, however, the view of Cowles pre-
vailed, though he had long departed from the scene. The
faculty grew increasingly conservative on curricular matters
and after Mahan left Oberlin in 1850 even the minor reforms
he had supported were abandoned. Hebrew was discontinued
and the study of Latin fully reinstated. Oberlin then had
essentially the same rigid classical curriculum as Yale,
Amherst, and Western Reserve. Wayland's and Mahan's
views only reached fruition at Harvard in 1869 and then
gradually spread to all colleges and universities.[42]

    Finally, Mahan felt that the classical curriculum was
superficial. He did not mean, of course, that the study of
the classics and mathematics was superficial--far from it.
He meant that the other topics and areas of study--political
economy, public speaking, and belles lettres, to name only

a few--were superfically done, either taught as part of
another course or incompetently taught in a brief course
by someone trained in another area. Instead of cheap sub-
stitutes he felt that the college curriculum should be enriched by the introduction of full courses in political economy, modern literature, modern history, art, public speaking, and so on, these courses to be taught be specialists in
the subjects. The crucial result would be that with a wide
range of competently taught courses not everyone could or
should be required to take precisely the same course of
study. The student, in short, should be able to mold, in
part at least, a course of study fitting his own specific requirements and abilities. Mahan, in short, was an early
proponent of the elective system eventually introduced at
Harvard by Eliot. Even after the reforms of Eliot had
spread widely through American colleges, the Oberlin faculty, still conservative on curricular matters, continued to
resist change until pressure was brought to bear by alumni
and trustees in the 1880's.[43]

      The practical and political issues facing Mahan as
president were of no small dimensions. To begin with,
there were the innumerable routine details of college life
to attend to, an enormous correspondence to cope with, and,
after the collapse of Arthur Tappan's silk business and the
Panic of 1837, financial problems to solve. Oberlin agents
in the field simply could not get enough donations to meet
the institution's barest needs, and there was no endowment
whatever. Faculty salaries were often not met in full and
often tardily. Sometimes part of the payment came in commodities rather than currency. The faculty members wrote
numerous letters to college officials and trustees enumerat-
ing in detail their plight. All supplemented their incomes,
for example, by taking in boarders or preaching in the winter term. As we have seen, Mahan entirely supported himself for a time by his winter preaching. Eventually William
Dawes and various trustees, supported by Mahan, proposed
that no one in the college receive a fixed salary but work on
the "faith mission" concept of dividing in appropriate amounts
whatever money the agents were able to collect. The faculty
members strenuously opposed this proposal and with the support of Lewis Tappan made the trustees abandon the idea.
The faculty was not happy with Mahan's support of Dawes
and the trustees.[44] In spite of believing that Mahan had a
greater facility in conviction than in conciliation, the judicious James Fairchild wrote in later years that Mahan's "administration of the college was, in general, successful, and

he gave his heart and strength to its prosperity without any
reservation."45

    There was, however, from the beginning a power
struggle between the president and faculty of the Institute.
Throughout its history the Oberlin faculty has had far more
power, and the president less, than at other colleges and
universities. This tradition began already during Mahan's
administration. It will be recalled that the Board of Trustees agreed that they would not interfere with internal matters of the Institute--that was explicitly insisted upon by
Finney and implicitly assumed by Mahan, Morgan, and the
Lane Rebels as a condition for their coming to Oberlin. The
faculty was to decide the policy for admitting students, ar-
ranging curricular matters, and so on. But, as it happened,
the faculty was just as insistent that the president have no
power to interfere with their decisions either. The president was to have no special power, his vote was to count
for one like any other faculty member, and while he carried
some issues by persuasion and the force of his personality
he was, on the whole, defeated on most issues. As we have
seen, he was opposed on curricular reform (and what reform did occur disappeared after his departure) as well as
on the faith mission view of salaries. We will see other
ways in which the faculty put down his ideas, including his
efforts to implement the rights of women students. The
president and the faculty sometimes had prickly sessions,
and the president more than once became exasperated with
his timid, cautious, judicious (which?) faculty. James Fairchild reported the following incident to Delevan Leonard:

          At a faculty meeting [Mahan] had laid down the
          law or announced a policy which the faculty sat
          down on to a man. When he arose, [he] said
          gentlemen I can't remain in such a place and left.
          They went on as though nothing had happened and
          did the business, and later he came back with a
          smile as though nothing had happened. 46

    Mahan was a member of the Board of Trustees, and
the faculty worried that Mahan might succeed in getting his
programs through by virtue of influencing the other members
of the board. The board had agreed not to interfere in the
internal management of the Institute, but it still had strong
policy forming power. Fairchild reported to Leonard that
in order to get the faculty viewpoint across to the trustees
they managed to have Henry Cowles appointed to the board

even though it was against the rules to have a professor on
it. Fairchild reported this matter to Leonard in later years
and his memory had failed him. Cowles was not appointed
as trustee until 1851, a year after Mahan had left Oberlin.
Still there is little doubt that the faculty desired the result
that Fairchild reported as a fact. Finney was appointed to
the board before Mahan left but Finney does not appear a
likely candidate for the role described by Fairchild. [47] He
more or less stayed aloof from the nitty-gritty of academic
life and, in any case, was likely to be off on a revival at
a crucial moment.

Professor of Philosophy

Being president of Oberlin was only a part of Mahan's
job and that not the most time-consuming one. He was as
well Professor of Mental and Moral Philosophy, this being
the top academic position in those days and traditionally
filled by the president of the college. A major part of Mahan's work was teaching philosophy and writing textbooks
and treatises in various philosophical areas. During his
Pittsford and Cincinnati years he had continued most diligently to study his favorite authors and was well prepared
for his classes. His superb speaking ability and his thorough
knowledge of mental and moral philosophy made his success
as a teacher almost certain. That he was a first-rate teacher, and popular even though tough, is clear: students who
took his courses were enthusiastic about them, and the tradition of his excellence as a teacher carried through gener-
ations of students who came to Oberlin after Mahan had left.
Even the faculty, particularly Fairchild, found him an outstanding teacher.

According to Leonard S. Parker, '38, "under President Mahan, I studied mental and moral philosophy, and
heard lessons never to be forgotten touching 'fundamental
principles.'" Mrs. Douglass Putnam, '39, Lit., said that
when "Mahan and Finney arrived we were awakened, stimulated, and instructed on subjects far beyond what occupies
the minds of the girls of the present day [1883]." W. M.
Barbour, '59, included Mahan as one of the "four grand men
... who came here to lead in the theological instruction."
"[They] have gone apart from us, but their impress is still
on this place and on this generation [1883]." J. L. Patton,
'59, said to Oberlin's Jubilee audience in 1883, "If there are
such men here in unbroken succession--men of the mind and

heart and spirit to follow Mahan and Finney ... and others
like them, then this will still be <u>Oberlin College</u> through the
coming decade."[48]

James H. Fairchild, whenever he had occasion to
write about Oberlin's history, never failed to praise Mahan
as a teacher. In his 1860 monograph on Oberlin history he
wrote that mental science and metaphysics was a prominent
specialty at Oberlin "due mainly to the influence of President Mahan, whose tastes and culture led him in that direction." In his classic <u>Oberlin: the Colony and the College</u>
(1883) he observed that Mahan was an enthusiastic teacher
and gave a powerful impetus to the study of philosophy at
Oberlin. "The whole school shared more or less in [Ma-
han's enthusiasm for philosophy]."[49] A. T. Swing, Fairchild's biographer, nicely sums up these estimates:

> President Mahan is spoken of with great loyalty
> by the early students as a powerful reasoner on
> the public platform, and as an inspiring teacher
> of mental and moral philosophy. And there is no
> question that he exerted a great influence not only
> on the student body but on the whole new life of
> the community. James Fairchild who was one of
> the brightest students in his classes has said of
> his distinctive work that "he gave an impetus to
> the study of philosophy at the time which it has
> never lost."[50]

Mahan was not only intellectually stimulating to his
students but cared about them personally. We have already
seen how he took students with him to debates out of town
and how he kindly, even affectionately, helped E. J. Comings to adjust to Oberlin life as a new student. When Sherlock Bristol had a lung infection during term and had to return to his home in Connecticut the president accompanied
him to Cleveland to see that he safely got aboard the steamer for Buffalo. According to Bristol, "his words of cheer
and words of love were among the most stimulating and hope-
inspiring I ever heard."[51]

It must not be supposed, however, that the president
always treated students gently and kindly. He suffered neither fools nor laggards gladly and could upon occasion be
devastating. Under the stress of administrative duties without presidential powers and under attack from outsiders (and
some faculty members again) for his views on reform, cur-

riculum, and religion, Mahan could even speak harshly to a
student without sufficient justification. While no such incident is documented, references are made to them by sources
which were entirely sympathetic to Mahan. [52] Nevertheless,
in spite of these incidents, we have seen that the president
was not only an effective but also a popular teacher of the
Oberlin Collegiate Institute--probably the most effective and
popular one in his day.

In 1840 Mahan had printed in Oberlin his Abstract of
a Course of Lectures on Mental and Moral Philosophy to be
used as a textbook for Oberlin students. In it, in embryonic
form, are the theses which would be expanded in the three
later philosophical books published during his Oberlin years:
A System of Intellectual Philosophy, 1845; The Doctrine of
the Will, 1845; and The Science of Moral Philosophy, 1848.

Mahan's Intellectual Philosophy was widely read and
went through many editions. First published in New York
City by Saxton and Miles, a second edition was published
by Harper and Brothers in 1847, and a revised and enlarged
version of the second edition was published by A. S. Barnes
in New York and H. W. Derby in Cincinnati in 1854. Reprintings continued at least until 1857 and probably longer.
Of this influential book Charles M. Perry, a recent scholar
in American intellectual history, writes, "Asa Mahan ...
read Kant and his successors with shrewd intelligence,
though after all his wanderings in forbidden territory he
came safely back to Scottish common sense. The reader
of his Intellectual Philosophy, published in 1845, is astounded at the accuracy of his knowledge and the keen-ness of
his criticism."[53] Significant as Intellectual Philosophy is,
however, for biographical purposes The Doctrine of the Will
and The Science of Moral Philosophy are more important.

The Doctrine of the Will also had a long publishing
history. It was first published simultaneously in New York
by M. H. Newman and in Oberlin by R. E. Gillett. A second edition was published in 1846 by J. K. Wellman of New
York and a third edition in 1847 by J. M. Fitch of Oberlin.
It was another successful book which Jabez Burns, a Scottish
clergyman, in his Doctrinal Conversations called a "most
complete vindication of the Freedom of the Will," an "in-
comparable book," and the best answer, along with Eli Noyes,
to Jonathan Edwards' arguments against free will. [54]

Mahan's Doctrine of the Will was particularly impor-

tant for religious purposes. As we have seen earlier, Mahan in seminary or soon thereafter already had accepted
New School views and so had already formulated various
arguments against Old School Calvinism. He articulated these
arguments and added many others in defense of free will in
his Doctrine of the Will, but he added something infinitely
more important. In this book for the first time he answered
Edwards' claim that Calvinistic determinism and human freedom, and hence moral responsibility, are perfectly compatible. Mahan's rebuttal of Edwards' view is a first-rate piece
of philosophical analysis.

         According to Edwards, freedom means the power or
ability to do as one pleases. One is unfree only if he is
compelled to do other than he wishes. A man is not responsible for what he is compelled to do, but he is responsible for what he does when he is not coerced. After all,
in such cases he is the one who did as he pleased and so
is responsible. Mahan objected that this argument confuses
several senses of the word freedom, a confusion made evident by comparing "freedom" with the concepts of servitude
and necessity. Freedom contrasted with servitude means
that a man can do as he pleases; he is not in chains or
forced by other constraints to do other than he would. Freedom contrasted with necessity means that a man can please
(or will) to do one thing rather than another; he is under no
constraint to will or choose the way he does in fact. Freedom in the second sense is what is required for the ascription of responsibility. Edwards allowed only freedom in the
first sense and offered it, irrelevantly, as sufficient grounds
for ascribing responsibility. Mahan summed up the point
succinctly: Determinism is identical with Fatalism "in its
worst form"; they both alike affirm that man can "do as he
pleases" and both agree that "man cannot but please to do
as he does."[55]

         The Science of Moral Philosophy was first published
in 1848 by J. M. Fitch of Oberlin and was reprinted as late
as 1884. In it Mahan criticized all teleological moral systems and defended a deontological one. Edwards, Paley,
and Bentham, though different in crucial respects, were all
teleologists because they insisted that only one thing is intrinsically valuable--be it pleasure, happiness, or well-being
for everyone, including God--and that all other acts and intentions are right or dutiful only insofar as they are condu-
cive to achieving this end. Mahan insisted, however, that
there are many basic rights and duties which cannot be re-

duced to one all-inclusive principle. Obligations, duties,
and rights depend upon perceiving certain "fitting relation-
ships." That maximizing happiness (or universal well-being) and justice are irreducible concepts, he insisted, follows from the fact that only virtuous people deserve to be
happy. [56]

     Mahan's deontological moral view throws much light
on his behavior, though we need to analyze the notions of
"deontology" and "teleology" more fully in order to see how
this is the case. Which view is more rigorous in its moral
demands? In one way teleology might seem to be more demanding since the utilitarian, the most important example
of teleology, seems committed to do all kinds of morally
heroic acts, such as giving almost all one's worldly goods
to the poor. In another way, however, the utilitarian is
less demanding. He will justify breaking moral rules if the
evidence strongly suggests that doing so will maximize well-
being. Although telling the truth in general is our duty since
it leads to good results, it would be wrong to tell the truth
on a specific occasion if the results overall would be painful.
On this issue the deontologist is more demanding; he holds
moral rules to be inviolable and so is inflexible about what
constitutes right or wrong in any situation. For him justice
is quite independent of good results, of well-being, and to
act justly often causes hardship and pain. Justice must be
done, so to speak, though the heavens fall. No one accepted
this consequence of the deontological position more strongly
than Mahan; indeed it would be closer to the truth to say he
embraced it. To some people Mahan's view of morality is
sublime and to others it is harsh, abrasive, and uncompromising. However one feels about the issue it is impossible
to understand Brother Mahan, either his inner life or what
he did, without giving great weight to his deontological motives. No one was more willing than he to do what he took
to be his duty even though the heavens fell. To emancipate
the slave, he thought, a person must be willing to risk losing all his goods and even his life. When enough people
feel that way, the slave will be emancipated. Teleologists
like Finney and Fairchild looked upon Mahan's views as
risky and fraught with the possibilities of disaster, as indeed they were. But perhaps the best way to judge as well
as understand people is to discover the risks they are willing to incur and why.

     Mahan's moral views also throw light on his relations
with Finney. In his Science of Moral Philosophy he devoted

the most space to expose what he took to be the errors in
the moral philosophy of his colleague. He showed great di-
alectical skill in arguing against Finney's version of Jonathan
Edwards' teleological ethics. His strategy was to show that
Finney's views were simply a variation of the principle of util-
ity and to press the attack from that vantage point. He realized,
of course, that the evangelist's views were not identical with
either Bentham's or Paley's utilitarianism, but he argued that
they all shared the common flaw of being teleological. 57

  Finney objected strenuously to the claim that he was
a utilitarian and had mixed feelings about Mahan when he
wrote to James Morison on January 5, 1851. He was not
quite able to hide his irritation behind his declarations of
affection.

> Have you read my Dear Br. Mahan's Moral Phil-
> osophy? If so you have noted the sad confusion of
> his mind on the question of the foundation of Ob-
> ligation. ... I was obliged to write a review of
> it for the use of the students, which I have in
> manuscript, but dislike to publish because I so
> much love Br. M. and because of my relations
> to him. ... I feared that Dear Br. M. would fall
> into confusion just as he did because in his former
> treatise [Abstracts of a Course of Lectures?] he
> had done so. But I am sorry to say that on this
> question his confusion rather increases than other-
> wise. 58

The judgment of subsequent scholars locates the confusion in
Finney's thinking rather than Mahan's. Finney was a gifted
evangelist, but as a philosopher or biblical scholar he was
not first-rate.

  Finally, in his classrooms and in his Abstract and
Moral Philosophy Mahan found many opportunities for incul-
cating in his students an enthusiasm for and dedication to
reform measures. He never tired of telling them that it
was the duty of a citizen "to regard the law of right or the
will of God as of supreme authority above all human enact-
ments." This doctrine is the "Higher Law" of Emerson,
Thoreau, and Theodore Parker, however their moral and
theological foundations for it might differ. "In his lectures
before the seniors Mahan trained himself and his hearers
for those remarkable series of debates on come-outerism
and war." Indeed, "the chief link between the Oberlin curriculum and the real world of reform societies and fugitive

slaves was through 'Mental and Moral Philosophy.'"59 Mahan, unlike Francis Wayland at Brown, was not content simply to speak the truth as he saw it and denounce injustice,
though even speaking against slavery, the subjection of wom-
en, and intemperance took courage in those early days.   Mahan acted on his principles even though the course of action
cost him dearly, just as it had in Cincinnati.

Anti-Slavery Activity

Mahan's attack on slavery had three parts: turning
the Visible Church into the True Church and thus making it
an antislavery instrument; creating new channels for combatting slavery within the Constitutional framework; and being civilly disobedient toward fugitive slave laws, whether
state or federal.   On all of these points Mahan and the vast
majority of the Oberlin community agreed.   However cautious
or conservative some people might have been on different
issues, the community was united in its abolitionism.

The Oberlin Congregational Church used numerous religious sanctions in its antislavery crusade.   No slaveholder
could preach or commune in the church, no transfer would
be given to any church which was not against slavery, and
after 1846 all fellowship was withdrawn from any people who
would lend their influence to sustain slavery.   Fellowship
was not withdrawn from a church that was itself antislavery
even if its ecclesiastical hierarchy had not declared against
slavery.   The members of the church cooperated fully with
the antislavery elements in other denominations, particularly
with the Free-will Baptists and the Wesleyan Methodists.
The antislavery church was wholly nondenominational and became an increasingly potent factor through the years in turning Northern sentiment in favor of the slave.   A denomination poorly represented in the antislavery church was the
Presbyterian.   Its congregations were the most affluent and
had the most to lose by the abolition of slavery.

The Oberlin Church strongly supported the Christian
antislavery conventions.   It was important, Mahan felt, to
have some strictly Christian antislavery society to offset the
notion that abolitionism was exclusively the affair of nonbelievers like William Lloyd Garrison.   In 1850 the Christian
Anti-Slavery Convention met in Mahan's old church in Cincinnati, by then renamed the Vine Street Congregational
Church.   In 1851 the convention met in Chicago and Mahan
and Finney were elected vice presidents.   Oberlin men and

women tried to keep the movement alive but by 1854 it had
lost most of its force. [60]   Part of the force lost was Mahan,
who departed from Oberlin in 1850.

Mahan's political activity in support of the abolition
of slavery consisted in helping form an antislavery third
party as an alternative to the Whigs and Democrats.   Brother
Mahan and the majority of the Oberlin community were originally Whigs, but they quickly became disillusioned.   In 1839
many members of the Whig Party in the Ohio legislature, including the member elected by Oberlin voters, had helped en-
act a strong fugitive slave law.   As a result, the formation
of a new political party was advocated at a meeting of the
American Anti-Slavery Society in Cleveland.   Both Mahan
and Finney spoke in favor of this proposal.   Garrison and
his followers objected because they refused to acknowledge
the Constitution as a moral document.   The society split on
this issue and those favoring political action, like the Oberlin community, formed the American and Foreign Anti-Slavery Society and the Liberty Party, which in April 1840 at
the convention in Albany nominated James G. Birney for
President.   Oberlin leaders supported the Liberty Party in
various ways and also continued to support actively various
antislavery societies on the local and state as well as national level.   In 1848 Mahan attended the Buffalo convention
at which the Free Soil Party was organized and Martin Van
Buren nominated for President and Charles Francis Adams
for Vice President.   The Oberlin people were partial to
Adams.   Again the Oberlin leaders supported this antislavery
party and they carried almost the whole of the community
with them this time.

Mahan had left Oberlin by the time the Republican
Party was formed but he supported it in Michigan, the state
in which the party originated.   In fact, in 1859 the party
members asked him to go to Cleveland to speak at the jail
in support of the Oberlin citizens who had been arrested for
aiding a runaway slave to escape.   Fortunately the jailer
was sympathetic toward the Republican Party and his captives.
He allowed Mr. Fitch, superintendent of the Oberlin Sunday
School, to teach his class in the jail yard one Sunday morning.   The leaders of the Republican Party encouraged Fitch
and the other prisoners and made political capital out of the
ensuing trial.   They staged an antislavery mass meeting in
the Cleveland Public Square in front of the jail yard.   Resolutions were passed and addresses were delivered by Asa
Mahan, Joshua Giddings, and Salmon P. Chase, Governor of
Ohio. [61]

Oberlin civil disobedience began in 1835, when the college was refounded, and consisted in the flouting of all fugitive slave laws whether state or federal. Oberlin was an extremely important part of the Underground Railroad. Through the years many hundreds of runaway slaves found shelter in Oberlin, some staying indefinitely and others stopping only long enough for arrangements to be made for their passage to Canada. Oberlin had the incredible record of never losing a single runaway slave to federal marshals. Most of the Oberlin community cooperated in this type of civil disobedience. Township funds were regularly set aside as part of the budget for taking care of runaway slaves. [62]

President Mahan's house was one of those, among others, in which runaway slaves were regularly hidden. Mahan is reported to have said that should the authorities attempt to capture the fugitives he and other members of the community would fight until the last, though this report came from Delazon Smith and may be exaggerated. [63] There is, however, probably a kernel of truth in it.

Some members of the community were disobedient in more militant ways. In the autumn of 1839 James A. Thome, a Lane Rebel who was now a member of the Oberlin faculty, went into hiding temporarily because of the role he had played in preventing an aged Negro woman in Kentucky from being sold into slavery. Three Oberlin students even invaded the South and helped slaves escape to Illinois. George Thompson and Calvin Fairbank were apprehended in this activity and spent substantial terms in prison. There is no indication that Mahan sympathized with these completely radical activities, and there is evidence that other Oberlinians, including Fairchild, were wholly unsympathetic to them. Indeed, the majority of the community disapproved of the course taken by Thompson and Fairbank, though by 1864 they came to look upon Fairbank as something of a hero.

Mahan was a relentless critic of Garrison. The editor of the Liberator, he felt, wrongly rejected the Visible Church altogether instead of helping to return it to the True Church and wrongly rejected political efforts to combat slavery on the grounds that the Constitution was an instrument of slavery. Mahan denied that it was a pro-slavery document, decried Garrison's secessionist views, and was himself a staunch Unionist. [64] In spite of his distaste for Garrison's view, he believed that Garrison and his adherents had a right to be heard anywhere, including Oberlin. The Oberlin faculty did not share his view. Stephen and Abby

Foster, ardent Garrisonians, wanted to speak at Oberlin in
1846, but on the whole only Mahan, blacks, and students
were in favor of it. Finney ridiculed Mahan for being willing to debate the Fosters, but Mahan believed that truth cannot prosper by ignoring its detractors and that a platform is
not free if open only to those who agree with what the audience already believes. [65] In his Baccalaureate Sermon on
June 18, 1911, President Henry Churchill King reminded his
audience of the origin of the Oberlin tradition of hearing all
sides of an issue: "What has not always been duly recognized [is that] thru President Mahan, and probably as the
direct result of his experience of the attempt to suppress
free discussion in Lane Seminary, it became a habit of the
new community to furnish a free platform for the full discussion of all pressing questions, whether social or philosophical, dietetic, political, moral, or religious; and the
intellectual life of the new community was thus [particular-
ly] stimulating. "[66]

    The debate between Mahan and the Fosters was stren-
uous and for the most part was a technical discussion about
the Constitution, though both sides engaged in ad hominem
remarks. Foster always described the clergy as a "brotherhood of thieves" and Mahan imputed the motives of hate and
injustice to Garrisonians. "Come-outerism" was like a huge
monster equipped with great claws "each armed with hellish
daggers." References to "hellish daggers" and the rough-
and-tumble of the debate in general fueled faculty views that
Mahan's language was too pungent and indiscreet, perhaps
even unchristian. The Fosters, however, viewed things differently. In a letter printed in the Liberator, October 23,
1846, they acknowledged that Mahan "was very gentlemanly
in deportment." They were not shocked by tough remarks,
either given or taken, and no doubt regarded Mahan as a
gentleman primarily because he fought for their right to
speak at all. "Professor Finney said the spirit of God left
the place immediately upon our entering it; and Professor
Morgan publicly declared that they should not have opened
the Chapel for us, had it not been for the colored people. "[67]

    Garrison himself, with Frederick Douglass, came to
Oberlin in 1847, and he and Mahan debated in front of a
sizable audience, each remaining unruffled throughout the
performance. Garrison wrote to his wife that Mahan "was
perfectly respectful, and submitted to our interrogations
with good temper and courtesy." "As a disputant, he is
adroit and plausible, but neither vigorous nor profound."

With a few exceptions to be noted later the Oberlin audience,
understandably, was wholly with Mahan. One member wrote
that "the reply of Prest. Mahan was masterly and dignified,
overturning and scattering to the winds every position of his
opponent."[68] It is interesting to note that not long after his
appearance in Oberlin Douglass deserted the come-outer
ranks and joined the growing group that advocated the fighting of slavery through political channels.

Mahan criticized Garrison again in 1849 while lecturing in England and Scotland. He spoke against slavery in
London, where he addressed a large audience in a room ad-
joining the Surrey Chapel, and in Glasgow, under the auspices of the Evangelical Union. While talking with the Reverend William Scott, Mahan, when asked about antislavery
activity in America, replied that much good work was done
by abolitionists who, unlike Garrison, did not alienate the
community by attacking the Bible and the Constitution. He
said to Scott that Garrison spoke one word for the slave
and two against the church. Scott understood him to mean
that Garrison spoke two words against the pro-slavery dimension of the church and not against the church in general.
Others understood Mahan as saying that Garrison attacked
the church in general, and they withdrew their support from
his organization and made their weight felt elsewhere.

After Mahan returned to the States he became aware
of the differences of opinion concerning what he had said
and quickly made it clear in a letter to Scott published in
the Glasgow Examiner, April 24, 1852, that Scott was wrong
and the others were right in their interpretation of his remarks. Concerning Garrison and the American Anti-Slavery
Society he wrote, "I believe that I give not only my own but
the almost, if not quite, undivided opinion of Christian men
in this country when I say that this Society, in its fundamental tendencies and aims is not, properly speaking, an
Anti-Slavery Society, but an infidel, no-human-government
movement, using the antislavery sentiment as a club with
which to strike down the Church and the State, and mainly
the former." Mahan said he was willing to join with infidels
in fighting slavery but he was not willing "to lend my countenance for a moment to a society which, masking itself as
an antislavery society, is in fact aiming to prostrate Christianity itself."[69]

Mahan sent Garrison a copy of his letter to Scott, and
Garrison reprinted it in the Liberator for June 4, 1852, along

with an attack on Mahan by R. Wright and a Report on the
Nineteenth Annual New England Anti-Slavery Convention where
Garrison had introduced a resolution condemning the letter.
The Report carried a detailed statement of the debate occasioned by the resolution.   Garrison commented "upon the
bitter and malignant spirit which characterized the letter."
Stephen Foster said derisively that when he was in Oberlin,
Mahan always referred to him as Brother Foster, quite different from the tone of his letter!   Lucy Stone criticized
James H. Fairchild because he was living in a house built
by money from his wife's slave-holding family.   The resolutions condemning Mahan were passed unanimously, but the
charge against Fairchild, which was never part of the resolutions, was not pursued.   In a later issue of the Liberator
Garrison printed a letter from Fairchild which showed the
charge against him to be wholly unfounded; and Garrison
added that the unjust charge "had been made without design
or malice."   The resolutions condemning Mahan and a covering letter by Garrison were sent to the editor of the Glasgow
Examiner, who published them in the issue for June 26,
1852, under the heading "Garrison V. Mahan."   The whole
Mahan-Garrison issue and the resolutions were scrutinized
in a tract published in England in The Friend of the Fugitive
and Antislavery Record by John Guthrie, a prominent Evangelical Union minister who strongly defended Mahan and criticized the resolutions.   The tract was reprinted in the Liberator for May 13, 1853. [70]

As we have seen, Mahan stoutly defended the right
of the Garrisonians to be heard at Oberlin even though in
his opinion they unjustly criticized Christianity and the Constitution of the United States.   And to begin with he had a
high opinion of the sincerity and honesty with which they pursued what he took to be mistaken goals.   He spoke sincerely
when he called Stephen Foster "Brother Foster."   However,
he came to doubt this sincerity which probably accounts for
the increasing vigor of his criticism.   On March 25, 1846,
Lucy Stone wrote to the Fosters that "Prest. Mahan and
Prof. Morgan have both spoken highly of you since you left."
Subsequently Stephen and Abby Foster circulated at Oberlin
a book attacking the observance of the Sabbath.   The book
was written by a man named Fisher and was full of inac-
curate references and unsupported statements.   In lectures
at Oberlin Mahan exposed Fisher's misquotations and questioned Foster's honesty in circulating copies of the book.
Disturbed about the incident, Lucy Stone wrote Abby Foster
on July 3, 1846:

> Up to that time Prest. Mahan had always spoken
> kindly, and highly, of you as honest seekers after
> truth, and uniformly called you brother and sister
> Foster, but now the tide is turned. Some of us
> have no less confidence in your integrity than ever,
> but we are sorry that you circulated the book be-
> fore you proved it. [71]

Mahan and Garrison were much alike; they were pervasively
honest and abrasively uncompromising. It would have mattered little to Mahan whether Foster had knowingly or unwittingly distributed an unworthy book. To act irresponsibly
in his eyes was little better than to act dishonestly.

Co-education and Women's Rights

Co-education was a part of Oberlin when the institution was founded in 1833 by Shipherd and Stewart. The higher education of women, however, was by no means part of
a women's rights ideology, and to so construe it is to mag-
nify the original scope of the founders' enterprise and to
miss the practical nature of their commitment to women's
education. The Institute began largely as a preparatory
school, or academy, with the idea that a collegiate and theological department might well be added as the younger students advanced and wanted the benefits of higher education.
With both the present and future in mind the founders requested, and received, a charter from the Ohio Legislature
that granted the right to educate on all levels (including a
"school for infants" which was short lived).

There was no problem about the preparatory department being co-educational since New England academies had
long taught boys and girls together. The public sentiment
was only against teaching men and women together. What
happened at Oberlin was more an unplanned evolution than
an ideological commitment. There was quickly a demand
for collegiate education and since women were already on
the ground it seemed impolite and arbitrary to send them
away immediately upon completion of the prep course. So
women stayed on for the college course, and others quickly
came only for the college course. The women attended the
same classes in science, philosophy, and so on and had the
same instructors as the men. However, they did not take
the full collegiate course; their program substituted modern
language and literature for much of the classical studies,

and this course of "Literary Study" was under the jurisdic-
tion of the Ladies Department consisting of a principal and
a board made up of the wives of professors.   The official
justification of co-education at Oberlin was that the presence
of women had a civilizing influence on men students and fa-
cilitated their education as well as prepared women for a
more intelligent fulfilling of their subsequent crucial roles
as wives of ministers and other useful citizens and as mothers of children upon whom the future of the fledgling country
depended. [72]

        In light of considerations like the foregoing ones sev-
eral recent commentators have concluded that Oberlin, after
all, cared little about the intrinsic worth of women and that
the institution has received undue credit as a pioneer in the
advancement of women's welfare.   This conclusion is a mistake particularly since these commentators act as if Oberlin
was as biassed as the rest of nineteenth-century American
society. [73] It must be kept in mind that while the "libera-
tion of women" was by no means a goal of the Oberlin community women in fact could get an education there that they
could get nowhere else.   Moreover, the community retained
co-education in the face of much opposition and criticism,
to say nothing of derision.   These rocks of fact withstand
a good deal of pooh-poohing.

        When Asa Mahan arrived in Oberlin he was not in
favor of co-education, nor were Finney and Morgan.   They
tended to accept it as a necessary evil since it was already
on the ground, and they did not intend to let it or anything
else stand in the way of accomplishing what they took to be
the important goals.   However, they were all quickly won
over after they arrived, though Mahan became the most ardent defender of co-education and the chief faculty champion
of its extension.   The first extension came when four women
of the class of 1837 petitioned to take the full college course
and to receive the A. B. degree along with men.   The women
were Mary Hosford, Mary Kellogg, Elizabeth Prall, and
Caroline Mary Rudd (who had followed Aunt Sally's call to
come to Oberlin).   John Morgan, who had become unaccount-
ably conservative since his defense of the Lane Rebels, opposed the idea, though a majority of the faculty, including
Mahan, approved of it for a variety of reasons including,
for some, the disinclination to refuse the request of admirable and noncontentious young ladies.   In the historic commencement of 1841, Hosford, Prall, and Rudd received their
degrees on equal terms with men, "the first bona fide A. B.

degrees ever granted to women." Mahan rejoiced at their
achievement and who can doubt that he took special pride
in loyal Sally Rudd's niece. It was still on his mind when
he wrote in his Autobiography in his eighty-second year, "I
here record the conviction that I have no occasion to be
ashamed to have it universally known that I am the first
man in the history of the race who conducted women through
a full course of liberal education, and conferred upon [them]
the degrees of A.B. and A.M."[74]

In spite of this advance there were numerous restrictions on women in all divisions of the Institute, including
ones prohibiting them from giving speeches in class in front
of men and from reading their own essays at commencement.
President Mahan and James Thome (Lane Rebel and subsequently professor at Oberlin) always favoring "mixed speaking," fought such discrimination, though without effect in the
short run. Thome allowed women to speak publicly in his
declamation class and was told by the faculty to desist. Mahan pressed for Lucy Stone to read her own essay at commencement but was overruled by a majority of the faculty.
The following year, 1848, he tried to get permission for his
daughter Anna to read her own essay on Wednesday with the
men of the class. "But the faculty moved straight along not-
withstanding, and voted that she have the usual alternative
of reading her own piece Tuesday, or of having it read by
some gentleman on Wednesday." Morgan, Dascomb, Fairchild, and other faculty members took dim views of "public
exhibition" on the part of women. According to Fairchild,
if consistency requires going forward and allowing women to
speak at commencement, "then decency requires us to go
backward." The faculty was irritated with Mahan for "agitating the minds of the students on questions which involve
the established order of the Institution."[75]

It might seem strange that what nowadays seems like
a trivial issue should have been taken so seriously by the
Oberlin faculty. However, the issue was far from trivial
in import, as Lucy Stone and Antoinette Brown, as well as
the faculty, saw clearly. These two Oberlin students of the
later 1840's, unlike the first recipients of the A.B. in 1841,
were dedicated advocates of the rights of women and were
acting on principle when they insisted on their right to speak
publicly. They saw public speech not simply as an accom-
plishment or means to self advancement, but as a weapon
vitally needed in fighting for the causes to which they were
committed. As Frances Hosford, historian of Oberlin's

women's history, comments, "the women who led the first
fight for public speech had not the faintest intention of giving parlor talks on parlor topics." Rather "they meant to
join the fight for temperance, abolition, women's rights--
in short, the war against vested interests, of all foes the
most merciless." Lest Hosford sound too favorable to Stone
and Brown we must attend to one of her many qualifying
comments. The two women, she writes, "made a problem"
for the college authorities. "Indeed we might spare some
sympathy for the men and women whose generosity had already gone far beyond the support of public opinion and had
reached the limit even of their own conviction."[76] They
were, however, no problem for Asa Mahan nor had he reached
the limit of his conviction.

In 1859, nine years after Mahan had left, the Oberlin
faculty finally agreed to permit women to read their own
essays at commencement along with men. However, there
were still restrictions. Women were restricted to reading
their essays; they were not allowed to deliver orations.
"This last stronghold," Hosford observes, "was more strenuously defended because it was the last." In 1870 Harriet
L. Keeler shattered the final restraint. At commencement
she started to read her essay and then discarding her manuscript proceeded to deliver the forbidden oration.[77] The
Oberlin faculty was far too polite to interrupt her, and so
a new precedent was established.

That Mahan was the leader of women's rights at Oberlin is further apparent on the issue of women's suffrage.
He not only favored it but was even sanguine about the possibility of getting the majority of men to agree to it. Speaking in Cleveland in 1853 he said, "if the women of this State
want the elective franchise, they can have it. I don't believe it is in the heart of man to refuse it." The proviso
"if women want it" is important. Mahan was never a radical and he tired of women's rights orators talking as if the
role of women in American society resulted from a conspiracy among men to keep them down. He advised the advocates of women's rights to concentrate on convincing the
majority of women to want and then to demand the opportunity to vote.[78]

Mahan's views on women's suffrage were by no means
those of the majority of the Oberlin community. James H.
Fairchild spoke for this majority and was still expressing
the same viewpoint in 1870. He wrote then that the law

should not be changed since it protects the majority of wom-
en in their right not to vote, "a right which they hold as
precious and sacred." If women enter politics they will be
associated with men "in late sessions, in midnight caucuses,
in committee rooms and in the hotels"; is this "likely to
prove refining and elevating? ... I cannot dwell upon this
subject, I only suggest it." The whole thrust of the wom-
en's rights movement is unhappy. In pursuing a profession,
women decline marriage. "Exceptions may be named to
this law, but they are so rare as merely to serve as re-
minders of the law." "There can be but one calling or
profession in a family, and nature has guarded against any
collision." Reformers who advocate suffrage and independ-
ence for women honor the institution of marriage in form
but nevertheless "still hold out to her aims and plans incon-
sistent with these conditions." "Her life-work comes to her
by a higher law, and no human power can make it otherwise."[79] Fairchild's sentiments are grating to the modern
ear and no doubt are not acceptable as a whole, and yet do
they not serve the useful purpose of reminding people on all
sides that for every gain there is a loss and that it is wise
to proceed cautiously and with full understanding?

What did Lucy Stone and Antoinette Brown think of
Oberlin? They appreciated what their alma mater had done
for them, though they were not without reservations. In
speaking at the Semi-Centennial celebration of Oberlin College during Fairchild's presidency, Lucy, after speaking
kindly of Oberlin for what it had done, launched her barb.
Why not go another step, she asked her audience, including
Fairchild, and stand for women's suffrage. Set women apart
from Jefferson Davis, she demanded. After all, the punishment for Davis as president of the Confederacy had been to
deprive him of the right to vote! At a women's rights convention in Cleveland Antoinette said, "Much as I owe to
Oberlin ... it is due to that Institution that these facts should
be made known, for they have the credit with many of rec-
ognizing full equality between the sexes, in the matter of
education, at least, and they do not wish that credit."[80]
President Mahan was another matter. In her "Reminiscences
of Early Oberlin" Antoinette wrote:

> Pres. Mahan was in office for two years after
> I entered college. He was liberal and criticized
> on that account. I used to air my pet opinions
> in my compositions and one of them was an ex-
> egesis of St. Paul's teaching, suffer not women

to speak in the church.   Pres. Mahan heard of it
and sent for it and had it printed in the next edition of the Oberlin Review [Oberlin Quarterly Re-
view], the first article I ever had printed.   Prof.
Fairchild rather objected and wrote an article on
the other side.[81]

In 1847 Antoinette went to see David Brokaw, an Oberlin
artist who was painting a portrait of Mahan.   On September
23 she wrote to Lucy Stone.   The informal relation between
president and student comes through strongly.

When I went in he [President Mahan] noticed me and
said soon after, "Some people use it as one argument that woman's mind is not equal to man's,
that she has never become eminent in portrait
painting."   "Yes," I replied, "but I have just come
to see if Mr. Brocaw [sic] will teach me how to
paint."   He laughed at me a little, wished me
success, etc., etc.[82]

Peace and Temperance Abroad

Two other reform movements that engaged Mahan
were efforts to eliminate war and intemperance.   He spoke
on these topics in the United States upon appropriate occasions but contributed most to them while abroad in 1849-50.

While Mahan and Finney campaigned against war as
a solution to international disputes, it must not be supposed
that either one of them was a pacifist.   Finney wrote that
there could be no reasonable doubt that "war has been in
some instances demanded by the spirit of moral law."   Mahan contented himself with justifying the use of force only
in self defense.   In his Science of Moral Philosophy he wrote
that "the use of force in self-defense is fundamentally different from revenge, and the Bible prohibits the latter only,
not the former.   The only question, then, is what are the
extent and limits of this right.   The principle which I lay
down ... is this.   Never intentionally put in jeopardy, for
self-protection, higher interest than those assailed."[83]

The pacifists and anti-war people kept an uneasy truce
and held numerous well organized international peace conventions during the 1840's and 1850's, the most successful one
of which was held in the fall of 1849 in Paris.   On May 30,

1849, the "friends of peace" in Oberlin met and elected
numerous delegates to the convention but eventually only
two went, Asa Mahan and Hamilton Hill, secretary of the
Institute. On July 18 the two men sailed from Boston aboard
the Canada. A great adventure far surpassing anything an-
ticipated lay ahead for Asa Mahan in France, England, and
Scotland. [84]

Mahan dutifully and capably carried out his responsibilities as representative of the Oberlin peace movement.
He spoke to numerous groups including the London Peace Society meeting in Exeter Hall. According to The Standard
of Freedom, November 3, 1849, Professor Mahan, who was
sitting on the platform with various members of Parliament
and members of the Established Church, upon rising to move
the next resolution was loudly cheered. He prefaced this
speech, as he did all sermons and talks abroad so that his
listeners would know where he stood on the key issue in
America, with the statement that he abhorred slavery and
was an abolitionist. At the end of his speech he referred to
the Free Soil Party convention held a year previously. "If
you meet any one of those thousands of men and women that
were there you meet one that is working for the realization
of [our] idea of the universal brotherhood of men--an idea
that must and will be realized. "[85] According to the newspaper account this statement was followed by loud and prolonged cheering.

The Peace Conference in Paris was quite impressive,
beginning with the impassioned opening address of the chairman of the congress, Victor Hugo. Among other speakers
on the first day was Mr. Cobden from the United Kingdom,
who had been on the platform with Mahan at the meeting in
London, and Mahan himself. Cobden defended the idea of
having a special board of arbitration whenever an international problem arose, while Mahan favored a permanent tri-
bunal to insure continuity and stability. The congress, however, kept to safe generalities and Asa felt that the proceedings yielded no definite or significant measures for accomplishing, as against praising, peace. [86]

President Mahan spent most of his six months abroad
in England and Scotland and divided his time between temperance and holiness sermons and lectures. He was genuinely
appalled by the amount of public drunkenness in the United
Kingdom. Along with other clergy he lectured on temperance to a capacity audience in Exeter Hall in early December

and later in the month preached several times in the Borough Road Chapel in favor of total abstinence.   One of his
sermons delivered there was published in a tract entitled
"Temperance and the Christian Church" and was highly
praised by the reviewer for The National Temperance Chronicle, March 1850.   In Scotland he had more requests for
temperance sermons than he could accept.   He preached on
this theme, at the request of the Scottish Temperance League,
at the Renfield Street Church, where "the house was crowded
to excess," and to the Wellington Street Church, where "the
Reverend gentleman received the hearty thanks of the audience."   In February 1850 the secretary of the Scottish Temperance League published a tribute to their American friend.
"The disinterested, cordial, courteous and Christian manner
in which you have advocated [our] claims in various parts
of our Island" and "the prompt and generous response you
have made to every application for your aid" surely "demand and receive the sincere acknowledgement of the friends
of temperance throughout the kingdom."[87]

In London, Glasgow, and Edinburgh Brother Mahan
preached the holiness message.   In London he lectured on
the Ninth of Romans at the Borough Road Chapel, Southwark,
and at the request of those who heard him his lectures were
published in 1850 as Lectures on the Ninth of Romans by
Ward and Company of London and reprinted by Peirce and
Company of Boston in 1851.   In the General Baptist Repository for March 1850 the reviewers declared, "we do most
cordially agree with the main argument of each subject."
Mahan was sponsored in London by the Reverend John Stevenson, and the American visitor managed to spark a revival
of substantial if not monumental proportions in the Southwark area.   Stevenson, who had long been influenced by
Christian Perfection, arranged to have an English edition
of the volume published in 1850 for which Mahan wrote an
introduction in which he answered some of the objections to
his doctrine of entire sanctification.   In Glasgow he preached
the holiness doctrine to congregations belonging to the Evangelical Union, a union of churches which had been earlier
influenced in the direction of the holiness movement by the
work of Charles Finney.   He preached at Fergus Ferguson's
East Regent Street Church and at William Scott's Pitt Street
Church, among others, and, as in England, was enthusiastically received.[88]

The question arises why Mahan was so successful in
preaching to English and Scottish audiences.   Why were the

groups to which he spoke more often than not overflow crowds?
Part of the answer is that he differed markedly from the
British clergy in his style of preaching, and the difference
was enjoyed. Mahan was straightforward and even blunt
but always interesting, all without a trace of the crudeness
usually associated with those "who speak their mind."

The sermons of the English clerics tended to sound
more like pieces written with an eye toward publication than
sermons designed to quicken the hearts of auditors beginning to daydream or grow increasingly sleepy. This fact
was almost wholly true of the clergy in the established
Church but was by no means unknown in the dissenting ranks
also. After all, the latter had to show the former that
while they did not wholly frown on "enthusiasm" they knew
its limits, and they also had to show that they could sprinkle
sermons with Greek and Latin literary allusions, like a cook
sprinkles dough with caraway seeds, quite as well as anyone in a parish church or cathedral. To use anecdotes,
stories, and parables--and worse yet, to draw them from
personal experience--was unheard of. And the best form
was always that of gentility, never a touch of bluntness and
always a gentlemanly reference to members of the audience
as "my dear friends" or "my beloved brethren." A cultural tone of voice was cultivated, even at the expense of
the people sitting in the back pews who, strain as they might,
could not quite make out what the good pastor was saying.
No doubt it was eminently worth hearing, and they often
consulted a friend after services who had brought an ear
trumpet along.

Into the midst of this ambience Asa Mahan forcefully
fell and shattered it in a way that the evangelicals would
never forget or cease to marvel at, as well as respect. A
writer for the Glasgow Examiner, October 20, 1849, appreciatively observed that Mahan's preaching "had more the
character of extempore teaching than of the essay pruned
and refined in accordance with the established canons of
literature." And "if preaching be intended to elucidate, and
render practical the great truths of Christianity there cannot be a doubt but this is an effectual method." It wasn't
that what he had to say was new or startling, not that at
all--his genius went quite the other way. Rather

> [his] manner of discussing, enforcing, and explain-
> ing the various truths of the gospel [was] so dif-
> ferent from what we are accustomed to hear, that

one could not but feel highly interested. The
hearer could not get listless, for his attention
was constantly kept awake by the abrupt, ener-
getic manner, the simplicity and familiarity of
the language, and the interest of the anecdotes....
This preacher eminently possesses the tact of securing the attention of his hearers, and can make
them imagine that they are harkening to something
perfectly new and conclusive, though they may have
heard the same ideas uttered perhaps fifty times
before.... His tones and gestures smack more
of the woods and prairies than of Oxford or Cambridge. Not that he exhibits anything like rude-
ness in either word or thought, but he speaks with
the free, straight-forward, dauntless manner of
an honest, earnest man, and a republican--of one
who cares less to please ears polite than to state
vigorously what he feels. [89]

When he preached, Mahan dressed plainly and wore
neither bands nor white neckcloth but a narrow black cravat
the ends of which trailed down his chest. When he spoke
no one needed to depend upon a friend with an ear trumpet
to know what had been said. "He seems to have a frame
of iron; nor is the irony feeling in any degree lessened when
you hear him speak. His voice is clear and sharp as the
sounds from an anvil, penetrates the remotest corners of
the church, and impresses one with the idea that he could
extort respect either in the church or in the valley of the
Sacramento [among the '49ers]." He never says "My beloved
brethren" but "Hearer, listen!" "Our conviction is that he
is a strong-minded, earnest, and good man, who will not
bend to circumstances, but who will make circumstances
bend to what he conceives to be right."[90]

Chapter 4

LEAVING OBERLIN

Serious trouble between Mahan and the faculty erupt-
ted in 1844, and even though a surface calm was re-established the ambience of Old Oberlin was never regained.
During his absence abroad in 1849-50 the faculty members
wrote a letter in which they suggested, not unkindly but
quite firmly, that Mahan would do well to resign as president. The letter was finally delivered to him shortly after
his return from England. After much thrust and parry, the
request was withdrawn; but the hostility remained. Thus it
was that Brother Asa resigned in August 1850, after fifteen
years of service to Oberlin, to found a university in Cleveland. Mahan's departure was an unhappy one indeed, and
quite different interpretations--one favorable and one unfavorable to Mahan--have been put upon it. Neither of these
interpretations, it will appear, is based on all the available
evidence. We will proceed in the following way: we will
reconstruct the chain of events that eventuated in Mahan's
resignation; amplify the events with background information;
describe the opposing interpretations, largely in the words
of their proponents; and criticize these opposing views. One
proponent does less than justice to the faculty, the other less
than justice to Mahan.

Dissension

In 1844 President Mahan was requested by a number
of the faculty to resign on the grounds that his constitutional
traits were so annoying that the faculty could not work with

him and that he was "the chief obstacle to pacification in
the Ministry around." The records do not reveal precisely
which members of the faculty made the request though they
do indicate that John Morgan and Henry Cowles were deeply
involved but that Finney was not among the dissenters. It
must have been a significant majority, however, or else the
request for Mahan's resignation would have been fatuous. [1]

That Mahan was an annoying person no one could
doubt. It was the nature of his irritating qualities that was
at issue. After all, Socrates, Jesus, Luther, and Wesley
had been exceedingly annoying people. An eloquent defense
of the president was mounted by John Keep, a non-resident
trustee; Edward Weed, one of the Lane Rebels; Samuel Cochran, brother of William Cochran who was probably one of
the complaining faculty members; and Sherlock Bristol, at
that time General Agent of the Institute. In a joint letter
to the faculty and trustees these four men expounded at
length on many points, all crucial, though the following long
quotation contains the ones most important for biographical
purposes.

> We have understood that one of the reasons as-
> signed for his [Mahan's] removal was his unpop-
> ularity with the Churches. We ask what Churches?
> Sure we are that in this city [New York] and vicin-
> ity, and throughout New England, he stands pre-
> eminently high. We do not believe that any other
> man living has a stronger hold upon the affections
> of the people of God in the region specified, and
> unless a strange reverse has recently taken place,
> we know that the same is true in the West. His
> little work on "Christian Perfection" has endeared
> him to thousands and thousands of Christian hearts
> .... There is no one who goes forth from Oberlin,
> not even Mr. Finney himself, who in every re-
> spect is more highly esteemed than Bro. Mahan
> .... Indeed, brethren, as a man of talents, a
> profound thinker, a skillful theologian and meta-
> physician, a preacher and Christian, in the public
> eye, Mahan is one of the most brilliant lights at
> your Institution....
> Another reason assigned for his retirement is
> the strong aggressive character of his mind and
> principles. This, in our estimation, is the very
> reason why he should remain--the very thing, to-
> gether with his piety, above all others, that qual-

ifies him preeminently to be at the head of such
an Institution--the secret of his power and hold
upon the public mind.... Diminish [Oberlin's]
aggressive spirit [by Mahan's departure] and you
diminish its power--take it away and like Sampson,
shorn of its locks, its might and glory will have
departed. Truth and reform will seek another
fortress from which to do battle with the giant
sins of the Church and the world.... You may
hold the same theories you do now, write beautiful and learned essays upon them, but if you
do not attempt to push them and make living converts to them, no one will care for them.... [T]he
aggressiveness of the President is the very com-
modity that of all things, Oberlin needs most, and
which losing, will see her error too late, when
no space for repentance can be found.

But it is said that these characteristics have
frequently manifested themselves in an unlovely
manner, and at times, greatly to the annoyance
of his fellow professors and others. This charge
to a considerable extent we are disposed to admit,
and doubt not, that Bro. Mahan ought to be faith-
fully labored with upon this subject, and that he is
bound to do all in his power to correct the evil.
Allow this charge, brethren, to its full extent, we
ask, is it a sufficient reason to justify the Faculty
and Resident-Trustees to vote the withdrawal from
their midst of one of the most talented, spiritual,
laborious, efficient and influential of their number
.... Suppose the coadjutators of Luther, coming
in contact with his rough corners and becoming
restive and impatient under their feelings, had got
together and voted it was the duty of the Great
Reformer to leave Wurtemburg. In what light
would history have looked upon their conduct? Ap-
plaudingly, think you?...

In our estimation, there are few men who have
made so great conquests, through the grace of
God, over those faults growing out of the constitutional traits of their minds, as Brother Mahan.
So much is this felt to be the case, that many of
our best families in this city are ready to board
him gratuitously, in order to have breathed over
their family circle the sweet and subdued spirit
he manifests. If you send him away from Oberlin,
we greatly fear the general impression will be,

that instead of his having a bad spirit, you did not
appreciate and were not worthy of him.   In addition we ask if nothing is to be pardoned to the man
in view of the position he has occupied and the
burdens thrown upon him the last ten years.
Placed as he has been at the head of a great and
complicated Institution, the executive part of the
government upon his shoulders, and most of the
time the Institution passing through the ordeal of
a furnace heated seven times hotter than it is wont
to be heated: is it wonderful that in the midst of
some important Faculty discussion the fires of
his intensely ardent earnest mind should have
burnt too rudely and scorched the finer sensibilities of some of his fellow professors, and at other times worn down with care and labor he should
have rebuked an erring student too severely, and
reproved a captious colonist too harshly?   As to
this part of the President's failings together with
his apparent overbearing spirit, we have always
supposed they grew out of the best side of his
character.   They spring from the great sincerity,
earnestness, firmness and devotion to truth, so
that in these respects we have been ready to say
"Ev'n his failings lean to virtue's side."   Besides,
we think the very severity complained of has been
of great service to the Institution.   We ask if in
the midst of such a mix'd population of colonists
and students professing so great a diversity of
character, there should not be some one in your
midst, whose terrible rebuke, all, and especially
the wayward, will fear and dread?[2]

. Sherlock Bristol defended the president vigorously by
writing long letters to the faculty and resident trustees, Hamilton Hill, Secretary of the Institute, and Henry Cowles.   In
truth Bristol was greatly drawn to Mahan and his opponents
alike, though his ultimate allegiance was no doubt to the
president who had taken him to the steamer in Cleveland and
spoken loving and encouraging words during the illness of
his student days.   He wrote appreciatively of the other faculty members but said that since they were critical of Mahan he would hold a mirror in front of them.   He admitted
the president had faults as well as virtues--harshness being
the main one--but observed, "If we must go back to by gone
years, how few could point to a life unsullied by grievous
faults. "   The faculty's "<u>lanceing</u> a healed or healing wound

illy becomes those who are scarred from head to foot."[3]
That sentence must have jarred the faculty members even
though it occurred in a matrix of moderate and unpresump-
tuous language.

        The upshot of the 1844 affair was that the faculty with-
drew its request in light of the opposition and in view of
Brother Mahan's statement that if the faculty should become
dissatisfied with his performance any time in the future he
would retire as president.   In spite of his conciliatory and
friendly words Mahan was deeply hurt by this effort to unseat him.   He had long thought that they all belonged to a
sort of salvation army, in spite of various differences, but
he saw now that this was far from the case.   He continued
to work diligently for Oberlin but no longer with the same
spirit of self-sacrifice.   He had the note for the $800 he
had loaned the Institute assumed by someone else, and he
officially requested back wages for college work done during
the off-term.   And yet, in the end, he still could not resist
Oberlin (for was it not an instrument of God's good work?)
and loaned the Institute more money.   He held three notes
against the institution when he left in 1850.[4]

        Following 1844 there was a continuation of disagree-
ment between Mahan and the faculty, a major dispute oc-
curring in 1846 over the issue of salaries.   Financial problems, chronic at Oberlin after the Panic of 1837, made it
difficult for the trustees to meet faculty salaries and outside debts.   In 1846 William Dawes became General Agent
and introduced a program of austerity, with which the other
agents, trustees, and the president agreed.   The austerity
began immediately after Dawes' appointment: John Keep was
named to consult with Finney and Cowles "relative to a re-
duction of their salaries."   The trustees said they would
"pay punctually to each Teacher a liberal salary so far as
is practicable" (it was rarely possible apparently, given the
faculty letters of complaint), but facing realities they added
"that it is material that we all practice a rigid economy."
They asserted they would not pay salaries to teachers absent on their own business or to those with a protracted disability.   The concept of austerity mounted.   As much of
faculty salaries would be paid as meagre resources permitted; but the faculty should not always expect to receive full
amounts.   Dawes, Mahan, and various trustees apparently
were approaching, though they did not quite reach, the "faith
mission" concept that regular salaries are in a sense irre-
ligious in import and that a person should be satisfied with

a certain share of whatever money God's mercy and man's
effort made available. As a further economy, it was decided to drop Hamilton Hill as Secretary of the Institute.[5]

The response of the faculty was strongly negative.
William Cochran resigned, and Finney threatened to go.
Lewis Tappan supported the faculty. Hill was not dropped,
and the faculty forced the trustees to change their policy.
Dawes resigned giving as his reasons 1) the lowering of
the spiritual tone at Oberlin and 2) the faculty's demand
that the trustees rescind the austerity program. The faculty members were displeased by the fact that Mahan had
agreed with the original policy of the trustees and agents.[6]

In addition to the salary issue, other disagreements
between Mahan and the faculty surfaced. As we have seen,
there were constant battles over curricular matters and in
1846 there was the hassle over the Fosters' right to speak
at Oberlin. In 1847 and 1848 Mahan pushed for the right
of Lucy Stone and Anna Mahan to read their own essays at
Commencement, by no means a superficial issue. The faculty was adamantly against it and suspected Mahan of enlist-
ing the support of the trustees in the battle of women's
rights. In July 1848 Henry Cowles wrote to his wife,

> We learned that the Trustees--last fall--voted to
> recommend to the Faculty to bring the young la-
> dies forward to read their own pieces Wednesday.
> Mr. Mahan took great pains to say that he had no
> agency in obtaining this vote. The Faculty ap-
> pointed a Committee of Conference with the Trus-
> tees in reference to this resolution, in order that
> they may have our reasons before them.[7]

In addition, there were the church trials in which
Mahan participated, much to the disgruntlement of some faculty members, including Finney, and townsmen. The Congregational Church of Oberlin (the only church in the village
and essentially a community rather than denominational institution) had elaborate trials in which members might be
admonished, suspended, or excommunicated if found guilty
of some moral dereliction. An accused person could have
a counsel at such trials and Mahan had acted in this capacity
several times and had been criticized for so doing. (Acting
as counsel automatically ensured the enmity of the person or
group of people who had brought the charges.)[8]

Finally, Mahan, as always, never relented in criticiz-

ing what he liked to call lukewarm Christians, those whom
he considered to be formalists and legalists in their attitude
toward God, Jesus Christ, and the Holy Spirit. And it was
clear to anyone with ears that the president considered the
bulk of his faculty (Finney, of course, excepted) to be that
sort of Christian. It was not by chance that one of his sermons was entitled "Lukewarm Professors."[9] He used it as
synonymous with "any person who professes belief without
deep commitment" but the double meaning of the phrase was
not lost on anyone. Even faculty members like Morgan and
Cowles who held a holiness view did not pursue the Higher
Life ardently enough (Finney again excepted). For Mahan
the feeling of the presence of God had to be renewed each
day, or sought for, in any case, and anyone who did not do
so had to be prayed for and sometimes admonished for sec-
ond-hand religion. Standards must be maintained at all costs.
H. E. Woodcock recalls that one Sabbath Fairchild preached
on the text "They set Dagon in his place again" and not finding the subject fruitful he stopped preaching long before the
usual time and sat down. "Brother Mahan arose and said,
'There are yet fifteen minutes,' and so he proceeded to finish Professor Fairchild's sermon." Swing, Fairchild's biographer, adds that thus "the congregation was not allowed
to form the habit of going before the accustomed time."[10]

In late 1848 the faculty had another try at unseating
Mahan, but the president had proved remarkably durable because of his many non-academic and student supporters. In
January 1849 Timothy Hudson, one of the faculty members
most deeply committed to removing Mahan from office, wrote
his colleague James Monroe:

> At one time, serious talk was had in certain quar-
> ters about asking the Prest. to resign his post.
> But it has ended as I assumed it would--in smoke.
> Tho' I fancy it alarmed the Prest. a little for the
> time. Mrs. Pelton has been getting up some par-
> ties at her house partly for the sake of promoting
> social feeling and partly to help support the Tavern
> [hotel]. Prof. Finney is out on such things. He
> paid Mrs. P. two visits laboring with her on this
> point. Both were firm. The faculty generally
> think with Mrs. P. that such gatherings properly
> conducted will do good.[11]

During the end of 1849 and the beginning of 1850,
while Mahan was in Europe, the faculty, however, began an
all-out campaign to unseat the president. They carefully

prepared a letter stating their case but hoped to avoid using
it. All those who wanted to get rid of Mahan wanted to do
it quietly. They felt certain that an open and public break
between the faculty and president could be harmful indeed to
the Institute. Finney was abroad, as well as Mahan, and
John Morgan wrote the evangelist asking him to contact Mahan in England and convince him to step down. It was not
that the faculty felt unkindly toward Mahan, he averred, but
that they simply could not work with him. While they ad-
mired and appreciated the good work Mahan had done in
England and Scotland, that fact did not change their views. [12]
Finney ignored the request, even though he had informed
his colleagues that he thought it best now that Mahan should
leave.

        The faculty members, having to act on their own but
still wanting much to avoid a confrontation with the redoubtable Mahan, sent their letter to George Whipple in New York
City asking him to present it to the president when he dis-
embarked. Whipple had been a Lane Rebel, subsequently a
faculty member at Oberlin, and was now the secretary of
the American Missionary Association. Whipple loved Oberlin and wanted to avoid anything that would harm it. He
thought Mahan should leave (for his sake as well as the faculty's) but the separation must be accomplished without a
harmful explosion. That could be accomplished, he thought,
because Joab Seeley, an Oberlin agent, had secured a call
for Mahan from a prestigious church in Newark, New Jersey.
Whipple and Lewis Tappan urged him to accept the pastorate
the prestige of which would explain his leaving Oberlin.
Needless to say, leaving Oberlin without "sifting things to
the bottom" was not the president's style. If he left Oberlin, people would have to know the real reasons. Whipple
returned the letter to the faculty unused. [13]

        When Mahan arrived in Oberlin he asked the faculty
to state their views. Ten days later he was presented with
the long-prepared letter, though it now bore a later date.
In the letter the faculty praised the president's "eminent
abilities as a preacher and public speaker" and "his talents
as a writer," but said he lacked "those peculiar gifts which
qualify for the presidency of a literary Institution." It
would be better for both him and the college, they thought,
if he would accept the invitation of the Newark pastorate.
On March 8, 1850, Mahan wrote to William Dawes, resident
trustee, "You are aware that since my return to Oberlin I
have received a request from my associates who are on the

ground to vacate my post as President of this Institution and
enter a new field of activity." Would the trustees inquire
into the matter? Dawes, Josiah B. Hall, and Isaac Jennings,
all trustees, replied on March 11 saying that the real problem was Oberlin's decline from original spirituality and its
increasing worldliness. They praised Mahan highly but said
he was not without faults, yet faults that were shared by
his critics. They declared that the vast majority of students,
colonists, and Oberlin friends afield would be shocked by his
departure. [14]

The faculty wrote Mahan a brisk letter concerning
his March 8 communication to Dawes. "Every assertion respecting the nature of our communication [with you] in your
letter [to Dawes] is entirely erroneous, and everyone of its
erroneous assertions is fitted to excite odium against us and
conciliate sympathy towards yourself." They chided him for
not saying he had asked the faculty for a statement of opinion
(a bit disingenuous since they had been trying to peddle the
letter since February), for not referring to the commenda-
tory part of the letter, for saying that the faculty had requested him to resign when in fact they had only suggested
it, for mistakenly saying that the faculty had made no specific complaint when in fact they had said he lacked the tact
and wisdom necessary for a college president. All of this
was so much chaff in the wind as far as Mahan was concerned. They had something else to say, however, that hit
Mahan hard. Mahan, they said, was apparently under the
illusion that Finney did not share their views. They had a
letter from Finney which showed undoubtedly that the evangelist shared their opinions. Indeed it was a blow. Mary
Dix Mahan as well as Asa had firmly believed that Finney
was still supportive as he had been in the past. [15]

Under Mahan's and Dawes' initiative a special meeting of the board of trustees was called for April 18 to consider the faculty's request--or suggestion or whatever--that
the president resign. To the board there appeared to be no
sufficient reason to ask Mahan to resign and the members
asked the faculty if they wished to press specific charges.
The faculty replied that it did not wish to do so but simply
reaffirmed the president's lack of tact and wisdom in dealing
with people. That scarcely came as news to anyone, including Mahan's friends on the board. The question was simply
this, then: Could the faculty and president manage to patch
up their differences and cooperate sufficiently for the continued progress of the Institute? It was suggested that the

faculty compose a list of grievances the correction of which
would provide the ground for hearty cooperation between the
two contending parties. [16]

In the meantime the board received numerous petitions from students, college agents, community members
(both black and white) to the effect that Brother Mahan must
stay. These petitions were signed by hundreds of people
even though some of Mahan's supporters refused to sign on
the grounds that the very nature of a petition was divisive
and would only add to the contention. [17] A petition signed
by twenty-five residents, including Alexander Steele and
Homer Johnson, physicians, Hiram Pease, brother of Peter
Pindar Pease, and William Plumb, lawyer, stated quite
bluntly that Mahan should go. The names of no faculty members appear on the petition. [18]

Of the petitions in favor of Mahan none is more instructive than the one signed by eighty-six black residents
of Oberlin, one of whom was John Copeland, the man destined to be involved in the Wellington Rescue Case and to
be one of John Brown's raiders at Harper's Ferry. The
petition, in the form of a letter to Mahan, includes the following:

> We have long looked upon you as being among our
> firmest and most able friends and believing the
> station you occupy to be a most favorable position
> for exerting a wide-spread and lasting influence
> for Humanity, we most earnestly desire and re-
> quest that you may continue in your present field
> of great usefulness.... Loving and respecting you
> as we do, and hoping that this expression of our
> feelings may be of some weight in your pending de-
> cision as the representative of a down-trodden race,
> we respectfully subscribe ourselves, Yours in be-
> half of Justice and Humanity. [19]

The "Basis of Hearty Cooperation," written by several
members of the faculty aided by trustees Peter Pindar Pease
and others, was vitriolic in its characterization of Mahan's
alleged faults. James H. Fairchild and Michael Strieby insisted on toning it down and reworked the document which
was finally accepted by the whole faculty. [20] The list of
faults ascribed to the president even in the toned-down version was a tough one and included these complaints:

1) He should see that his self-esteem has amounted

to self-conceit and has led him to over-rate both
his natural abilities and his moral attainments,
and that under the same influence he underrates
the ability and character of his brethren; 2) He
should see his tendency to attribute unworthy motives to his brethren and promise to do so no
more; 3) He should see his tendency to set forth
himself and the institution at Oberlin in a boastful
manner and thus exhibit us in an attitude that is
odious to God and man; 4) He should be aware of
his tendency to deal in wholesale denunciation of
the church and the ministry and to publish anecdotes unadvisedly, derogatory to the character of
individuals; 5) He should see his tendency to make
strong positive statements amounting, though not
intended, to misrepresentation as to matters of
fact on points where he is committed and promise
to guard against it; 6) He should be aware of his
liability, in his popular political discourses to assume an attitude and use language unbecoming to
a Christian minister and the President of a religious Institution; 7) He should be careful not to
leave his work in the Institution without consultation and arrangement with his brethren, thus embarrassing our operations and burdening the other
Instructors; 8) He should refrain from agitating
the minds of the Students on questions which involve the established order of the Institution; 9)
He should refrain from committing the Institution
to sentiments which he only holds or which are
contrary to the views of his brethren; 10) He
should not act as counsel in cases of discipline
before the Church in Oberlin, or interfere in such
a way as to endanger the harmony of the Church.

The faculty said that if the President acknowledged these
faults and agreed to amend them they would be content to
continue to work with him. [21]

In a joint meeting of the board and faculty Mahan
heard the specific complaints read, happily agreed to remedy the deficiencies and, according to John Morgan, "seemed
really desirous of pursuing a course which would give us
joint satisfaction." The community in general knew only
that the quarrel had been patched up and were much relieved
at the outcome. There was much rejoicing among the students and townspeople as well as among the host of Oberlinians who had gone out from the Institute to do God's work

in the way propounded by Mahan and Finney.   Soon after
the special session of the board Mary Dix Mahan invited
the whole faculty to supper, and Mahan was cordial. [22]
John Keep was delighted that the Oberlin team remained intact and that the Mahans did not feel bitter toward anyone.

The Break

That Asa Mahan accepted the faculty's list of grievances is surprising, to say the least.   Indeed, it is absurd
to think that, taken at its face value, he agreed with it in
the slightest.   And yet not one commentator has made any
effort to explain what he really thought about the list or to
explain the wild discrepancy between what he really thought
and what he did.   It might be supposed that he simply acquiesced in what he did not believe in order to remain as
president of Oberlin, but such a supposition is surely mistaken.   Such conduct would have been entirely impossible
for a man who was honest in a most fundamental and pervasive way.

What in fact did Mahan think of each of the items on
the list? [23]   He was quite willing to admit that self-conceit
had been a past sin, his greatest sin, but he sincerely believed that as a result of his second blessing this sin had
been crucified.   He no longer cared about the opinion of
men but only the judgment of God.   Concerning self-conceit
and boasting about himself and the college as a present sin,
he felt he had been misunderstood.   To be sure, he emphasized how many people had been converted as a result of
his preaching and how Oberlin was a great instrument in
the hands of God, bringing light to the children of darkness.
However such statements are wrongly construed if taken as
evidence of present self-conceit and boasting.   He repeatedly
wrote that he took no credit whatever for what he or Oberlin as an institution achieved; the results were achieved by
the in-dwelling Christ, the fullness of God, the presence of
the Holy Spirit.   Neither he nor anyone else at Oberlin
achieved anything in the supernatural sphere; all was the
result of God's work.   We might add that unless one takes
Mahan seriously on this point there is a real problem in
understanding Finney's behavior.   Without Mahan's distinction Finney's Memoirs and much of his other writing appear
to be nothing but unbridled egotism.

As far as items 2 through 5 were concerned, Mahan

was perfectly willing to admit that he had not acted perfectly in many ways.   No doubt he had committed blunders, but
they were mistakes of judgment attended upon lack of knowledge in given cases and were not evidence of a will uncon-
secrated to God.   Only God has infinite knowledge and wisdom and any finite individual is bound to make mistakes.
No man can act perfectly since this implies infinite wisdom;
any man, however, can walk in the ways of God and exhibit
a will generally disposed to eschew evil if only he will pray
for the presence of the in-dwelling Spirit.   Mahan certainly
believed that his will was generally disposed to eschew evil
ways.   As we shall see, this distinction between a holy will
and limited knowledge was not only used in the present context but became Mahan's defense of the holiness view in
general when critics of it pointed out some of the shortcomings of himself, Finney, Morgan, Cowles, and other
believers in sanctification scattered throughout the country
and the world.

        Concerning the charges of "attributing unworthy mo-
tives to individuals" and dealing in "wholesale denunciation
of the church and ministers," Mahan pointed out that he had
written many books and numerous articles for the Oberlin
Evangelist and Oberlin Quarterly Review and he challenged
anyone to show by specific references that they exhibited
any such tendencies on his part.   Moreover, the students
whom he had influenced did not show this tendency toward
denunciation either, which one might expect if their mentor
indulged in it.   He denied burdening other faculty members
with his classes when he was absent in England.   It was
standard procedure for the faculty to cover for each other
when there was an absence.   He himself had taught Finney's
classes in his absence for a longer period of time than he
himself had been in Europe, for which he received not a
farthing in recompense while Finney drew his college salary
as well as remuneration for his work as a revivalist.

        He had not "agitated" students unless his talks on the
importance of the Bible in college education is to count as
agitation.   Concerning the "fault" of representing his own
views as those of the Institute, he wrote that he had not
done so anymore than T. C. Upham, Sir William Hamilton,
or C. G. Finney had when, as independent thinkers, they
published what they regarded as true on their own exclusive,
individual responsibility.   The restriction on his acting as
counsel in a church trial he accepted "as a condition of
peace."   "But what had I done to occasion the demand that

I should give such a pledge?" After all, John Morgan had
previously acted as counsel in such cases and "for a long
time subsequent, Prof. Morgan, at least, maintained strongly that no one had a right to object to my doing as I had
done."24

Now that it is clear what in fact Mahan thought of
the list of grievances the question why he acquiesced to the
faculty demands requires an answer more urgently than ever.
It is a story with numerous complications but it began with
a talk Samuel D. Porter had with Mahan immediately before
the special meeting of the board in April 1850. Porter was
the "infidel" converted by Finney in the Great Rochester Revival, and he had been named a trustee of Oberlin in 1844.
Like most of the trustees, with the exception of Peter Pindar
Pease perhaps, Porter wanted both Mahan and the faculty to
stay at Oberlin. The problem was how to reconcile them,
either in substance or appearance, but preferably both. It
seemed wholly unlikely that Mahan would accede to the faculty demands even in their modified form, so Porter, wholly
on his own, urged the president to accept the document and
recommended to him "not to be fastidious about the 'wording'
of the Document." "Some words or phrases might be ob-
noxious in their verbiage or form of expression," Porter
continued, but he "ought not to make a stand about words
...." Porter also said that none of them, including John
Keep, were without faults.25 In addition, Mahan and Mary
Dix Mahan, who was present during the conversation, understood Porter to say that the trustees would let Mahan
know how they understood the document, as if there were
a surface and an esoteric interpretation of the document
possible. Though Porter acknowledged that he had said not
to take the wording seriously and that all of them had faults,
he had not intended to imply, he wrote later, that the import of the document should not be taken seriously. He insisted that when he had included John Keep among those, including himself, who had faults he had not meant the fault
of self-conceit. He was astounded that the Mahans thought
a latent meaning possible in such a clear and unambiguous
document; and, in any case, if the trustees had intended to
communicate to Mahan the meaning they affixed to the document why had they not done so?26

We are now in a position to reconstruct at least partially why Mahan subscribed to a document the articles of
which, taken at face value, he disagreed with entirely. The
point was that he did not think he had to take them at face

value. Given Porter's loophole--"don't fret about the wording" and "we all have faults"--Mahan assumed that the trustees were telling him that they knew perfectly well that this
document was another episode in an ongoing contest between
the president and faculty and that all he had to do was agree
to the document and thus achieve the goal they all wanted,
namely, the advancement of Oberlin. He knew that most of
the trustees valued his service even though they sincerely
believed he had faults--a view held, he realized, even by
his closest backers on the board like William Dawes, F. D.
Parish, and J. B. Hall. Mahan did not need any delegation
from the faculty to tell him what he felt he already knew--a
view completely reinforced by Porter's visit, since Porter
was not one of his strongest backers. At the time he must
have been cheered by Porter's visit, reassuring as it was .
of what he already understood the situation to be.

     This reconstruction, however, is only partial since
Mahan also sincerely believed that the document could be so
construed that he was confessing only to errors of judgment
(which he was quite willing and happy to do, believing as
much as anyone that he, along with everyone else, made
such errors) and not confessing to evil traits of character
or propensities of the will. Surely, however, Porter was
right in saying that the document was unambiguous and that
the charges clearly were more than errors of judgment. To
be sure, Mahan made changes, insisting upon past tenses,
so that self-conceit could be construed as a frailty of his
past rather than present character, but he was rattled and
failed to change the tense in the latter part of item 1.27
But even so, the document seems utterly straightforward.
Why, then, did Mahan finally accept it? He did so in part
because he was deeply upset by the dispute and in a dis-
traught state of mind tended to read into the document what
he wanted, in part also because he loved Oberlin so dearly
as an instrument of God that he would have signed anything
to stay.28   And, in any case, would not the trustees know
how it should be read?

     For all these reasons (complexly interwoven and not
separated in their workings as we have separated them for
conceptual clarity) Mahan agreed "happily" to accept the conditions for a "hearty basis of cooperation." The result is
known--the community was cheered and relieved that the
president and faculty, all of whom they respected, would
continue to work together for the good of Oberlin. However,
it can come as no surprise that an agreement reached on
such flimsy foundation could not last. Some of the faculty

were honestly convinced that things had been patched up but
others remained unconvinced skeptics.[29]

From April to August a series of events occurred
that eventuated in the resignation of the president at the annual meeting of the board in late August. It did not seem
to the Mahans that the friendly gesture of their faculty supper
was reciprocated. Indeed, it appeared that some of the faculty
members and their wives snubbed Asa and Mary, though such
events, while contributory, were not decisive in their decision
to leave, a decision extremely difficult for both of them.[30]

In the early summer an attractive alternative emerged.
Thirza and Brewster Pelton, under pressure from Finney,
had decided to leave Oberlin. Thirza had promoted the idea
of a women's seminary in conjunction with Oberlin at the
special meeting of the board of trustees in April but nothing
came of it. She decided to establish such a seminary in
Cleveland and she and other individuals proposed to Mahan
to start a whole new educational enterprise in Cleveland, of
which the seminary would be a part, an enterprise that would
be a full-fledged university and would incorporate in all its
departments Mahan's advanced theories of education. Needless to say, the idea was attractive to the beleagured president, but was it only an idea? No, it turned out that money
had already been raised by George Clark and Mrs. Pelton
in Boston and elsewhere. The idea could be achieved; could
Mahan be persuaded to become the president of the new university?[31] As attractive as it would be to select a faculty sympathetic to his educational views, Mahan held back. Oberlin was
an instrument of God, and he still hated to leave it.

In early July John Keep wrote a letter to Mahan the
contents of which unfortunately remain unknown. On July 9
Charles Finney, the evangelist's son, wrote his father,

> Pres. M. rec'd a letter from Mr. Keep a short
> time since couched in as [he?] says very insulting
> language and I understand that the committee to
> whom he referred the letter said they could not
> blame him for leaving, should he do so at once.
> Mr. George Clark is not here at present but is
> soliciting funds for the new Inst. at Cleveland.
> Everything is so unsettled here at present and the
> very existence of the Inst.... so doubtful, that I
> would much prefer to go to Yale and graduate if
> for no other reason.[32]

It was certainly a hard decision and a hard summer for the
Mahans.   Caroline Mary Rudd Allen wrote her husband on
July 23 that "Mrs. Mahan called on us this week, she is
all worn down." "I do pity her, she is very nervous" and
"she said nothing about leaving and of course I did not."[33]
Even as late as July 28 Mahan had still not finally made up
his mind, though he now definitely leaned toward leaving
since the new university was gaining momentum.   On that
date W. W. Wright, a previous member of the faculty, wrote
George Allen,

> [The] President preached this a.m. and Prof. Mor-
> gan this p.m.   Nothing more definite about Pres.
> leaving....   Trustees have been appointed [for the
> new university] and Pres M informally invited to
> take the Presidency.   It is said to be his present
> expectation to accept.   Prof. Morgan says that he
> (Prof M) looks upon the whole affair with not a
> little solicitude.   Should it go on, he thinks it
> would be likely to injure this Inst.   The Pres will
> probably take no decisive step until the next meet-
> ing of the Board of Trustees of this Inst.[34]

There were still efforts to persuade Mahan to stay
and to persuade the trustees not to let him go.   On August
13 Uriah Thompson, only days before being named a trustee
himself, headed a petition to the board which read,

> The extent to which this community sympathises
> with the different parties in the Board of Instruc-
> tion is indicated by the number of petitioners in
> their behalf whose names were presented at your
> last meeting--the petitioners on one side amounting
> to twenty four, and on the other to about six or
> seven hundred.   And this we believe is a fair in-
> dex of the feeling abroad....   It cannot reasonably
> be expected in the present state of society that
> any public man with strong decided executive tal-
> ents, who is the fearless champion of progress
> and reform in all that pertains to human welfare,
> should find none to oppose him....   We would re-
> spectfully suggest ... a return to the Original
> Policy and spirit of this Institution....   Our desire
> is that both the Prest. and Professor Finney may
> as formerly labor together in this Institution.[35]

It was not to be.   On August 26 Asa Mahan sent this terse

note to the trustees, "Brethren, I hereby present to you my resignation of the presidency of this college. Yours respectfully, A. Mahan."[36] It was all over, and Asa and Mary were soon to leave for Cleveland.

Different Interpretations

In his biography of Finney, A. M. Hills presents Mahan in a favorable light and explains his departure from Oberlin as a result of hostile action by those faculty members, including Fairchild, who opposed the doctrine of holiness. In his History of Oberlin College R. S. Fletcher characterizes Mahan in less than flattering ways and explains his leaving Oberlin as a result of personality defects. Neither seems to have captured either the full flavor of the conflict or the complexity of the man. We shall let each commentator speak for himself and shall criticize each in turn.

According to Hills, Mahan was a great spiritual leader who aggressively defended and pushed the doctrine of sanctification.

> [This activity], of course, aroused opposition to the college; this, in turn, led those in influence in the college who were formal in religion and cold toward the doctrine of sanctification, to oppose him at home. They wanted peace with those who opposed the doctrine of holiness; and this man was betrayed to formal professors and a Christless world, and practically forced to resign from the presidency in 1850. That was the darkest day, I believe, that ever came to Oberlin; from which may be dated the beginning of her fatal spiritual decline.... [Finney] had been in England for a year when Mahan resigned. It is evident that he had no part in bringing it about. On his return to Oberlin, in 1851, he was elected to the presidency of the college, and filled the place until 1865, when he, in turn, was asked to resign; ostensibly, on account of his age; possibly, for the same reason that Mahan's resignation was secured .... Fairchild was his successor in the office, -- a cool, almost contemptuous, rejecter of both the doctrine and experience of sanctification. He was a man of large intellectual gifts, but unusually devoid of spiritual power.... It is well to notice

that the outside opposition to Oberlin never did her
the slightest harm.... She was betrayed by those
within her own fold. [37]

In his biography Hills included a statement, along
similar lines, by Sherlock Bristol. Some members of the
faculty (Fairchild, Dascomb, and Hudson) did not relish the
doctrine of sanctification, Bristol wrote, and they "felt restive under its demands and restraints." They persistently
and continually talked to other members of the faculty and,
as Bristol observed, "a continued dropping wears a rock."

> I knew these men one and all, and how assidu-
> ously they worked. During a winter vacation,
> while Mahan was absent in Boston, Providence,
> and New York, these home critics drew up a pa-
> per, and, by strong efforts, persuaded a majority
> of the Faculty to ask him to resign. It almost
> broke his heart.... I have no more doubt that it
> was want of spirituality that generated the opposi-
> tion and fed it than I have that I write this account
> of the matter. Nor have I any doubt of that action
> being a great sin against God.... The retrograde
> steps of Oberlin were due to the persistent carp-
> ings and criticisms of men in the Faculty, college,
> and town [including Fairchild], who had small ex-
> perience in spiritual things. So chronic it became,
> at length, that better men at last yielded, and con-
> sented to Mahan's departure, and with him the
> doctrine of sanctification, for the sake of peace!
> Oberlin's "Old Guard," Morgan, Finney, and
> Cowles, and many sanctified students, will mourn
> this concession for many a day. [38]

To begin with, Hills' explanation, with Bristol's support, of why Mahan left Oberlin is too one-dimensional to
be accepted as adequate. That some members of the faculty
and community tried to get rid of Mahan because of his holiness views is quite true, but, as we have seen, there were
many other issues that caused dissension also, including the
curriculum, the right of anyone to speak on campus, wom-
en's rights, the relative powers of the president, faculty,
and trustees, lack of tact, forceful criticism of "lukewarm
professors," and so on. It must be kept in mind that Hills
and Bristol were wholly committed to the holiness movement
and saw events as filtered through that perspective. We do
not mean that as a special criticism of them, since no doubt

everyone has a special perspective. The crucial thing is
to look at an issue from a number of perspectives and thus
come closer to the truth.   True, the sanctification dispute
was an important factor in Mahan's leaving but is by no
means explanatory taken by itself.   After all, Morgan and
Henry Cowles were thoroughly committed to the holiness
viewpoint and yet they were two of Mahan's most persistent
and earliest critics.

Furthermore the suggestion that Fairchild was contemptuous toward sanctification and at the heart of a conspiracy to unseat Mahan does not sound like Fairchild's
style. We must be careful, of course, since Hills and
Bristol knew Fairchild well and, in fact, were well acquainted with the events in question. It is true that Fairchild
threw his weight against holiness. He wrote that it came
to be "more and more a matter of doubt whether the seeking of sanctification as a special experience was on the whole
to be encouraged"[39]--but that sort of remark, often repeat-
ed by Fairchild, scarcely seems contemptuous. And the
quiet, fair-minded portrait of Fairchild that emerges from
other sources does not suggest a man who would keep cajol-
ing his peers until he had ground them down and pressed his
views on them. Moreover, as we have seen, Fairchild,
along with Strieby, played the role of mediator and toned
down the first draft of the faculty document on the faults of
President Mahan. It does not follow from our discussion
that Fairchild was not firm in his opposition to Mahan.   Indeed he was, and to that extent Hills and Bristol are right.
They are also right in thinking that there were people who
were contemptuous of the doctrine of sanctification and of
Mahan personally, but such a group did not include Fairchild.
Homer Johnson, the physician farthest from the homeopathic
viewpoint, in a letter to G. N. Allen actually accused Mahan of being a hypocrite and made fun of his holiness views.[40]
That sort of attitude was shared only by a small number that
included Horace Taylor, who had returned to Oberlin after
serving his jail term and who, Fairchild felt, remained a
blackguard to the end of his days.[41]

Finally, Hills is mistaken in saying that Finney had
no part in bringing about Mahan's departure. It is a fact
that Finney refused to write the president, asking for his
resignation, as Morgan asked him to do. However, he did
write the faculty to the effect that he was on their side, a
point which the faculty quickly and effectively used against
the president. Finney was a cautious person and committed

to the greatest happiness principle and was bound to find
Mahan unpalatable. Finney never wholeheartedly embraced
any reform except the regeneration of souls through revivals.
What the faculty reported him as saying was this: "[Mahan]
is a Christian man, and in many respects a useful and lovely man;--upon the whole honest and well meaning, but possessing certain characteristics which are highly calculated
to undermine and finally to annihilate confidence in his discretion, and even in his piety where there is a want of intimate acquaintance."   And yet, as in so many other cases,
Finney's feelings were ambivalent.   Had they not been com-
rades-in-arms?   "May the Lord direct" for "I cannot bear
to have anything done that shall injure a hair of his head."
To James Morison he wrote, "I shall feel his loss, but I
suppose the step of his resignation was upon the whole,
wise."[42] In fact there was a big blowup between Finney
and Mahan in 1854, much to the horror of their mutual
friends.   However, the mutual affection and respect between
the two that had existed in earlier years was re-established
between them fairly quickly, and it was no doubt this outcome that obliterated from Hills' mind the fact that during
the crises of 1850 Finney was indeed involved.

According to Fletcher, Mahan was not so much the
leader of a significant religious movement as he was the
proponent of a heresy that was another oddity, about on the
same level with Grahamism, that characterized early Oberlin, an oddity, moreover, that soon died out after Mahan's
departure from the scene.   That departure he describes
mainly as the result of flaws in Mahan's character.

> There was never any doubt about Mahan's high
> moral principles, his sincerity, and his devotion
> to the truth, but out of these virtues grew his
> chief shortcomings.   He was imperious; he was
> egotistical; he was overbearing; he would brook no
> opposition nor criticism.   In the heat of argument
> he would often overstep the bounds of good taste
> and good manners.   Mahan was the sort of man
> who made firm friends and bitter enemies, unfor-
> tunately, many of the latter....   As a result of
> his highhanded methods in meetings of the faculty
> and his cruel and tactless personal allusions in
> public and in private the number of those who felt
> themselves personally aggrieved steadily increased
> ....   Dawes and the President thought the teach-
> ers should accept with gratitude what funds could

be collected and not expect always to receive their
full salaries. Mahan's salary was fully subscribed,
but others were not so lucky, and Mahan "most entirely objected to any part of the money subscribed
for him being appropriated to any other use whatever than for himself.". . . The testimony taken
[in the Gillett case] occupies some hundreds of
manuscript pages. President Mahan, as council
and as witness, threw himself, with his usual precipitancy, unreservedly on the side of G   . . . .
As a result of this episode, by the beginning of
1849 the relation between the President and the
faculty had again become tense. . . . George Whipple and Lewis Tappan talked to [Mahan on his return from Europe] heart-to-heart, urging him to
accept the [Newark] call and retire from the presidency quietly, "in such a manner as would not exhibit to the world a quarrel between the members
of the faculty." But Asa Mahan was not so easily
to be set aside; when he reached Oberlin he never
said a word about his call to the Newark Church.
It had been previously decided to present him a
statement upon his arrival, advising his resignation. Such a formal statement signed by all of
the faculty was prepared the last of February and
presented to him on March 5, 1850. . . . Instead
of resigning, Mahan gathered his henchmen about
him and fought back. . . . When George Whipple,
one of those who had been most prominent in taking action with regard to the President, visited
Oberlin a little later, Mrs. Mahan invited him and
all of the families of the faculty to her house for
supper. It was agreed that Mr. Mahan was very
cordial. . . . As the weeks went by it became increasingly apparent that the settlement of April
had not been a settlement at all but merely a
truce. . . . Late in August came the regular annual meeting of the Board of Trustees. Mahan presented his resignation, simply stating that he had
already accepted the presidency of the new institution in Cleveland. . . . Thus quietly was the long
conflict between President Mahan and the faculty
concluded. [43]

Fletcher's explanation of why Mahan left Oberlin is
also too one-dimensional to be acceptable, though his defect
is quite the opposite of Hills'. That personality factors

were involved no one doubts but they must not be emphasized to the neglect of the ideological and religious disputes
between the president and the faculty and the ongoing power
struggle between the two camps. [44]   Hills emphasizes the
struggle over sanctification too much; Fletcher emphasizes
it too little.   Fletcher, in fact, exhibits no fundamental understanding of the holiness tradition in American Protestant
thought.   He treats sanctification as an Oberlin heresy which
was an oddity like Grahamism which soon died out at Oberlin.   Nothing could be further from the truth.   The tradition
was sustained at Oberlin by the students of Mahan and Finney through the 1860's and well into the 1870's and outside
of Oberlin much longer.   Moreover, just as sanctification
was dying out at Oberlin under Fairchild's presidency, it
burgeoned in the United Kingdom and the United States and
became one of the dominant strands in evangelical Christianity everywhere during the latter half of the nineteenth century.   As late as the 1930's Benjamin Warfield, like his
predecessors at the Princeton Theological Seminary during
the previous century, wrote a lengthy critique of the Oberlin doctrine of scriptural perfection.   To construe Oberlin
perfection as a heresy which soon died out would be like
construing John Wesley's concept of Christian perfection as
short-lived heresy.   No, Oberlin sanctification was not a
passing fad but became a significant part of the ongoing
Wesleyan concept of the second blessing. [45]

Moreover, Fletcher does not do justice to the one
dimension he emphasizes.   He begins promisingly when he
writes that Mahan's shortcomings grew out of his virtues,
for, as we have seen, in certain ways such a claim is correct.   That Mahan was imperious, tactless, and pushy no
one can doubt any more than they can doubt that they are
the defects of his virtues of sincerity and devotion to the
truth, which meant for him the ever-renewing experience
of sanctification and the absolute demands of conscience,
which is God's eternal law writ on men's souls.   But it is
difficult to see that being egotistical, overbearing, and brook-
ing no opposition were the natural consequences of Mahan's
high moral principles, sincerity, and dedication to truth.   Indeed, it is not clear at all that these were his defects.

As we have already seen, that Mahan was egotistical
and overbearing in a personal way may well have been the
interpretation of those who neither shared nor understood the
consequences of his deep commitment to sanctification and
his deontological views of morality.   And as far as saying

that Mahan would tolerate no opposition, a characterization
which gives a dictatorial flavor to his role at Oberlin, the
evidence is overwhelmingly against such a characterization.
He was overruled in his efforts to modernize the curriculum, to have women read their own commencement essays,
to justify Hudson's role in the Norton case, to marshal support for criticizing clergymen who were lukewarm professors, and so on; and he would have been unsuccessful in
bringing the Fosters to Oberlin had it not been for the support of the black population of Oberlin--or so John Morgan
thought.   Mahan did not like the constant opposition--there
can be no doubt about that.   But to say that he would not
tolerate opposition is amusingly false.   Indeed, the president's lack of power makes such a statement meaningless
rather than simply false.

     Fletcher says that Mahan acted in a rude and tact-
less way toward the faculty but presents only one substan-
tiating example and that in a footnote.   There he quotes
from "Notes Upon Talks with Pres. Fairchild" recorded by
D. L. Leonard: "At a faculty meeting [Mahan] had laid
down the law, or announced a policy which the faculty sat
down on to a man, when he arose, said, Gentlemen, I can't
remain in such a place and left."[46]   Fletcher neglects to
add that Leonard also wrote in the same place that Mahan
returned not long after with a smile on his face.   Why not
refer to the whole episode if it is to be referred to at all?
The truth is that Mahan was both an irritable and a loving
person and his rebukes should not be construed either as
given in anger or as leading to grudges.

     Why Fletcher should connect rudeness and tactless-
ness is not clear.   That Mahan was tactless is unquestion-
ably true.   Perhaps the most instructive instance of it was
Mahan's rising in church, saying there were still fifteen
minutes of the service remaining, and finishing Fairchild's
sermon.   What an embarrassment it must have been to the
diffident, quiet Fairchild and to many of the members of the
congregation.   The crucial question is not whether Mahan
was tactless but what mainly caused it.   The answer again
lies in those aspects of Mahan's character inadequately de-
lineated by Fletcher--namely, in Mahan's over-eagerness to
lead his people into what he took to be the ever-refreshing
waters of the second blessing and to push them into accepting what he saw as the dictates of conscience.

     Fletcher construes George Whipple as one of the

prime movers in getting rid of Mahan in 1850 as if he were
an antagonist in the same class with Steele, Johnson, Pease,
Hudson, and Dascomb. Whipple in fact was a life-long
friend of Mahan, as the correspondence between G. D. Pike
and Whipple in the archives of the American Missionary Association reveal. [47] The point is that Whipple had affection
for both the faculty and Mahan but loved the Institute dearly
and felt that for the sake of peace within the Institute and
for the welfare of Mahan himself he should accept the prestigious Newark pastorate.

Fletcher simply says that Mahan would often overstep
the bounds of good taste and good manners and make cruel
personal allusions in public and in private but gives no examples. Such an allegation is useless unless documented so
we know what counts for Fletcher as bad taste and manners
and cruel allusions. No doubt finishing Fairchild's sermon
would count as bad taste and manners for most people, but
to Mahan and others not to have done so would have been
shirking his duty to God and the rest of the congregation.
That Mahan rebuked what he took to be the sins of others
quite specifically, in public and in private, there can be no
doubt. We know that he did so in the case of Horace Taylor
before Taylor's "fall."[48] Was Mahan's conduct cruel? Perhaps so, but to him it would have been infinitely more cruel
not to have rebuked Taylor and others, for in Mahan's eyes
their immortal souls were in jeopardy and a rebuke might
help save them. (In Taylor's case it would seem that nothing
helped.) It must also be kept in mind that after the rough
and tumble debate with the Fosters they wrote that Mahan
"was very gentlemanly in deportment." They were not
shocked by tough remarks, either taken or given, but regarded Mahan as a fair and calm opponent. They also respected the fact that he was the only faculty member who
fought at all for their right to speak at Oberlin.

Other defects in Fletcher's description of Mahan's departure from Oberlin include the following: 1) He fails to
refer to the July 9, 1850, letter of Charles Finney to his
father in which the former reported that the committee members who read Keep's letter to Mahan said they could not
blame Mahan if he were to leave at once. Charles' letter
proves nothing conclusively but suggests what clearly was the
case, namely, that Mahan's leaving was a complex affair involving faults on all sides; and such a letter should not be
ignored by ascribing Mahan's departure to his own personality faults. 2) Even more importantly, Fletcher makes no

effort to explain why Mahan would agree to a document which
in fact he thought to be false in parts and unjustly restric-
tive of his rights in others.   Not to do so portrays Mahan
as accepting the interpretation of the faculty and antagonistic trustees like Pease and hence admitting to fundamental
character faults.   The explanation of why Mahan agreed to
the document is contained in his long letter to the Oberlin
trustees of August 15, 1854, and in Samuel D. Porter's long
letter to the same group of December 2, 1854. [49]   They are
both in the Oberlin College Archives, and it is puzzling why
Fletcher did not use them.

In line with his negative characterization of Mahan,
Fletcher portrays him as selfish, saying that the president's
salary was fully subscribed but that he most entirely objected to any part of that money being used for other purposes.
To impute selfishness to Mahan is so far to miss the character of the man as not to be understandable.   The documents we have cited thus far in characterizing the man, and
those to come, all testify to his complete unselfishness.
Not even his Oberlin critics accused him of selfishness in
any list of faults they assembled through the years.   The
document used by Fletcher to ascribe a selfish attitude toward salaries on Mahan's part is a letter from Joab Seeley,
an Oberlin agent, to Hamilton Hill, Secretary of Oberlin,
dated July 23, 1846. [50]   From this source, however, it becomes clear not only that Mahan objected to the procedure
of re-allocating funds but that Hill, who reflected the faculty
feeling, completely agreed with him on this issue.   Many
salaries were specifically subscribed and no one wanted Seeley to use any money subscribed toward one purpose used
for another.   This document does not support Fletcher's
ascription of selfishness to Mahan, and the corpus of documents speak overwhelmingly against such a characterization
of him.

Finally, Fletcher is simply mistaken in his characterization of Mahan's role in the Gillett trial.   Neither as counsel nor witness did he throw himself "with his usual precipitancy, unreservedly on the side of G___."   In fact, he was
not Gillett's counsel at all, and as a witness played a minor
role in the vast proceedings of the trial.   There are hundreds
of pages of written testimony and church records concerning
this trial and when they are read in their entirety a story
quite different from Fletcher's emerges. [51]

In 1846 Lucy Gillett had abandoned her husband Robert

E. Gillett and their children because she thought that in the
eyes of the Lord she was no longer married to Gillett and
because she became enamored of Second Adventism, which
was odious to her husband. She was excommunicated by
the Oberlin Church. Her relatives (not her husband) committed her to an asylum in Utica, New York and she was
readmitted to the Church on the grounds of insanity. In the
meantime Gillett had engaged Lois Ingraham, a widow with
a child of her own, to live in the Gillett home to take care
of his children as well as her own. Gillett's parents also
came to help. The services of these people were especially
needed since Gillett was a businessman who was away from
home for months at a time and unable to care for his children himself. When Lucy was released from the asylum she
was willing to live with Gillett as a sister, but Gillett refused to receive her back into the household. For this conduct, as well as other alleged misdemeanors, including improper conduct toward ladies, Peter Pindar Pease brought
charges of unchristian conduct against Gillett in the Oberlin
Church. Mahan felt the charges and innuendos of improper
relations between Gillett and Mrs. Ingraham totally false
and no doubt was prepared to act as counsel for Gillett.

Finney definitely did not want Mahan to act as counsel for Gillett, not because he was ill disposed toward Gillett
but because in acting as counsel in previous cases Mahan
had incurred--in one case especially--the wrath of the opposing side. He and Pease thought that Mahan should not
act as counsel in church trials because any criticism of him
personally had an adverse effect on the religion which Mahan so prominently represented. Finney suggested that Pease
tell Mahan they thought it inadvisable for him to act as counsel for Gillett and to explain the reason behind their request.[52] He did so, but Mahan discovered that Pease wanted to have the Church appoint Dr. Alexander Steele as Gillett's counsel. Pease thought Steele would be objective, but
Mahan knew perfectly well that Steele in 1844 had himself
preferred charges against Gillett, charges of which the latter
had been acquitted. Mahan thought Pease was acting strangely and no doubt he would have agreed to be Gillett's counsel
had the defendant asked him; however, Gillett, not wanting to
get Mahan involved in a messy case, never asked him to be
his counsel.[53] It had been proposed during a meeting of the
Church Council that Mahan be appointed by the Church as
Gillett's counsel, a motion which was voted down. The Council agreed that Gillett should choose his own counsel, and he
decided, as the reams of testimony show, to be his own

counsel.   Almost the whole population of Oberlin testified at
least once during the trial, and the testimony of Mahan and
Mrs. Mahan in this huge literature is quite minor. 54

        The result of this account of the trial is that Fletcher
is wrong in writing that Mahan as counsel and witness threw
himself with his usual precipitancy into the proceedings of
the trial.   Even for his restrained behavior, however, Mahan suffered.   People like Steele, Cowles, Johnson, and
others who were against Gillett were disgruntled with Mahan
for supporting Gillett; and people like Finney, Pease, and
others were displeased that Mahan would have been willing
to act as Gillett's counsel. 55

        The upshot of the whole discussion of Fletcher's treat-
ment of Mahan is simply that it is not only one sided but
inadequate.   There are other deficiencies, including his use
of pejorative terms like Mahan's "henchmen," but we shall
not pursue them here.

        It is painful to be critical of Fletcher since on the
whole his History of Oberlin College is a first-rate piece of
work, and any scholar interested in any aspect of early Oberlin history is deeply indebted to Fletcher's careful preserva-
tion of documents and his discovery of crucially important
new ones.   One can still deeply appreciate Fletcher's scholarly achievements without in some cases and certainly in
the case of Mahan accepting at face value any longer everything that he wrote.

Chapter 5

CLEVELAND

The Rise

In 1850 Cleveland was a town of approximately twenty-
one thousand people; it was confined to the lake front, and
cows munched grass tranquilly on the Public Square. Ohio
City, now the west side of the metropole, was its twin sister. Mahan was no stranger to either town, having preached
often in both places. He was most familiar with the Third
Presbyterian Church of Cleveland, the pastor of which, Edwin H. Nevin, was a friend who shared Asa's distaste for
strident denominationalism. South of Cleveland, where the
University was to be built, the area was mainly uninhabited.
The floor of the Cuyahoga River Valley separated the lake
town from the "Heights" south of it, and the valley in the
spring was a lush meadow where violets grew abundantly and
the river itself was perfect for swimming and fishing. The
new Cleveland University would overlook the valley, town,
and lake. The site was undoubtedly a beautiful location for
a home or farm, but whether it was a good location for a
university remained to be seen.[1] In the beginning everyone
thought it was perfect. It turned out to be quite otherwise.

With his usual energy Mahan began the promotion of
the university. Numerous advertisements for it appeared in
the Cleveland newspapers, including The Daily True Democrat, an editor of which, John C. Vaughn, was a friend of
Mahan. And a letter by Mahan and William Slade, prominent Cleveland attorney and former governor of Vermont,
outlining the plans of the new venture appeared in Horace

127

Greeley's New York Tribune.   The advertisement stressed
that arrangements were being made to secure an able faculty. 2   Mahan gave numerous fund-raising talks including several at the prestigious Stone Church.   He gave several lectures to the Board of National Popular Education and delivered the main address to the American Association for the
Advancement of Education, which met at the First Presbyterian Church.   He used these occasions to promote the
university by expounding the "new view of education" which
it exemplified.

        The "new view" was in part a critique of the classical
concept of liberal education and the delineation of a more
permissive alternative, just what Mahan had advocated during Oberlin days; but it was, in addition, the formulation of
the concept of a university in contrast to a college.   Unlike
classical education there would be no one fixed course of
study which all students, whatever their interests, tastes,
abilities, and future plans were, must take.   There would
be numerous areas of study and the student would choose
one area to pursue intensively.   With the advice of parents,
students would also be permitted to choose broadening "elec-
tives."   There would eventually be professional schools of
medicine, engineering, and so on that would draw on community doctors and technicians for teachers.   In all areas
popular lectures would be given for the community as well
as the students.   As a further way of breaking down the
isolation of academia the continental style would be followed,
students living and eating in the community.   It was not the
job of a college or university, he thought, to provide dormitories and serve meals; it should provide a good education
and let the student live a normal, uncloistered life.   Moreover, degrees would be conferred not with reference to the
actual time spent in study but as indicators of actual achievement demonstrated by proficiency in recitations and examinations. 3   Mahan was indeed ahead of his time, for this enlarged concept of "the new education" had intimations not
only of Eliot at Harvard but of Gilman at Johns Hopkins and
Hutchins at Chicago as well.

        Mahan's talks on education received wide newspaper
coverage, and the one presented to "the National Educational Convention" was printed in full in a special edition of the
True Democrat.   Not all of the educators, needless to say,
were attracted by these innovative ideas but most of the
townspeople, no doubt appreciating the concern for the community in the new view, were quite attracted to this new way

of looking at education.   That the Ohio State Journal endorsed the new university seemed like a good omen.[4]   That
wealthy and influential Cleveland businessmen became members of the Board of Trustees seemed even more promising
than good omens.   Included among the trustees were William
Case, mayor of Cleveland; Truman P. Handy, banker; George
Mygatt, banker; Elias Merchant, engineer; John C. Vaughn;
Samuel Starkweather, lawyer and jurist and mayor of Cleveland several times; Richard Hilliard, merchant; James M.
Hoyt, attorney; Edward Wade, member of Congress; and
Hiram V. Willson, a federal judge.[5]

The trustees and Mahan agreed that Cleveland University should start as soon as possible and not remain in lim-
bo while the new campus was being built on the bluff south
of the city.   Classes opened late in 1850 in the Mechanics
Block at the southeast corner of Ontario and Prospect Streets,
and the first commencement, at the end of the first term,
took place in August 1851 at the Melodeon.[6]   The commencement was held in this downtown hall because the new campus
was still far from being finished.   That any students at all
were ready to graduate after one term might seem surprising, but there were three seniors who had transferred from
Oberlin.   The hall was crowded with townspeople who had
come to hear Mahan's official inaugural address.   Predictably
the title of the address was "The Comparative Merits of the
Old and New Systems of Liberal Education."   Predictable as
the title was, the president always had a new point to make
or a new way of making an old point.   Among other things
he said to his audience,

> It is hardly necessary to allude to the objection
> often urged against the new system, that it will
> make one-sided men, men well educated in some
> one direction and not at all in others.   In reply,
> it may be suggested that it may be as well to have
> men with one side well developed and polished, as
> to have them with no sides at all, to have men
> well educated in some specific direction, as to
> have them poorly educated in many and well in
> none.   But why should we suppose such a result
> from that system?[7]

The result that Mahan envisioned was a many-sided man, one
who knew one subject well and thoroughly, and hence had
depth of knowledge, and one who knew other subjects less
well but still not superficially, and hence had breadth of
knowledge.

At the same time that the university started classes
in the Mechanics Block, the Western College of Homeopathic
Medicine opened its doors in the same building. Its able
faculty included Edwin C. Wetherell, Charles D. Williams,
Lewis Dodge, and Storm Rosa, among others. The sharing
of quarters brought the two institutions into close and friendly relations, and Mahan was asked to deliver a series of
lectures to the college. These friendly relations were a
boon to Mahan several years later when, as we shall see,
his financial resources became quite straitened. During
the time the university remained downtown the Mahans lived
on Pittsburg Street and enjoyed the conveniences of living in
a larger community. 8

Promoting the new university was an arduous job but
no single occupation ever seemed able to absorb the abundant
energies of Asa Mahan. He seemed almost like a force of
nature that went flowing on and on either obliterating or by-
passing the obstacles in its way. By way of filling out his
days he often preached at the Third Presbyterian in Cleveland and the Presbyterian Church in Ohio City. Nevin's
church was liberal, to say the least, since one Sunday Mahan preached in the morning and James Freeman Clarke, the
Unitarian minister, preached in the afternoon. 9 At a conference at the Tabernacle Church on the topic of church fellowship Nevin, A. B. Bradford, Joseph Gordon, and others
resolved to withdraw fellowship from members of proslavery
churches. President Mahan spoke against the resolution and
"Nevin expressed surprise at his worthy friend's views."
Surely Nevin and the others had good reason to be surprised
because it was not the sort of view they had been accustomed
to hearing from their friend. What had changed Mahan's
mind on this issue? His most compelling reason was that
"to condemn any man in a wrong position is to sit in judgment upon him, which was not the province of any Christian
brother." Mahan may have been right as far as Christian
doctrine was concerned but surely he never consistently practiced what he preached on this occasion. If there was anything Mahan was incapable of doing it was refraining from
judging people. A writer for the Weekly True Democrat reported, though certainly not impartially, that "Mr. Gordon
spoke some three quarters of an hour in taking up and answering, to the great satisfaction of the audience, the very
strange arguments and objections of Mr. Mahan."10 Whether
Mahan continued to hold to this view of church fellowship
the records do not reveal, although they do reveal that his
espousal of it on this occasion did not disrupt his own fellowship with his clerical friends.

In addition to his preaching, attending conferences, and promoting the university Mahan lectured at the Western College of Homeopathic Medicine and at the Mercantile Library Association in Empire Hall, addressed the delegates at a temperance convention held in the courthouse at Ravenna, and spoke at a Kossuth meeting at Kelly's Hall, a gathering described in the newspapers as "full of spirit." He was also active in the Western Home and Foreign Missionary Association, and he and Nevins were elected vice presidents of the organization at a meeting held in the Tabernacle Church in October 1850.[11]

Early in the Cleveland years Mahan, always the philosopher, began to revise in a substantial way his System of Intellectual Philosophy. It proved to be an arduous task and was not finished and published until 1855. A. S. Barnes and Company of New York City was the publisher. In his Prefatory Note to the new edition, written in August 1854, the author noted that "some of the most important chapters have been so entirely rewritten and remodeled, as to render the present [book] in some important respects, a new work on Intellectual philosophy."[12] He had assiduously reworked the chapter on "Sense," among others, since he was persuaded that a correct analysis of the "perception of the external world" is absolutely fundamental to any right system of mental science. That he not only carefully reworked various chapters but substantially added to them is attested by the fact that the previous edition of 330 pages was expanded in the 1855 edition to 476 pages.

During the Cleveland years Family Mahan remained a close knit group even though Anna and Lucy were now grown women. In 1849 Anna had married William C. North and the young couple had taken up residence in Cleveland. So the family was reunited when Asa and Mary and the rest of the children moved to Cleveland. Lucy, nineteen when they moved, was married to George H. Wyman in 1854. Theodore was fourteen, Mary thirteen, Sarah ten, Elizabeth seven, and Almira four. Asa and Lucy kept their special bond, as did Mary Dix Mahan and Theodore. Elizabeth adored her brother, and she and Theodore were destined to share a tragic ending.[13] Asa and Mary Dix were as much in love as they had been when they chatted so happily in the parlor of Theodore and Lucy Strong's home in Clinton. Asa was as robust as ever, but were the rubs and bumps of life beginning to grind down the spirited Mary Dix? She still was the hub of family life and everyone depended upon

her love, judgment, and good sense; they did not yet notice
the tired look about her eyes.

The Fall

The main Hall on the Heights was not quite completed
when Cleveland University moved its quarters there early in
1852. Lovely though the view was, the location was quite
isolated and inconvenient. There were no stores, and the
handful of people who farmed in the area had to go to Cleveland for their supplies. Unfortunately there was no bridge
spanning the valley so people either had to drive an incredibly long way around in horse and buggy or else walk down
the bluff, across the valley, and into town. Add to this
problem the fact that there was no mail delivery on the
Heights and one can appreciate an early resident's humor-
ous description of it as "an inaccessible and impossible sort
of place, only known to a few bold and venturesome explor-
ers."[14]

Family Mahan moved into their new home near University Hall, and the students began to arrive in increasing
numbers. Attracted by the advantages of the school and its
lovely surroundings, other families began to move to the
Heights, and a number of houses were built. As planned,
part of the university land was sub-divided into numerous
building lots and a few streets were laid out, streets that
still exist and bear the names of trustees and appropriate
academic entities--Starkweather, Jennings, Pelton, University, College, Professor, and so on.[15] It hardly seems like
an accident that the latter two names were included, since
Mahan lived for fifteen years at the corner of College and
Professor Streets in Oberlin.

The prospects for success of the venture on University Heights, as the bluff was now called, were bright indeed.
William Slade had accepted the pivotal position of secretary-
treasurer of the university, and as former governor of Vermont his prestige carried over to the new institution. Also
a political and legal figure promoted the image of the university as relevant to the world outside of academia. The
same things can be said of the members of the Board of
Trustees, the list of which reads like a Who's Who of Cleveland political, commercial, professional, and industrial life.[16]
Mahan, William Dawes, and George Clark had been successful in soliciting funds from influential people in Boston,

Providence, New York City, and elsewhere in the East.
The faculty included professors of music, natural science,
modern languages, mathematics, elocution, oratory and
belles lettres, and mental and moral philosophy.   The in-
cumbents, on the whole, had decent credentials and the professor of oratory and belles lettres was first rate--James
A. Thome, Lane Rebel and erstwhile faculty colleague of
Mahan at Oberlin.   There were thirty-seven students enrolled, a few of them part-time, and the prospects for more
were good.   At the commencement held in June 1852 eight
of the thirty-seven, five of whom were former Oberlin students, were granted degrees.   The commencement exercises
were held at the First Presbyterian Church since no meeting hall existed on the bluff.   Indeed, the main building was
still uncompleted.[17]   Friends of the university were sanguine about the completion of a fine physical plant.   Surely
next year commencement would be held on the home grounds.

        The expectation that the university would prosper and
blossom, given its encouraging beginnings, seems quite reasonable.   And yet in mid 1852 the last advertisement for the
school had appeared in the local newspapers, and in December of that year Mahan resigned as president.   The Cleveland Herald reported that "it is now confidently expected his
place will soon be filled by Rev. Edward Beecher, of Boston."   "Meanwhile the University will continue its operations
under the charge of its Professors."[18]   However, it turned
out otherwise.   There was no new president, Beecher or
anyone else, and there were numerous resignations, replace-
ments, and ultimately vacancies on the Board of Trustees.
The institution was moribund for several years and then disappeared entirely.   The Cleveland Directory, always a bit
out of date by the time of publication, tells the story.   In
1853 Mahan is still listed as president, in 1856 the university is listed as inoperative, and in 1857 no mention of it
occurs at all.   By that time the building on the bluff had
been purchased by Ransom F. Humiston and became the
Cleveland Institute, or Humiston's Institute, a first-rate
preparatory school that flourished for a number of years.
The university did not last long but as William Ganson Rose,
the historian of the city of Cleveland, wrote recently, it
was "a brilliant effort that was a generation ahead of its
time."[19]

        What had happened to blight such a promising insti-
tution as Cleveland University?   The collapse had numerous
causes but we will be content in pointing out several of the

more prominent ones. To begin with, the location, lovely
and picturesque though it was, did not fit the needs of an
institution that in concept was an urban university. The
bluff was completely isolated from the city until the Seneca
Street bridge was built in 1856 and that was too late to help
salvage the school. The idea was to have community members attend lectures and have professional men give lectures,
but how in the world could these Clevelanders shuttle back
and forth on an impossible and often impassable trail? And
the university was to follow the continental plan of having
students live and board in the community. Unfortunately the
community on the Heights was too small to sustain a student
body of any size, and the Cleveland community was inaccessible to the students just as the school was to the townspeople. It was altogether a hopeless situation from the beginning. If the university had remained downtown the chances
of its success would have been greater, though still not very
great.

       Another problem, closely connected with the previous
one, was the composition of the Board of Trustees. Impressive as it was, and representative of huge amounts of
capital, it turned out to be more of an ornament than a
working force. The members were enthusiastic about the
new concept of an urban university but they did not see how
Cleveland University was going to achieve this status; indeed,
it was not even within the city limits of Cleveland but was
a part of Brooklyn Township. [20] However, these men had
vision and unlimited resources and they could have transformed the bluff to the south into the cultural center of
Cleveland that the later University Heights to the east eventually became. That they did not produce the transformation
is a matter of fact. That they would have done so had there
been no interfering conditions is difficult to say. Unfortunately, there were two interfering conditions of monumental
proportions.

       There was some marginal financial dealing that caused
Mahan and many members of the board to lose confidence in
the university. It is difficult to say precisely what the nature of these dealings was since the records of the university were destroyed, or in any case have never been un-
earthed by the careful search of various scholars, including
William Ganson Rose. There are several scraps that whet
one's appetite. According to the Cleveland Herald, December 13, 1852, "All controversy in relation to the Lands have
been compromised, as we understand, and the University
secured in the possession of a fine building and some seven-

ty acres of land. "21 How did the university property shrink
from two hundred and seventy-five acres to seventy, what was
the nature of the compromise, and why was any compromise
necessary? To these questions there are no complete and detailed answers. Rose remarks that "although the records have
disappeared, it is reasonable to believe that when the university
encountered financial extremes, land holders who speculated on
its success declined or were unable to help. "22

        Mahan described the land speculation disaster in his
Out of Darkness into Light and that description is helpful,
though it is only a larger scrap and leaves many interesting
questions unanswered.

> The basis of the endowment of [the university] was
> a tract of land of two hundred and seventy-five
> acres, most propitiously located in the immediate
> vicinity of the city of Cleveland, Ohio. This pro-
> perty, which promised to render the university a
> better endowed institution by far than any other in
> any of the Western States, was obtained, and by
> written covenant was held, by myself and two other
> individuals in trust, for the purposes named. By
> the trustees of the university, and by the trustees
> in trust, a power of attorney was given to one of
> the latter to lay out this property into city lots,
> and sell the same for the benefit of the institution.
> After matters had proceeded for a time, the trus-
> tees and community were utterly astounded by the
> disclosure of the fact, that, under that power of
> attorney, all this property had been disposed of
> for private speculation, the house which I had built,
> and in which my family was residing, being in-
> cluded in the sale, no deed having yet been con-
> veyed to me. By a bogus-settlement, against
> which I recorded a written protest, and for which
> the trustees afterwards expressed the deepest re-
> gret, the ruin of the university was consummated. 23

There is every reason to accept this description since Mahan's reports of other highly charged events tally closely
with surviving documents--the records of the Pittsford Church,
minutes of the Board of Trustees of Vine Street Congregational Church, Lane Seminary, Oberlin College, Adrian College, and so on. In any case, no one ever challenged Mahan's veracity no matter how critical of him they may have
been in other ways. But the description, no doubt true as

far as it goes, does not go very far. Who was the person
given the power of attorney?   Precisely whose money paid
for the two hundred and seventy-five acres in the first place?
One commentator says that Brewster Pelton and John G. Jennings bought the land but no documentation is given for this
claim. [24] Even if it were the case that these two men bought
the land, it would not necessarily follow that they used their
own money rather than funds raised for that purpose.   If
they did use their own money then the chances of misunderstanding all around were unlimited.   Unfortunately, the answers to all of these puzzles remain unknown.

          Oberlin College dealt Cleveland University the second
jarring blow.   Dawes, Clark, and Mahan had numerous
friends from whom they had solicited funds for Oberlin in
the past.   In seeking funds for the new university they did
not neglect any source including these old friends.   They
approached these Oberlin donors and asked them to switch
their support, explaining why they thought the university was
educationally superior to Oberlin and criticizing Oberlin for
its "sad declension in purity."   By the latter they meant that
the governance of the college, because of Finney's absence,
had fallen into the hands of members of the faculty like Fairchild and Dascomb who, taking a dim view of the holiness
viewpoint, were encouraging what Mahan took to be a formal
and legalistic view of religion.   Dawes, Clark, and Mahan
initially were successful in getting Oberlin donors to switch
their support to the new university as well as in attracting
increasing numbers of Oberlin students to the Heights. [25]
Timothy Hudson and Hamilton Hill, who had been two of the
most ardent campaigners against Mahan, became convinced,
and convinced others, that the very existence of Oberlin was
at stake.   They were also incensed by the claim that Oberlin was declining in purity, rightly or wrongly reading personal dimensions into it as well as religious ones. [26] To
forestall Oberlin's demise (surely they must have been pan-
icky in envisioning this) some Oberlin people, precisely which
ones remains unknown, made public Mahan's April 1850 "Confessions" and showed it specifically to Slade and various
backers of the university who lived in Boston.   Having no
understanding whatever of the context of this document, Slade
was appalled when he read it and withdrew as secretary-
treasurer and took substantial support with him.   Various
Boston merchants who had pledged large amounts to Cleveland University refused to pay them. [27]

          It is impossible to say when Mahan learned what

Oberlin had done, but his outraged response did not come
until August 1854 when he wrote the trustees of Oberlin that
they had violated in a very flagrant manner both Christian
and worldly moral principles when they made public the private document of April 1850. It is the same long letter in
which he explained in what sense he had agreed to the faculty demands to mend his ways, an explanation we have discussed in detail earlier. Porter's reply was essentially to
this latter point but does not explain why the trustees and/or
faculty did not consider the document private to the Oberlin
community or why they felt justified in making it public. In
accepting Porter's statement the faculty and trustees added
no explanation of why they felt justified in showing the document to Slade and the Boston donors; they simply endorsed
Porter's view of the conditions under which the document
was presented and presumably accepted. That Mahan was
correct in insisting that the document was private is confirmed by John Morgan, who wrote Finney, "This paper was
not to be construed as charges submitted for the adjudication
of the Trustees; and if the attempt at an adjustment failed
no use was to be made of the paper on either side to the
prejudice of the other." Mahan requested that his letter be
placed in the records of the college and that copies be sent
to those to whom his "confessions" had been disclosed. [28]
Mahan's letter, along with Porter's reply, was dutifully put
in the college records, but it is doubtful that a copy of the
letter was sent to Slade or anyone else. The Oberlin faculty probably preferred to leave that task to Mahan.

When Mahan left Oberlin the college owed him money
on a note he held and also some back wages. The latter
was not unusual since the college owed back wages to everyone on the faculty. He wrote a pleasant and polite letter
from Cleveland in the fall requesting that he be reimbursed.
The repayment of the note was amicably taken care of by
Uriah Thompson, a newly appointed member of the Oberlin
Board of Trustees. The matter of the back salary was de-
ferred. After the document was made public Oberlin felt
the sting of Mahan's much more pressing demands. Some
payments were made, but by 1855-56 the trustees ignored
his continued claims. [29]

Mahan was especially furious with Finney because he
felt betrayed by his old comrade-in-arms. He was appalled
that the revivalist, as President of Oberlin, had allowed the
1850 document to be made public. He said that the moral
decline at Oberlin was particularly marked in Finney's case.

Finney in turn passed along uncomplimentary remarks about
Mahan. Lewis Tappan was horrified at the break between
the two men. He told Mahan that "Mr. Finney will either
confess to you that he has wronged you or will give substantial reasons for the course he has pursued." He was
even a bit cool to John Keep, suggesting to him that there
used to be a praying force at Oberlin to raise all needed
supplies. He wrote Thome that Finney was probably as
well aware of his unfitness for the presidency as anyone
else--the office, Tappan felt, had been thrust upon him. 30
Tappan made inquiries and got mixed results. At the time,
however, Tappan was close to Finney (he had once been
harshly critical of him and would drift away from him in
the future) and wanted to side with the revivalist. John G.
Fee, a Kentucky educator and abolitionist, provided him with
the occasion.

        According to Fee, Mahan had reported the following
incident: Finney in conversation with a beautiful woman had
remarked to her, "You have the prettiest foot and ankle in
Cleveland." Tappan exploded and read the riot act to Mahan, informing him that he was simply spiteful toward Oberlin for obvious reasons and was full of self-conceit. (Theodore Weld had reprimanded Tappan more than once for his
tendency to reach highly adverse judgments on the slightest
evidence). Still Tappan worried. Could Finney have said
such a thing? He inquired of George Clark, who had returned to live in Oberlin. Clark replied that Finney probably had said it. 31 Tappan was agitated to the depths of his
being. Monstrous, he cried, to think that Finney could have
said such a thing by way of a compliment. He could only
have meant it as a reproach to a woman who had exposed
herself in an unladylike way! Tappan was obsessed with
thoughts about Finney and the Cleveland lady, repeatedly returning to the incident in letter after letter. 32 Poor Tappan
had contracted a bad case of foot-and-ankle disease. And
the pity of it was that he so little knew his fascinating and
complicated friend. Finney was eccentric and outgoing, a
fact realized by those who loved him best. Indeed, they reported Finney saying things similar to the remark above.
According to Alfred Vance Churchill,

            Finney loved a beautiful gown. Not infrequently
            would he speak to a member of his flock of his
            pleasure in some felicity in the color or cut of
            her dress, or perhaps in the arrangement of her
            hair. It was not so much a compliment as a can-
            did expression of pleasure. 33

In the summer of 1855 Mahan and Finney had a meeting and mutually agreed to "bridle the tongue," much to the
relief of Tappan, who wrote Thome that "we all hope that a
cessation will be had of all difficulties." As the years passed
much more happened than the clearing up of a quarrel; the
old respect and even affection between the two crusaders for
holiness was re-established. Mahan ever after referred to
Finney and his work favorably, indeed glowingly, constantly
discussed his sermons appreciatively, and reprinted his articles in the pages of The Banner of Holiness and Divine
Life, two holiness journals edited by Mahan and published
in England. He referred to Finney and himself as com-
rades-in-arms. In his Memoirs Finney gave a positive characterization of Mahan, and he genuinely meant it. The original manuscript of the Memoirs is highly instructive. There
are sentences and paragraphs deleted, both by Finney and
by Fairchild, who edited the manuscript for publication, for
fear that they would give pain to the person written about or
to that individual's relatives and friends. There are no such
deletions in the case of Mahan. And in writing a compas-
sionate missive concerning Mahan and his family during a
time of sorrow in 1863, Finney solemnly said, "God bless
him."34

Both before and after the blowup the students and people in general who had been brought into the holiness movement by Mahan and Finney could never choose between them;
they loved them both for quite different qualities. According
to W. E. Lincoln, an English admirer of both men,

> Like a gently flowing river, blessing and making
> green the land it flowed through; so was the preach-
> ing of Mahan. This man was calm, loving, quiet,
> charming men to God. Finney was a storm, like
> the lightning and thunder of a dark, cloudy tem-
> pest. His eye and glance of indescribable power;
> it pierced you through and through, bringing to
> those who encountered its accusing sternness a
> picture of that eye, which on the judgment day,
> shall cause sinners to call on the rocks and moun-
> tains to hide them from its accusing glance.35

Though she only lived in Oberlin as a child, Frances Willard,
the great leader of the Women's Christian Temperance Union,
recalled Mahan and Finney in a strikingly similar way. In
an article in The Woman's Journal (1885) she wrote of the
old church "where Prof. Finney and Pres. Mahan used to
preach, both of whom furnished my earliest ideas of the

clergy--and lofty concepts these were--of men who, in their
day, were without superiors in the American pulpit." "Shad-
owy yet indelible are my recollections of the calm and state-
ly president, sharply contrasting with the fiery, white-eye-
browed burning-eyed preacher, Charles G. Finney, who
paced to and fro like a caged lion."[36]

That Mahan and Finney each respected the power of
the other's preaching is clear from the fact that each named
the other when asked who was the greatest speaker they
knew. W. E. Lincoln, the one who asked the question of
each, thought they were both right.

> We in England, who heard them, and also such
> men as Cobden, Bright, Gough, Beecher, Wendell
> Phillips and Bryan hold that their opinion was ful-
> ly justified. Mahan poured forth the Love of God,
> and charmed and shamed men from sin to holiness.
> Finney poured forth the fiery indignation of God
> against sin, and by sternest logic left men justly
> condemned by a righteous, yet merciful God. The
> true analysis of their power was, that both lived
> "in the Spirit."[37]

The Aftermath

After the collapse of Cleveland University Mahan was
out of a job, had lost most of his personal assets, and still
had a large family to support. How was he going to take
care of his loved ones? Moreover he felt himself cut off
from previous associations and had a deep sense of isolation,
loneliness, and alienation. These were trials of his faith
and they genuinely did shake him. And yet God, he felt,
had a reason for this disaster and humiliation and would not
forsake him. In Out of Darkness into Light Mahan referred
in several places to his plight.

> Standing in the midst of these ruins [Cleveland
> University] with a large family upon my hands, and
> with no visible means for their support, I found
> myself more completely insulated from former as-
> sociations than I had ever been before, and under
> the darkest cloud with which I could be over-shad-
> owed.... At the same time, "the light of the di-
> vine countenance" was so far withdrawn that all
> my afflictions pressed with great "heaviness" upon

all my susceptibilities, providential disappoint-
ments defeating all my plans and efforts for relief. Such were the temptations, trials of faith,
and chastening to which I was subject. Such, on
the other hand, were the divine helps and strength-
ening by which I was sustained during all that period. God gave me the most absolute inward assurance that my interior and outward life was fully approved of Him, that these sufferings were for
an end of infinite moment to me, and were preparatory to greater fruitfulness in the kingdom of
grace than was otherwise possible; that the im-
mutable condition of ensuring this personal good
and divine fruitfulness was that "the corn of wheat"
must at that very time "fall into the ground and
die;" in other words, that until God, in His own
time and way, should send deliverance, I must remain in absolute submission and content in the
centre of the divine will, entertaining no desire
or choice that the pressure of affliction should be
less severe or of shorter continuance than God
should choose.... Tribulation, affliction, and
sorrow, even unto "great heaviness," now became
sacred in [my] mind's regard; and one desire and
choice possessed [my] whole being--namely, to
have nothing occur but as God willed. [38]

Between 1853 and 1855 Mahan managed to support his
family in a variety of ways which included preaching, public
lectures at the Melodeon, lecturing at a mercantile or commercial college, and writing. Most significantly his cooperation with the Western Homeopathic College in the early days,
when Cleveland University and the college shared quarters in
the Mechanics Block, bore fruit. In the spring of 1853 he
was named president of the Homeopathic College, and the
financial picture, though not fine, was less bleak. The college trustees appointed him president not only as a matter of
friendship, of course, since Mahan's previous presidencies
had given him a great deal of administrative experience. [39]
Whether he also gave lectures at the college as he had done
in 1850-51 remains unknown. There is little reason to believe that this job brought him much cheer or warmed his
heart appreciably; he never referred to it in any of his auto-
biographical writings. He presumably looked upon it as a
stop-gap measure and no doubt during this period of his life
was grateful for small mercies.

Mahan gave a course of lectures at the Bryant, Spen-

cer, Lusk, and Stratton mercantile college on "Reminiscences
of Travel in Europe" and also lectured on "Political Economy." This mercantile college was the precursor of the
present-day Bryant and Stratton commercial colleges. He
gave frequent courses of lectures at the Melodeon, one of
which concerned "The Evidences of Christianity." A series
consisted of a week of evening lectures. The Melodeon was
the cultural and entertainment center of Cleveland in the
1850's. It was a store building that had a part fitted up as
an auditorium where concerts, lectures, and large social
events were held. The popular tastes of the time were
charmingly catholic. People streamed into the auditorium
to hear lectures by Wendell Phillips and George William
Curtis as well as by Mahan; they also crowded into the Melodeon to witness the marvels of P. T. Barnum--exhibitions
of Chinese fires, the hydro-oxygen microscope, and the dissolving views. [40]

    In spite of his feeling of isolation from old circles,
Mahan in fact was still active in the old ways and his talents
were used as they had been in the past. A convention met
at the First Presbyterian Church in Ohio City in October
1853 to organize a Congregational Congress and early the
next year convened again at the Plymouth Church in Cleveland. President Mahan and H. B. Spellman, the Cleveland
Leader reported, were appointed delegates to the annual
meeting of the state conference in June. Two resolutions
were passed: 1) to protest slavery (which became the third
article of the constitution of the congress); and 2) to solemnly protest the Kansas-Nebraska Bill. [41]

    Mahan attended the Women's Rights Convention held
in Cleveland on October 5, 6, and 7, 1853. William Lloyd
Garrison, Abby Kelley Foster, Antoinette Brown, and Lucy
Stone were also among the participants. Yes, Garrisonian
attacks on religion did come, as Asa knew they would. Why,
he wondered, must they always attack religion when they
speak in favor of women's rights. He spoke accordingly,

        And now let me say how, should the conviction
        once obtain that the principles which this society
        advocates are in any form unfavorable to the prev-
        alence of that dearest of Books, or that you are
        attempting to put them in that position, you will
        meet a rock. Any cause that strikes upon that
        rock will be broken, and any cause on which that
        rock descends will be ground to powder under it. [42]

He also wearied of hearing men denounced as the ones who
held women in subjection. He told the audience that in his
estimation the majority of men were in favor of women's
suffrage. The real job, he said, was to convince the majority of women to want to vote and to demand that right.
Moreover, there is nothing intrinsically wrong with any person being in "subjection." Everyone, even a free citizen,
he pointed out, lives under numerous restraints that are
wholly understandable and desirable. Subjection to civil
authority and family needs are crucial for the success of
any decent society. Do not seek freedom from restraints,
he told his audience, but rather demand that restraints be
justly distributed to all citizens. [43] Needless to say, not
everyone in the audience enjoyed hearing this sort of talk.
Imagine saying all these things at such a convention! Mahan's courage must have been monumental.

        Mahan's views on women's rights were far in advance
of most people's, but, as his remarks at the Cleveland Convention show, he was no radical on this issue. He supported
co-education, women speaking in public, and woman suffrage
but also felt that a family, just like a good government,
should have a head, and that should be the husband. But
what if the husband is not just and fair?--that is a crucial
question which Mahan neglected to consider explicitly. It
is difficult to believe, however, that he would insist upon
any absolute right of a husband to be head of the family.
He apparently had reservations about Paul's "subjugation"
themes or he would not have sought out Brown's exegesis
of Paul for publication. [44] And could he have missed the
implications of his own views on civil disobedience toward
an unjust government for the marriage relation? It is difficult to think so. Mahan's remarks at the Cleveland Convention can best be interpreted as warnings to other supporters against what he took to be the negative attitude toward religion and authority of any kind exhibited by the Garrisonian supporters of women's rights. [45]

        During this period Mahan became aware of the great
influence that spiritualism was exerting: mediums, séances,
and spiritualist literature abounded on all sides. Believing
as he did that mediums did a disservice to revealed Christianity, Brother Asa entered the lists once more in defense
of what was closest to his heart. In February 1855 he entered a debate on "Spiritualism," the proceedings of which
were later published. More significantly he wrote a 466-
page critique of spiritualism entitled Modern Mysteries Ex-

plained and Exposed, published simultaneously in Boston,
Cleveland, New York, and London. The Cleveland Leader
reported that the book was an immediate success; certainly
it was widely read and reviewed.

The reason for the success of the book was that it
appeared to readers to be a reasonable alternative to the
wholesale denunciations of "paranormal" claims as frauds,
on the one hand, and the naive acceptance of all such claims,
to which the spiritualists gave their own peculiar interpretation, on the other. Mahan rejected many of the paranormal
claims as fraudulent but found some sufficiently authenticated
by reliable witnesses to demand acceptance by a fair-minded
person. But he argued that such events did not require the
hypothesis that departed spirits were the causal agents. He
believed that all such events could be explained "mundanely"
by communication between minds of the living people involved.
Included in his "mundane" explanations, however, were not
only hypnosis but also the equivalent of what would now be
termed extra-sensory perception. For him the latter was
still a "mundane," or naturalistic, explanation since it requires no hypothesis about the existence of supernatural
spirits. 46

On the whole, Modern Mysteries was reviewed favorably, though S. B. Britten replied to Mahan in a tract entitled the Telegraph's Answer to Rev. Asa Mahan. There
were sporadic forays on both sides and eventually in 1875
Mahan wrote his Phenomena of Spiritualism Scientifically Explained and Exposed published by Hodder and Stoughton in
in London. 47 The book was welcomed in holiness circles
and by the Christian community in general. In a long review in The Christian Ambassador the author concluded: "We
hope that [Mahan's] calm and vigorous exposure of one of
the silliest delusions of modern times will command a wide
circulation, and save many strong and weak-minded persons
from wasting life in the pursuit of puerilities." In The
Original Secession Magazine the reviewer, alarmed by the
many votaries of spiritualism and impressed with Mahan's
critique, concluded: "We freely recommend this volume to
the attention of those who desire to know the mysteries of
spiritualism, and would seek to guard the simple and unsus-
pecting against its evil effects." Indeed, "it will amply re-
pay attentive perusal."48 Whether S. B. Britten and the
Telegraph again replied remains undetermined in the annals
of this strand of Asa Mahan's life.

In Cleveland, as elsewhere, Mahan pondered the

the scriptural basis for the holiness viewpoint. It is impossible to understand this central dimension of the man's
life unless it is fully appreciated that for him holiness was
no philosophical or theological doctrine but a Biblical message. In Christian Perfection and the numerous other books
on sanctification soom to come Mahan employed a two-pronged
strategy. First he argued that the promise of holiness is
explicitly contained in certain passages of the Bible; second,
that the passages traditionally cited to justify the sold-in-sin
view of man (Romans 7 always leading the list) have been
misunderstood. The meanings of these passages are still
being debated today but will be passed over here since the
correctness or incorrectness of any religious view or commitments is not at issue in this book. However, it is very
important to discover and state the principles that governed
all of his exegetical discourses, both because they are instructive in their own right and because they show that Mahan never ceased being a philosopher at heart. While holiness was not a speculative matter but a Biblical one, it has
no claim to acceptance if it is not arrived at in a rigidly
consistent and thoroughly rational way.

Considering the Scriptures to be a unity, Mahan, like
Augustine, would not allow a single passage to be so interpreted as to contradict the general teaching of the Bible.
Like Wesley, he interpreted the more obscure texts in the
light of the clear ones. He always interpreted in the light
of the context and according to the author's avowed purpose,
if such was evident. These principles were prominent in
his treatment of Romans 9. He also considered the historical context or setting of a passage. With reference to his
exegesis of Romans 7 he said, "to put any other construction upon these words is to forget that this epistle was written to Greeks and Romans who universally understood said
words in this one sense." He always sought to understand
the thrust or the sense of a passage, but he would not allow
a sense which was contradicted by the actual words employed.
He interpreted Scripture according to its commonsense
meaning. "That meaning I refer to, which most naturally
suggests itself to plain and unlettered men, reading the sacred
text without note or comment, and with their judgments un-
biased by preconceived opinions. For such minds the Bible
was written; and its import to them, in the state referred
to, is in accordance with 'the mind of the Spirit.'" He
thought that construction best "which would, by all mankind,
be put upon the same language, if found in any other book
but the Bible." Figurative words he treated as figurative,

but always sought to attach to them the meaning which they
were best adapted to convey. [49]

In his treatment of the text, Mahan frequently referred
to the original languages, consulting however many versions
as seemed to be required in a given case. He sought to in-
terpret grammatical constructions and phraseology according
to their common usage both inside and outside of the Bible,
a method employed by William Barclay in our own day. In
determining the import in the New Testament of an apostolic
quotation from the Old Testament, he always sought the answer in the import of the passage in its original setting.
Furthermore, he taught that principles of interpretation must
be uniform. For example, the word "dead" in the phrases
"dead in sins" and "dead to sin" must be so interpreted as
to carry the same import in both passages. In interpreting
the moral injunctions of both Testaments, Mahan sought to
understand them in the light of the law of love, on which,
according to Jesus, he pointed out, hangs all the law and the
prophets. [50]

A final principle of interpretation employed by Mahan
on occasion was an appeal to the Apostolic Fathers. In the
areas of freedom of the will and entire sanctification particularly he felt that unanimity of teaching among the Fathers
was a certain indication of the doctrine which the Apostles
intended to teach. In his later Misunderstood Texts of Scripture he wrote that for nearly four centuries after the Scriptures were written "the entire Primitive Church had no sus-
picion that these [misunderstood] passages have any bearing
whatever against the doctrine of full salvation from condemnation and power of sin in this life, or in proof of the opposite doctrine." On the contrary, "that Church, with won-
drous unanimity, put the identical construction upon these
passages, which the advocates of the doctrine of the Higher
Life now do."[51] Brother Asa felt that the Christian Church
had gone down hill from the freshness and fullness of power
of its early day. The desire to recapture that freshness is
the key to understanding most of what Mahan had to say about
"the second blessing."

Chapter 6

MICHIGAN YEARS

Jackson

Late in 1855 the fortunes of Asa Mahan and his family turned upward. In October he was called to be pastor of the Congregational Church in Jackson, Michigan, where he served until the spring of 1858. The Jackson Church had had a somewhat turbulent past--the church had been fire-bombed once because of the temperance sermons of one of its pastors--but with Mahan as pastor, surprising as it may seem, it experienced a tranquil period. Mahan's activity was straightforwardly pastoral, but not any the less interesting than his more colorful periods.

The church was organized in 1841 by the Reverend Marcus Harrison and thirteen members. For several years worship services were held in the "Session House," a small, plain wooden structure with rough-hewn floor boards and simple benches for pews. A later, new church building, occupied for sixteen years, though not grand was a marked improvement. It had brick veneer, a porch, a tower with a clock facing four ways, and a new bell that the town used on week days to announce that court was in session. It has been described as a "quaint and beautiful little church" and was the building used by Mahan during his Jackson pastorate. Only two years after he left, this edifice was demolished and a larger, stone church of modified Gothic design, still in use, was built.[1]

The main drama of the Jackson years was Mahan's

147

installation as pastor in May 1856, months after he had assumed and performed his clerical duties. The council which
assembled to interrogate the new pastor was large for such
an occasion, comprising over thirteen members who came
from all parts of Michigan. The council was drawn from
such a wide area because the General Conference of the Congregational Churches of Michigan was meeting in Jackson,
and it was so large because the crucial question had been
raised in Conference, "[Should] an individual known to all
the world as holding and teaching the doctrine of Scriptural
Holiness be installed over one of the leading Congregational
Churches in the State of Michigan?" According to Mahan,
a friend helped save the day. Mahan wrote that a Mr. Aiken
had testified that his uncle, Dr. Aiken of the First Presbyterian Church in Cleveland, thought highly of Mahan and endorsed him fully for any pastoral or academic duties. "I
therefore earnestly advise the Council to instal him as pastor over this church, and this Conference to welcome him
as one of your members," which was accordingly done. [2]
According to the editor of the Jackson American Citizen,
the positive result was due to Mahan's own performance:

> The examination ... was probably the most thorough,
> searching and satisfactory examination ever made
> or sustained in this State. It was supposed that
> the candidate was largely imbued with what are
> familiarly termed the "Oberlin Heresies"; hence
> the Council pressed its orthodoxy in every con-
> ceivable shape, point and manner, and with the
> utmost pertinacity; but without eliciting anything
> schismatic or heretical. It was well and proper
> that the Council should do this, as it was expected
> and hoped of them, and also due to Prest. Mahan,
> and gave him an ample and fair opportunity to set
> himself right before the ministry and people at
> large. Mr. M. sustained himself admirably in all
> points, and vindicated his theory, belief and char-
> acter in every particular. The examination lasted
> during Monday evening and the whole of Tuesday
> morning until the dinner hour. The Council de-
> clared themselves satisfied and the candidate ac-
> cepted for installation.... [The] right hand of fel-
> lowship was appropriately and feelingly bestowed
> by Rev. John D. Pierce [and] Rev. H. D. Kitchell
> delivered an eloquent ... charge to the People after
> which the Doxology was sung by the congregation
> and benediction by the Pastor. [3]

In addition to his regular pastoral duties Mahan became very active in the Jackson (County) Congregational Association and the General Association of Michigan, members
of which had queried him so carefully at his installation in-
terrogation. In the Jackson Association he served on the
Missionary Committee, the group charged with revising the
Articles of Faith with the intention of bringing them into line
with those of the General Association of Michigan, preached
at the Lodi meeting from I Peter 1:7, helped evaluate the
preaching and pastoral work of Rev. Beriah King of Napoleon
(at King's request) and, along with other members of the
committee, rendered a favorable verdict, served on a committee to investigate instances of Sabbath desecration, administered the Lord's Supper at the Dexter meeting, and at
that meeting was voted to present the associational sermon
at the next meeting, which, however, as it happened, he
was unable to do since by that time he had moved on to
Adrian. At the General Association of Michigan meeting in
Owosso he was appointed to a committee to report at the
next annual meeting on the expediency of raising a fund for
the benefit of indigent widows and orphans of deceased Congregational ministers. By the time he went to Adrian he
was so strongly entrenched in the General Association that
he was elected Moderator of the group in Detroit on May 19,
1859. [4]

On the whole, the parishioners of the Jackson Congregational Church were liberal-minded, and they and their
pastor got along well. On March 12, 1857, the editor of
the American Citizen reported that

> The members of the Congregational Society made
> a visit to Rev. Asa Mahan and family on Friday
> evening last and left with them as a token of good
> will and esteem the sum of one hundred and thirty
> odd dollars. It was a pleasant time--just such a
> reunion as tends to bind the hearts of pastor and
> people more closely together, and cultivate good
> feeling and harmony with all. May all parties live
> to enjoy many more such, and may they all be as
> pleasant, and the offerings be as richly deserved. [5]

That the editor was objective in his attitude toward Mahan
is evident in the fact that he could not help but twit the par-
son about his democratic tendencies, carried, the editor felt,
to an extreme. The problem arose at the church whether
the congregation should face the pastor or the choir when

the latter sang. The choir sang in the balcony and hence if the congregation were to "face the music" it required turning around and facing the rear of the church. Such movement, however, was not easy for the ladies who found it difficult to rotate inside their hoops. A bountiful supply of printed ballots were provided one Sunday morning, two to each person (why two is not explained), which stated the alternatives, "face the Pulpit" and "face the Choir," with appropriate places to mark one's choice. The Citizen reported that hoops came out ahead; the vote was not to revolve.

> It is said that some of the society who believe in "squatter sovereignty" refuse to acknowledge the decision as binding, but whether they will be able to stem the tide is uncertain. The great importance of this decision has induced us to report it for the information of the public, and to warn strangers or absentees to be on their guard against violating the etiquet of the sanctuary, or placing themselves in an awkward position.... We propose that a vote be taken upon a few other equally important questions--the proper and fashionable mode of entering and retiring; whether a person shall be allowed to wriggle round in their seat, scratch their head, adjust their wigs, or make up faces at their neighbours during service.[6]

Mahan, in fact, knew much better than the editor of the Citizen how unwise it would have been to decide unilaterally on the hoops issue.

It must not be supposed that Mahan's energies were exhausted by the ordinary round of duties and activities. He always had lectures to deliver and there were diverse audiences that were eager to hear him. To the Young Men's Association at the chapel of the Union School he spoke on "The Cathedrals of Europe," which, having been enthusiastically received, he followed with "The Palaces of Europe."[7] Brother Mahan certainly got a lot of mileage from his European sojourn of 1849-50; little did he realize that he would spend the last fifteen years of his life in England. Of course, he also spoke on educational themes, for his heart, despite his ministerial success, remained in academia. He thought about educational matters as much as ever. Frequently he used his Sabbath evening sermons, devoted to practical matters of the church in it worldly dealings, as a sounding board for his educational theories. The editor of the Citizen, who followed Mahan closely, reported:

His definitions and illustrations of what is known
as fashionable education and life, though searching
and severe, were eminently just and proper....
His views in regard to the education of the youth
were, as those of an old and experienced teacher
and educator, of more than ordinary interest and
entitled to more than ordinary weight. He regretted, and justly, too, the general laxity of home
government and family education.... Who can take
the place of the parent in the inculcation of habits
of industry and correct and refined morality and
deportment?... He remarked that children were
sent to school too early and too much. The only
care is to have the child out of the way of the
parent. [8]

Asa and Mary Mahan were those rare parents who liked
their children, as well as loved them, and enjoyed a sense
of corporate felicity when the children were close by.

Upon a subsequent speech of Mahan's on education the
Citizen remarked, "His great idea was that the aim of education ought to be to awaken thought; induce action of the
mind; and that textbooks and lessons therein should only be
used as instruments to awaken this activity of the mind 'to
know.'" To such modern sounding views the editor was in
full accord: "It is not often that we hear truth so boldly
spoken, which comes home to the vital part of our educational system, probing deep, but with a health-giving efficiency,
which if followed up would work a reform in our schools of
untold benefit."[9] Mahan would soon have another opportunity
to put his educational theories into practice, though at the
time he spoke there was no reason to suppose such a thing
was close at hand.

While at Jackson Mahan re-established his ties with
academic circles by lecturing to the literary societies at
Michigan Union College at nearby Leoni, a village a few
miles east of Jackson. This small college had been founded in 1845 by the Wesleyan Methodists only two years after
they had separated from the Methodist Episcopal Church
primarily over the slavery issue. In 1845 Dr. Orange Scott,
head of the Wesleyan Connection, as the group was originally called, toured Michigan and reported that the Leoni Institute (as Michigan Union was first named) had over two
hundred acres of land and fifty or sixty students. Since the
Wesleyan Methodists were strongly antislavery, it was no
accident that Michigan Union built up and fostered an aboli-

tionist sentiment for which it was becoming well known. Indeed, a sister and brother of one of the founders of the college, John H. Ellis, had been Oberlin students, so the abolitionist stance of the young college had more than one
source. 10

That Mahan was far from forgotten in the academic
world is attested to not only by his warm reception at Michigan Union but also by the fact that Hillsdale College, another pioneer Michigan college, awarded him an honorary Doctor of Divinity degree in the spring of 1858. The recognition no doubt cheered him. 11

Adrian

In the spring of 1858, in addition to the recognition
by Hillsdale College, Mahan received a pastoral call from
the Plymouth Congregational Church of Adrian, Michigan.
It was a larger congregation (Adrian was then larger than
Jackson) and would give him wider opportunities to be of
service to a community and to the reform causes which he
still heartily espoused. Moreover, the Plymouth pulpit was
traditionally characterized by its freedom of speech. These
considerations prompted Mahan to accept the call even though
there are no indications that he was dissatisfied at Jackson.
The Plymouth congregation was enthusiastic about Mahan and
being a very liberal group of people they scarcely felt the
need of Conference reassurance. Indeed, it was such a liberal congregation that eventually it ceased being Congregational. The church lost members to the Presbyterian and
Baptist Churches, while the core of the group, itself gaining
members, became the First Methodist Protestant Church and,
in the twentieth century, combined with the First Methodist
Episcopal Church to form the present-day First Methodist
Church of Adrian. 12

Family Mahan was quite excited about the upcoming
installation at Plymouth Church. Anna came from Cleveland
for the big occasion. On the train she met her old Oberlin
friend Mary Rudd Allen--much to their mutual surprise and
delight--and after a fine talk about old times Anna insisted
that Mary come to Adrian for the ceremonies, which she accordingly did. Mary wrote to her husband,

> We were well paid, I assure you. It did us good
> and they were so glad to see us. Today Mr. Mahan

is to be installed and the State Association meets
there. Delegates from other states [are] expected.
Even from Connecticut. Mr. Cochran (Samuel)
preaches [the] sermon--some expected Mr. Finney.
We left Jackson at four and were here at seven.
We might have gone on last night at ½ past 9 but
we were tired out and Mrs. Mahan being acquainted directed us to this good House, told us to let
them know she sent us and we would be most kindly cared for.13

It must have worked, for Mary wrote that "everything so
far has been delightful." "We seem to be 'first served'
all about." Oberlin ties are binding, and Mary Dix Mahan
always seemed to be loved on all sides--that seems to be
the message of this happy encounter.

In Adrian, Brother Mahan met his pastoral obligations
with his usual vigor. There were sermons to be preached,
children to be baptized, marriage ceremonies to perform,
the sick to visit, and, in addition, the work of being Moderator of the General Association of Michigan Churches. He
was eventually appointed to prepare a Manual of Congregational principles and rules of order for the Association, and
he preached to the members at the Port Huron meeting in
1860.14 Mahan, as always, delivered antislavery speeches.
The editor of the Weekly Watchtower took a dim view of
such activity. According to A. W. Kauffman,

When Mahan was preaching abolition at Adrian, the
editor of "The Adrian Weekly Watchtower," who
credited himself greatly for the amount of patri-
otism he said he possessed, was deploring the fact
that ministers were departing from the preaching
of the Gospel in their advocacy of abolitionism.
"Nice Negro-theorists," he called them. He was
exerting himself to give prominence and spice to
cases of alleged abduction of white women by Negroes, which cases he very ambitiously reported
in the columns of his paper.15

There is no record of Mahan's aiding runaway slaves or en-
gaging in any other acts of civil disobedience during this period. There was less need for it now, no doubt, since the
slavery issue was fast coming to a head in national politics.
Though active in the Republican Party, he held no prominent
office in county or state conventions and caucuses of the

party that had been founded in Jackson at about the same
time that he assumed his pastorate there.

Mahan's useful, if routine, life lasted scarcely more
than a year.   There was, as usual, another big adventure
on its way, this one involving Michigan Union College.   Even
before he left Jackson, the Leoni institution had been in financial difficulties.   Now the difficulties had blossomed into
a crisis and Mahan was very soon to play a crucial role in
rescuing the college.   The Wesleyan institution had financial
problems because the membership of the denomination had
been seriously depleted.   The Wesleyans had left the Methodist Episcopal Church because the latter had not taken a
stand against slavery.   Soon after their departure, however,
the M. E. Church split into Northern and Southern factions;
and the former, since it declared itself antislavery, attracted
many Wesleyans back to the fold.   With the drop in membership, the Wesleyans found it difficult to sustain their colleges.   Moreover, being strong temperance advocates as
well as abolitionists, the Wesleyans felt that Leoni, with a
big distillery, did not provide the sort of ambience proper
for a Christian college.   It was embarrassing to them to
have their college located in "Whiskey Town."   The decision
was finally to move the college to a more wholesome environment and one which would provide the required endowment.   The trustees offered to move the college to Jackson
or Adrian, depending on which of the two places should raise
the higher amount over the minimum of $25,000 and provide
a site of ten acres of acceptable land.   The Citizen pushed
hard for Jackson and the Adrian Daily Expositor pressed for
its town. 16   Influential citizens in each town pulled in the
tug of war, but Jackson was no match for Adrian since Asa
Mahan was now in Adrian, and he could pull harder than a
Clydesdale.

Why should Jackson benefit from Leoni's loss when
Adrian was a more appropriate spot?   That was the question
Brother Mahan asked his fellow citizens.   Under his spur
they replied, "Why indeed!" and, eager to outstrip Jackson
and reap the advantages that a college brought to a town in
those days, they rallied to his appeal for support.   Mass
meetings were held, committees appointed, and a canvass
for funds made all within the period of six weeks.   The efforts produced remarkable results: a desirable piece of
ground and the $30,000 to meet the charter requirements.
Mahan's initiative was rewarded and Michigan Union College
transferred operations to Adrian and on March 28, 1859,

reincorporated as Adrian College.   Of the new Board of
Trustees six prominent businessmen represented the town
while six Wesleyan ministers and laity represented the church.
They had little difficulty in deciding who should be the first
President of Adrian College.   Without him there would have
been no college, and only he had outstanding scholarly and
educational qualifications.[17]   Asa Mahan found himself president of a college once again.

Adrian College

        With the exception of a short interval midway in his
tenure Mahan was President of Adrian from 1859 to 1872.
The reason for the interlude is extremely interesting, re-
flecting as it does denominational strains within Methodism,
but an examination of this reason will be postponed until the
following section.   For the moment we will be concerned
with the whole spectrum of Mahan's presidency.

        The campus, the land for which had been donated by
L. G. Berry and D. K. Underwood, was a mile or so from
the center of town, and the building program began as soon
as Michigan Union committed itself to the Adrian move.   Two
buildings were ready for occupancy in November and classes
began on December 1, 1859.[18]   In his inaugural address--
by now a familiar sort of art form to him--which he delivered in the Plymouth Church, Mahan reserved for himself
as president the right to freely discuss any topic, and he
also emphasized the justice and educational value of co-education.   According to the editor of the Daily Expositor,

> [Mahan] urged the co-education of the sexes as
> both proper and judicious, and announced his in-
> tention of being none the less a citizen, none the
> less a man, none the less entitled to think and
> speak on all the topics of the day, because he
> was a minister, or the President of a College.
> He should continue to exercise the same freedom
> in regard to all this which he accorded to others.[19]

        It might seem that by 1859 defense of co-education
was unnecessary and that Mahan was harping on a favorite
theme for old times' sake.   Nothing, however, could be
further from the truth.   There had long been special problems besetting co-education in the state of Michigan, and
that for peculiar reasons.   The state officials of public in-

struction, eager to push forward the fortunes of state supported institutions, showed little friendliness to religious colleges like Michigan Union, Hillsdale, Kalamazoo, Olivet, and
now Adrian, and tried to prevent these church colleges from
conferring degrees. Since it was these church colleges that
were ardent supporters of co-education, the animosity toward
colleges competing with state institutions carried over to co-
education. The hostility toward co-education shown by the
state did not last long, but because of the opposition to them
the church colleges did not achieve equal rights in higher
education until the Enactment of 1853, and they had to be
alert to guard these rights. Mahan found himself in the
middle of the same old battle again, and once again he effectively used the same weapons as in earlier years--name-
ly, speaking in defense of co-education both from the pulpit
and at public meetings and by producing a product from a
co-educational institution that upon acquaintance inspired confidence. 20

          The character of student life was much the same as
at Oberlin. Mahan and the rest of the faculty expected the
students to act according to the same dictates of conscience
that should govern their behavior in everyday life, quite
apart from being a member of academia. As at Oberlin,
there was no formal deference paid to professors, no seg-
regation by classes, and no hazing. Student pranks were
at a minimum and the relation between students and townspeople a wholesome one. Mahan wrote that the only time
the students invaded a townsman's property was to drive off
a herd of cows that had wandered into a lot and was wreak-
ing havoc with the fruit trees. 21 In later years, when the
Methodist Protestant Church assumed control of Adrian College, the trustees pressed for more formal and rigid rules,
and, as we shall see, Mahan was not happy with this turn
of events.

          As an administrator Mahan, as at Oberlin, had no
special powers, though he was more successful in carrying
the faculty with him by force of character than heretofore.
It was only in 1882 that the college president at Adrian was
awarded special powers. When Mahan officiated "the president [of the college] aside from presiding on campus and directing school affairs was merely another individual at board
meetings." In 1882 the trustees voted that the president
should "exercise supervision over all local affairs of the
College" and "direct all the working forces of the College
and carry forward aggressive measures for increased pa-

tronage and in advancing college interests." His classroom
labor was not to interfere with these executive duties.   So
it was that Asa Mahan, when he carried a point, did it by
moral suasion and not by administrative fiat. [22]   That the
role of professor of philosophy should be diminished and not
allowed to interfere with executive duties would have appalled
him.   The most important thing that a president of a college
did, in his opinion, was to elucidate and drive home to students the eternal verities of philosophy and religion.

    In addition to being president, Mahan was, of course,
Professor of Mental and Moral Philosophy.   He was as usual popular with the students and was well portrayed in the
Semi-Centennial Souvenir, Adrian College and elsewhere.
There are no instances of altercations with students recorded; indeed, the only complaint that the students playfully advanced was that the president's handwriting was so bad that
they had grave difficulty in deciphering his written texts.
According to the Souvenir, "Dr. Asa Mahan was an author
of repute as well as an educator of renown, [though] the
boys of 1858-1868 still groan, as they tell of those lessons
assigned them from his manuscript text book, yet in press,
saying that Greek text was easy beside his script."[23]   We
may add that never was a complaint more thoroughly justified.

    Mahan also published philosophical and theological
works of considerable merit during his Michigan years, the
most notable probably being his Science of Logic (1857), Science of Natural Theology (1867), and The Baptism of the
Holy Ghost (1870).   At the moment we are concerned only
with the first two volumes; Baptism of the Holy Ghost will
play a prominent role in later discussion.   In his Logic Mahan owed most to Kant, Sir William Hamilton, and William
Thomson's An Outline of the Necessary Laws of Thought.
In his use of the Euler diagrams he followed Thomson very
carefully, including the use of dotted lines which Thomson
introduced and which do not occur in Euler's famous Lettres.
In addition to the Eulerian diagrams, Mahan gave extended
accounts of the line diagrams of J. H. Lambert, Hamilton's
"scheme of notation," and tables of valid forms according
to Thomson and Hamilton.   The most interesting of these to
a contemporary reader is Lambert's system, where Mahan
follows Thomson's exposition closely. [24]   Mahan's analysis
of non-standard propositions and arguments and of fallacies
is an especially penetrating part of his logic book.

    Mahan's Science of Natural Theology represented God

as the Unconditioned Cause, that is, the only thing with
necessary rather than contingent being, and, as revealed in
creation, both infinite and perfect. Natural theology was
again the theme of his Ingham lecture, "Theism and Anti-
theism in Their Relations to Science," in which he wrote
that "long before the year 1900 shall roll round ... the
great unbelievers of the present era--unbelievers such as
Parker, Emerson, Mill, Spencer, and Huxley--will be known
only as the bewildered sophists of the nineteenth century."
Mahan did not mean unbelievers only in the religious sense
but also those philosophers who denied the existence of mental and physical substances. Nowhere did the good doctor
exhibit his commitments to Scottish commonsense philosophy
more charmingly than in this lecture.

> I once ... saw a mother very much perplex her
> little child with this form of sophistry: Every
> creature which has two feet is a biped. You are
> a biped. A goose is a biped; therefore you are
> a goose. The child was perplexed; yet it abso-
> lutely knew that it was not a goose.

To a phenomenalist like Mill, he continued, the proper reply
is this:

> Your reasoning is quite plausible. It utterly fails,
> however, to induce that absolute assurance that I
> have, that I, myself, exist as endowed with the
> powers of thought, feeling, and willing, and that
> matter is before me as possessed of the qualities
> of extension and form. I conclude, therefore, that
> you are acting the sophist with me; and I know
> well that I should make a goose of myself if I
> should judge otherwise.[25]

The Ingham lectures, delivered at Ohio Wesleyan University,
were a prestigious series, and to be invited to deliver one
of the lectures was a significant recognition of philosophical
scholarship and/or contributions to religious thought. Other
lecturers included three Methodist bishops, the president of
the School of Theology at Boston University, the president
of Drew Theological Seminary, the editor of The Christian
Advocate, and the Olin Professor of Rhetoric and English
Literature from Wesleyan University in Connecticut. The
lectures were published in 1873 in Cleveland by Ingham,
Clarke, and Company (and in New York and Cincinnati by
different publishers) under the title A Course of Lectures on
the Evidence of Natural and Revealed Religion.

Of all Mahan's writings one of the most interesting
is an unpublished manuscript (now in the Adrian College
Archives[26]) consisting of sermon and lecture notes, skeleton
outlines of articles, and maxims and aphorisms covering a
wide range of topics. The whole of it was not written at
Adrian, though much of it was. The very lengthy manuscript
volume was started in the Oberlin days and concluded at
Adrian, as manuscript references to current events testify.
By the nature of this work there is no order or system but
ideas are recorded seriatim as they occurred to Mahan, and
various topics are re-examined innumerable times as the
years passed. There is much in it that overlaps his published work--indeed, the outline of much of what he published
occurs here--though there is a large amount of new, seminal
material, particularly in the maxims and aphorisms. The
manuscript begins with pagination but fairly soon that disappears. We will present only a few of his fascinating entries,
of necessity in seriatim order without page references.

> The world is a vast labyrinth in which almost every-
> one is running a different way, and almost every-
> one manifesting hatred to those who do not run the
> same way (do I?).

> It is better that the mind should move though in a
> wrong direction, than that it should stagnate in er-
> ror under the brooding night of superstition.

> God has put into the hand of every man a price
> fully adequate to the purchase of the entire uni-
> verse. It is always at his option to give or with-
> hold the boon. The price is himself. When a
> man will consent to part with himself, to say, "I
> am not my own," I belong to God and the universe,
> then in the highest sense of the term, he possess[es]
> all things.... If on the other hand, he keep[s] back
> even "a part of the price," he not only lose[s] God
> and the universe but himself also.

> To be truly blessed we must fervently love.

There follow long disquisitions on the will, emotions,
government, forms of prayer, inspiration, faith, moral government, atonement, sanctification, immortality, and liberty
of the will, all topics to which he returns again and again.
In discussing the liberty of the will, he formulates a devastating criticism of Edwards with incredible economy of
words.

1. There is no freedom at all where [Edwards]
has placed it.   2. It gives no ground for the distinction between natural and moral powers.   3.
Mean are deceived by it.... As soon as it is
shown, that men cannot choose differently from
what they do, and having chosen cannot but act as
they do, all will say, then we are not free.   They
suppose that phrase "we can do as we choose"
really means that we have the power of choice.

After lengthy discussions of the relation of the sensibility to
preaching, the planning of sermons, extemporary versus
written sermons, the idea of perfection, and another tour
through mental and moral philosophy in general, Mahan offers choice advice about the conduct of religious controversies:

A Christian minister must never strive for mastery
in arguments.   Consequently he must avoid everything which has the appearance of unfairness....
No advantage should be taken of the weakness of
an opponent.   In general the object should not be
merely to answer the arguments and objections of
an opponent, but to elucidate the subject.   There
should be the absence of a trifling spirit.   Sar-
casm and even ridicule [are] sometimes proper.
Yet all should bear the stamp of serious earnestness....   Never undervalue the weight of an opponent's argument.   Never attribute to an opponent
views which he don't [sic] admit....   Isolate the
real question at issue.   State it just as it is, and
then join issue upon that.   Never assume anything
secondary as the main question....

On the whole this advice seems unmistakably sound and on
the whole Mahan followed his own advice in his numerous
religious controversies.   He was genuinely fair in his polem-
ics and always went to the heart of an issue, and so on,
but it is difficult to believe that he kept his first rule up-
permost in mind.   No, it must be admitted, his strivings
for mastery in argument were not rare or even uncommon.

Curricular innovations, it might well be expected,
played a large role in Mahan's presidency of Adrian; here
was his third and clearly last opportunity to put his advanced theories of education into practice.   There was a
new look about the course structure at Adrian but not nearly

as much as expected.   We need first to describe what was
new and then to explore the reasons why there was nothing
even approximating Mahan's theoretical anticipations of the
educational wave of the future.

In addition to its classical course leading to the A.B.
degree, Adrian also instituted at the outset a scientific course
leading to the B.S. degree.   The latter embraced a fuller
course of mathematics and natural science than that included
in the classical course and added modern foreign language
and literature and English language and literature.   Ancient
language and literature were omitted except that in the first
year the student had the option of taking Latin and Greek.
It must not be assumed that the B.S. curriculum first appeared at Adrian.   At Indiana Asbury University (now Depauw), an institution of the Methodist Episcopal Church, a
B.S. degree already existed, and no doubt elsewhere as
well; but the genius of Adrian was to make it a respectable
program.   At Indiana Asbury the B.S. degree was granted
to those students who took all the courses required for the
A.B. except for Greek and Latin.   Since no additional
courses were required it was a cheap degree and few students entered the program.   Even in 1859 when the program
was reorganized and became more popular and respectable,
four of the required courses during the freshman year were
of preparatory rather than college grade.   Moreover, to
take the place of the omitted classical courses more practical ones, and none in language and literature, were added.[27]

At Adrian in addition to classical and scientific courses there were "Elective Studies" and the "Teacher's Class,"
the former consisting of courses in commerce and other vo-
cational areas, and the latter a course in teacher training.
There was also a strong music program of a practical nature (to train piano teachers, choir directors, and so on)
that was not a part of the liberal arts program, though the
latter aspect was by no means wholly absent.   According
to the College Catalogue, 1864 "For the benefit of such as
do not intend to complete a Collegiate course, instruction is
given in such branches as are requisite in practical business, and in preparation for teaching common schools, either
by a selection of particular studies from the regular departments, or by the formation of special classes, as occasion
may require."   "Special instruction is given to classes in
Vocal and Instrumental Music, Painting, Drawing, etc."[28]
Adrian also had a preparatory department.

Mahan's imprint is clear on the Adrian curriculum

both in the enriched form of the B.S. degree and in the diversity of practical courses that served the very practical
needs of an ever-expanding democratic society. He never
managed to introduce the elective plan in the collegiate courses, though he did not ultimately fail since it was partially
adopted the year immediately following his retirement. That
there were no more curricular innovations than there were
in the collegiate courses is understandable, since these courses played a minor role in the life of the college. The number of students pursuing A.B. and B.S. degrees was rela-
tively small; the bulk of the students of college age were in
the commercial, teacher training, and music courses. The
overwhelming percentage of the students were in the preparatory department; without that department the college would
not have existed at all. The educational need of frontier
Michigan life was basic education rather than collegiate courses. If college education was marginal it is easy to understand why Mahan never tried to implement the idea of a modern university that he had had in mind for Cleveland.[29] That
implementation required an urban environment and vast resources, conditions that never meshed for Mahan throughout
his life. In addition, implementing educational theory was
further hampered at Adrian by chronic financial difficulties
and from denominational strains within the fabric of Methodism. As we have seen, the Wesleyan Methodists were in
control at Michigan Union and had half of the trustee slots
at Adrian. Eventually Adrian became an institution controlled by the Methodist Protestant Church. The Wesleyans
and the Protestants tried to cooperate at Adrian but they
never managed it. The strains, as we shall see, became
quite intense and were further exacerbated by personal ani-
mosities that had nothing to do with denominational matters.

The Troubles

In order to understand the problems at Adrian it is
crucial to be acquainted with the background and context of
problems in Methodism generally. It will be recalled that
the Wesleyans withdrew from the Methodist Episcopal Church
because the latter would not declare against slavery. After
the M.E. body split into Northern and Southern groups and
the former denounced slavery, the ground was, to some extent, cut from under the Wesleyans and many returned to
the parent body. This decline in membership was one reason why the Wesleyans could not adequately sustain their institutions of higher learning.

The Methodist Protestant Church separated from the
M. E. Church even earlier than the Wesleyans, though the
reason for separation was different. From the beginnings
of Methodism in the United States under the auspices of
Francis Asbury, reformers within the parent body had insisted upon lay representation in church government. The
M. E. clergy were unimpressed and even expelled certain
leaders of the faction that chose to challenge the traditional
rights of the clergy. The "democrats" among the Method-
ists--that is, those who objected to the hierarchical government of the church--separated from the parent body and
formed the Methodist Protestant Church "for fellowship and
Christian service."[30]

Although the Methodist Protestants had different grounds
from those of the Wesleyans for leaving the M. E. Church,
there was a certain affinity between them since the latter
also took a dim view of hierarchical church government.
The two denominations tried hard to cooperate, even to join
forces, but they were never successful. Nowhere was their
effort to work together more sustained than at Leoni and
Adrian. There is some evidence that the two groups even
shared a building at the Leoni Institute, and a close connection was clearly assumed when Michigan Union was re-
established at Adrian. According to the Adrian Evening Expositor, February 4, 1859,

> There was a large meeting at [Bidwell's] Hall on
> Monday evening, to take into consideration the es-
> tablishment in Adrian of the great central College
> of the Wesleyan and Protestant Methodists....
> Prof. McEldowney addressed the meeting [concern-
> ing] the wishes and plans of the society with which
> he was connected [Wesleyan]. A short statement
> of facts, as we understand them, is as follows:
> the Wesleyan and Protestant Methodist denomina-
> tions contemplate a union....[31]

The contemplated union did not occur and Adrian began as a Wesleyan college; half of its trustees had to come
from that denomination, the other members of the board to
be prominent citizens of Adrian. However, while the town
had done its part by providing land and an endowment, the
Wesleyan Methodists could not adequately support the college.
It was Michigan Union and Leoni all over again. Sentiment
arose, strongly endorsed by Mahan, to ask the Methodist
Protestants to join the Wesleyans in supporting Adrian College

and making a cooperative venture of it.   The Adrian town
trustees, along with several Wesleyan trustees, voted in October 1862 to invite the M. P. Church to become involved at
Adrian with equal rights and responsibilities.   Mahan happily
extended this invitation to its Collegiate Committee.   Two
prominent members of the M. P. Committee in Ohio attended
the trustee meeting in June 1863 in response to the invitation,
but the matter was dropped abruptly by the board of trustees,
much to the annoyance of President Mahan, who saw no future for the college without financial assistance from the
Protestants.   The measure was dropped because, after all,
it was reported there were "Wesleyan objections in several
quarters."[32]

    Mahan continued to cooperate with the Methodist Pro-
testants in Ohio to gain their support.   It was clear that if
these Ohio Methodists were not allowed to support Adrian
they would start their own colleges; indeed, they proceeded
with Mahan's help to investigate sites in Mansfield and Spring-
field, while the President of Adrian engaged in a highly successful fund raising effort in their behalf.   Mahan spent so
much time in Ohio helping the Collegiate Committee of the
M. P. Church that the Adrian trustees declared the presidency
of Adrian vacant and appointed John McEldowney to succeed
him.   Adrian fortunes further declined.   At this point the
trustees inquired if Mahan could swing the support of the
M. P. 's away from their new projects to Adrian.   Mahan
thought under certain conditions they would agree.   He was
reappointed president of Adrian in 1867.   In 1868 legal transfer was made, with the Wesleyan trustees participating, and
the Methodist Protestant denomination assumed full control
of Adrian College, a control it continued to exercise into the
twentieth century when the Episcopal and Protestant branches
of Methodism reunited.[33]

    This account gives a useful overall view of the trou-
bles of Adrian College but it masks the severity and intensity
of denominational and personal conflicts.   It would be less
than honest if we did not pursue this unhappy story in considerable detail.   There is nothing to relate that dishonors
the memories of committed Christians but there is much to
reaffirm what is so well known, that fraternal strife is the
most unhappy and painful kind.

    The best way to reconstruct the quarrels is to follow
closely the chronology of events as presented in the Trustee
Minutes of Adrian College, 1859-1922, Minutes of the Wesley-

an Methodist Church, Michigan Conference, and letters by
Mahan and Luther Lee. Lee was a Wesleyan minister, ardent abolitionist, and, briefly, professor of theology at Leoni. In 1853 he had preached the ordination sermon when
Antoinette Brown became pastor of a church in South Butler,
New York. Both Lee and John McEldowney had been presidents of the Wesleyan institution at Leoni for short periods.
McEldowney came to Adrian as soon as Michigan Union re-
located; Lee came later and stayed for only a brief but stormy
period. 34

        June 17, 1862--Mahan is asked by his board of trus-
tees to help prepare a plan to submit to the Methodist Protestants "asking the cooperation of that denomination in the
endowment and support of this College on such terms and
conditions as shall hereafter be approved of." October 1--
Mahan is introduced to a meeting of the Wesleyan Conference, is invited to a seat of honor, and participates in an
"interesting discussion" of the annual educational report.
He is appointed "corresponding delegate" for the next annual
meeting. October 22--The Adrian Board, including the Wesleyan trustees, decides to ask the M. P. Church to become
"joint cooperators" at the college and to have "equal rights
and responsibilities." Mahan, McEldowney, and a trustee
have their fares paid to Cincinnati to confer with M. P. officials. June 19, 1863--M. P. committee comes to Adrian
to make plans for the cooperative venture. July 3--In a
surprise move the Wesleyans oppose collaboration, and the
M. P. committee, still at Adrian, is so informed. The committee members leave and begin preparations for their own
college in Ohio. Adrian trustees "indefinitely postpone" collaboration. Mahan keeps in close touch with M. P. Collegiate
Association in Ohio. 35

        Coincident with the Wesleyan change in mood is their
pressing for the appointment of Luther Lee as Professor of
Theology at Adrian. July 3, 1863--Trustees appoint Luther
Lee Professor of Theology. Later this action is reconsidered
and the proposal tabled. September 28--Wesleyan Conference
reaffirms its support of Adrian College and says Wesleyan
members of board have been "misinformed" about the interest of the conference in its institution of higher learning.
April 15, 1864--Lee is unanimously elected to theology post
at Adrian College. Wesleyans receive Lee on transfer from
Syracuse Conference and unanimously elect him president of
Michigan Conference. 36

        In light of the Wesleyan withdrawal from collaboration,

the continued poor financial support, and the rise of Lee's
influence, Mahan wholeheartedly turns to the M. P. Collegiate
Association and helps them raise funds and locate a site for
a college in Ohio. September 12, 1864--Mahan is absent
from Adrian board meeting, and the trustees vote to request
Mahan's resignation. He is actively working in Ohio, they
point out, and "his absence seriously embarrasses Adrian."
Time passes and they do not hear from Mahan (his letter of
resignation was not delivered) so they declare the presidency
vacant. January 23, 1865--The Wesleyan Conference wants
McEldowney named president and Lee conveys this sentiment
to trustees. October 20, 1865--There is a difficulty between
Mahan and McEldowney, now president, about what the college owes Mahan. A committee is appointed to investigate
the matter. [37]

The financial resources of the college dwindle further
and are insufficient for continuing the institution. October
24, 1865--Adrian trustees adopt a resolution asking M. P.
Church, in good faith, to join the Wesleyans in mutual support of the college. November 1--Mahan and McEldowney
correspond and Mahan lays down the conditions for M. P.
support. The Articles of Association must be revised "as
to allow the Board of Trustees to be elected by the General
Conference of the United Churches." The trustees agree.
January 10, 1866--Trustees of the M. P. Collegiate Association meet with Adrian Board to work out details. March 8--
Mahan returns to Adrian as Professor of Mental and Moral
Philosophy, and John McElroy, M. P., is elected to the faculty. [38] However, the two boards cannot agree and cooperation breaks down.

Amidst the denominational difficulties personal flare-
ups occur. There is tension between Mahan and the rest of
the faculty, on the one hand, and Lee and McEldowney, on the
other. June 13, 1866--Lee charges Mahan with spreading rumors about McEldowney and Miss M. H. Pomeroy, assistant
teacher in the English Department. June 15--Mahan appears
before Board to explain the case "as a Christian brother" and
"to set himself right upon questions including the interests of
the College." All members of the faculty agree that they can
cooperate. "Miss Pomeroy declines answering questions just
now." A committee of three, headed by Lee, exonerate McEldowney and Pomeroy; they were together on business matters.
November 29--Mahan and the rest of the faculty (except Lee and
Pomeroy) request the resignation of McEldowney; in close
vote the trustees decide not to ask for his resignation.

Board decides to have two Wesleyan and two M. P. trustees
resign and to appoint citizens of Adrian in their places.
November 30--Mahan resigns as Professor of Mental and
Moral Philosophy. December 3--L. G. Berry, most prominent of the local trustees, resolves, in light of the failure
of cooperation between the two denominations, that the Methodist Protestant Church be asked to take control of Adrian,
a motion that passes 6-3, Lee, McEldowney, and Rice cast-
ing the negative votes. Mahan withdraws his resignation.
February 2, 1867--Lee and Judge R. R. Beecher appoint a
committee to discuss the proposal with the M. P.'s.   February 15--M. P.'s indicate their willingness to assume control of college. February 28--The board unequivocally ac-
cepts the M. P. offer. Lee resigns and trustees write that
"so far as we know, he has discharged his duties with ability and fidelity."   McEldowney is no longer president. March
1--Mahan unanimously elected President of Adrian College.
August 16--The honorable R. R. Beecher is appointed to
correspond with Rev. John McEldowney, "in view of obtain-
ing from him all books, papers, documents, and records,
etc. belonging to the College." Late in 1867 the Wesleyan
Conference re-asserts its right to control Adrian College
and vows readiness to retain this right. [39]

        June 25, 1868--The Adrian trustees amend the Ar-
ticles of Association so that thirty members of the board
are to be appointed by the Methodist Church (the designa-
tion M. P. is temporarily dropped in Michigan and elsewhere). R. R. Beecher is appointed a committee of one
to obtain "peaceably if he can, forcibly if he must" certain
books of account now in the hands of Abel Whitney, Esq."
In 1868 the Wesleyan Conference announces that it has been
displaced at Adrian College and holds that since this was
done without the consent of the denomination all rights and
control still belong to it. The educational report of 1869
refers to Adrian College having passed from their control
"by strange processes."[40] Lee and McEldowney return to
the Methodist Episcopal Church.

        Tangled as this skein of events certainly was, there
can be no doubt that all parties acted with honorable intentions. Had the Wesleyans had sufficient financial resources
to sustain Adrian there would have been no problem in the
first place. It is a pity that the ranks of this denomination
were decimated so soon after its founding and its resources
thereby depleted. The local trustees were the ones who finally played the decisive role in bringing to an end an un-
workable situation.

In his second presidential term, under M. P. auspices,
Mahan discovered that the financial situation was still not
wholly cheering, a chronic difficulty, it would seem, in academia.   Fortunately the college procured two important gifts
in 1870, $20,000 from J. J. Amos of Rushville, Indiana,
and $10,000 from W. H. Hamilton of Wenona, Illinois.   Ma-
han moved at a trustees meeting to expand the Literary Society library into an adequate college library, and the motion was adopted and implemented within the limits of the
resources of the college, [41] an implementation begun while
he was president and continued after his retirement in 1872.

During his second term Mahan wrote Baptism of the
Holy Ghost, based on a course of lectures delivered to the
Senior class.   It was published under Methodist auspices in
New York in 1870.   Despite Phoebe Palmer's hesitation in
publishing it, the book was widely read and numerous further
printings required, much to the pleasure of Mrs. Palmer
and no doubt to the author as well.   John Bate published it,
with Finney's short Enduement of Power appended, in London in 1872.   C. Challand's French translation of Bate's
volume was published in Switzerland in 1889 and reprinted
as recently as 1963.   Mahan's book became a classic in the
literature of the holiness movement and it was repeatedly reprinted by religious publishing companies throughout the nineteenth and twentieth centuries.   It is still reprinted currently by several presses.   It should be noted that Bate took
editorial liberties with the manuscript, changing American
expressions into English ones and occasionally changing sentence structure.   The original edition is the one that should
be read and used in any further reprintings. [42]

During his second term two innovations by the M. P.
trustees bothered Mahan.   The first concerned college discipline and the second the administration of examinations.   The
Laws and Regulations of Adrian College, thirty-three in number, were printed in the 1869-70 Catalogue.   Some of the
rules were general and others quite specific: "No visiting
rooms of opposite sex on pain of expulsion" and "No Society
may continue its exercises after half-past nine in the evening without special permission."   There is no explicit reference to surveillance but "all unexcused delinquencies will be
registered by [the] faculty."   Should the number reach six
during one term "the student shall be admonished, suspended,
dismissed, or expelled."[43]   There is no explanation of the
presumably subtle distinction between dismissal and expulsion.
Also, stiff study hours in their rooms were imposed upon the

students. The trustees, however, decided that all this was
not sufficient. At the July 1, 1870, board meeting the members of the committee on the government of the college reported:

> ... while they are pleased with the general good
> order and harmony that prevails in each depart-
> ment of the Institution, and most heartily endorse
> the published "Laws and Regulations" of the college
> and believe their strict enforcement will necessar-
> ily contribute largely to the good of the students
> and the honor of the Institution, [they] would at the
> same time respectfully and kindly suggest the pro-
> priety of the adoption of the following: that the
> President and the Principal of the Preparatory De-
> partment, either personally, or by proxy, see that
> lights are extinguished in students' rooms at cer-
> tain hours in the evening and also that students be
> required to be in their respective rooms at a given
> hour, not later than 10 o'clock, p.m., unless by
> special permission. [44]

Apparently the trustees did not think that Mahan was a strict
enough disciplinarian and he, in turn, felt that the attitude
of the trustees was too rigid and likely to promote the old
animosity between students and faculty that had existed at
Hamilton in the old days and which he had worked so diligently to avoid at Oberlin and Adrian.

The question of administering examinations arose at
the same board meeting. The committee on governance proposed that the faculty have annual public, oral examinations
of students in addition to the written examinations. It was
no accident that this recommendation closely preceded the
following observation. "We believe that the Students, and
especially those preparing for the ministry, ought to be made
as familiar as possible, while pursuing their studies, with
Methodistic forms and usages, for reasons that must be apparent to all."[45] The point of the oral examinations each
year was clear: it gave a check on the orthodoxy of the
views held by Adrian students. It seemed obvious to the
trustees that the point of a Methodist school was to produce
scholars who viewed the world from its particular standpoint.
Certainly this public check by oral examination was not
unique to Adrian. At Indiana Asbury, Conference visitors
attended the oral examination of students and at such times
made specific criticisms and suggestions. "In 1856 the

Southeast Conference instructed its visitors to 'inquire closely whether there has been ... any departure from the usages
or teachings of Methodism.'"[46]

It is clear that the trustees doubted Mahan's commitment to institutionalized Methodism. He had always been a
member of the board of trustees, and often president of it,
during his first term; but he was, with one exception, pur-
posely excluded from the board during his second term. A
motion by a member of the board to elect Mahan was rebuffed. [47]

The trustees were certainly correct in their suspicions
that denominational purity was something Asa Mahan never
sought. He was completely ecumenical and remarked that
the path into a church should be no narrower than the entrance into heaven. It might be supposed that Mahan reached
his ecumenical views as a result of somewhat bruising en-
counters with presbyteries, associations, and conferences in
the past, but such a supposition would be erroneous. Mahan already had rejected denominational loyalties in the early
days at Oberlin. He stated his position in a sermon on
church fellowship preached at Oberlin in 1836, and he never
deviated from that position one iota throughout his long life:
"I do not set up for greater purity in doctrine than God: or
profess to be more select in my friendships than the Holy
Ghost." "Indeed, the imperfections of all Christians render
the toleration of some differences in doctrine essential to
the very existence of a church." To what extent are differences to be tolerated? "I answer, no greater agreement in
doctrine is required, as a condition of Church fellowship
than God requires as a condition of salvation."[48] Mahan was
only committed to the holiness movement which, in fact, was
wholly interdenominational.

Mahan was seventy-two in 1871 and growing a bit
weary of being a college president. Perhaps remembering
Oberlin he decided to resign while he was still a winner.
His letter of resignation was read at the June 22, 1871,
trustees meeting. The trustees genuinely wanted him to
stay, at least a while longer, and a committee of three was
appointed to discuss the matter with him. The committee
reported "that after a free consultation with the President,
his consent has been obtained to continue his Presidency to
the close of the college year only upon the condition that he
can be assured that his wishes will be respected by this
Board to be relieved of the responsibilities in an honorable

way, and that he will not be violently or forcibly ejected."[49]
In fact, Mahan stayed until 1872 and replacing him turned
out to be a long and bungled affair, but no part of our story.

Mahan was needlessly worried about the manner of
his exit from Adrian. Rarely has a college perpetuated its
feelings of gratitude toward a president as warmly and continuously as Adrian has for Mahan. In 1877 the first president was awarded an honorary LL.D. degree in light of his
services to Adrian College and to education in general, as
well as to philosophy and religion. Moreover, the honorary
degree was no mere "in-house" token award. In 1874 Professor A. W. McKeever took a stand in the board for raising the standard in giving honorary degrees. Each case, it
was voted, must lie over one year before any action could
be taken. At the same time the awarding of the M.A. degree in cursu was abandoned.[50] So it was a genuine honor
and a mark of deep respect when Adrian conferred upon its
first president in 1877 the honorary degree of LL.D. This
recognition warmed the good Dr.'s heart. But this was only
the beginning of a long line of recognitions by Adrian that
he never lived to witness. He is presented as the towering
leader in the Semi-Centennial Souvenir of Adrian College;
commencements have been dedicated to him; a classroom
building was named in his honor; and in the stunningly beautiful chapel on the present-day campus he is memorialized
as the central figure in one of a series of stained glass win-
dows that depict the beginning and evolution of the Protestant
Revolution.[51]

Disaster and Recovery

The years from 1862 to 1865 were ones of deep trial,
sorrow, and grief for Asa Mahan. Theodore Strong Mahan,
who had asked his father in the Oberlin years to tell him
stories of "dear Jesus," was destined not to survive the
Civil War. He was mortally wounded at the Battle of Fredericksburg. General A. E. Burnside planned to advance
southward against the Confederacy from a secure base at
Aquia Creek. However, General Robert E. Lee, anticipat-
ing the attack, occupied Fredericksburg, Virginia only twelve
miles away; and from this impregnable position rebuffed the
frontal charge that Burnside rashly began on December 13,
1862. Theodore, an infantry captain, was badly wounded as
he led his men in this hopeless attack. He was taken to the
home of his eldest sister, Anna Mahan North, in Cleveland

since he was unable to endure the longer journey to Adrian.
His mother and father rushed to his bedside and, though
Mary Dix Mahan nursed her son devotedly, he died six
months later.   Mahan wrote of Theodore:

> On occasion of the first great battle where he was
> present, he rose from a sick-bed, and, contrary
> to the absolute prohibition of his physician, as
> first lieutenant led his company into the scene,
> and remained with them during the day, leading
> fifty-six men into the battle, and sixteen out of it.
> Into the next great battle into which, as captain,
> he led his company, he himself received a fatal
> injury, from which he died some six months af-
> terwards.   And such a death!   He seemed to "see
> the heavens opened, and the Son of Man standing
> on the right hand of God," the Son of Man holding
> out to the dying one "a crown of life."[52]

Having buried their son, the parents returned to
Adrian, where Mary quietly died several months later.   She
had fatally overtaxed her strength in caring for Theodore
during the last months of his illness.   Was it possible that
she was gone, the hub of family life and the support of every
member of her family?   The resourceful Mary who fought
the good fight in Pittsford, Cincinnati, Oberlin, and Cleveland?   Yes, everyone has a breaking point.   For Mary, losing Theodore twice was too much to bear.

Mary's funeral was attended by the entire student
body of Adrian as well as by relatives and friends, old and
new.   The editor of the Daily Expositor wrote,

> And so has passed away one of far more than or-
> dinary merit, an intelligent, refined, and thought-
> ful woman, exerting an influence in all the circles
> in which she moved....   Possessing that quickness
> of perception and ready tact which is a character-
> istic of the best of her sex, she was ever doing
> good in ways unseen and by means unknown to
> most or all but none the less [powerful] for that....
> She was an active and wise helper and counselor
> to her honored husband, through a long, laborious,
> and eventful life....   Her presence was felt to be
> a blessing....   [She died partly of grief over the
> death of her son.]   She endured patiently and un-
> complainingly but the wound was too deep for hu-
> man mending.[53]

The Oberlin community mourned her loss, perhaps as deeply as anyone. Finney had the article from the <u>Daily Expositor</u> reprinted in the <u>Lorain County News</u> of November 11, 1863. He felt that "it will much gratify the numerous friends of President and Mrs. Mahan in this place to see it in your paper."

> All who knew Mrs. Mahan can testify to the truth-fulness of this notice. We, who have best known her, can bear the fullest testimony to her many excellent traits of character. She was indeed a most judicious wife and mother, and as a Christian lady she was always exemplary. [Finney wrote that he must not indulge his feelings about her excellencies.] I have received two letters from the President in regard to the death of his wife. He is, as we should all expect, greatly sustained by the grace of our Lord Jesus. His inward consolation abounds under his outward sore bereavement. God bless him and his bereaved children and all that know them here will say, Amen.[54]

Mary Dix Mahan was buried at the side of Theodore in Cleveland.

To complete the family tragedy, Elizabeth Mahan, who had been particularly close to her brother and mother, grieved unrestrainedly and, despite efforts to revive and sustain her, died not long after her mother. Her death, her father recorded, was not as "rapturous" but was as "peaceful" as that of her brother. In his sorrow Mahan wrote that under these bereavements "my whole soul was melted and flowed out like water." He could not tell which was the chief cause of his tears, "the great sorrow on the one hand, or the unspeakable joy of the Lord on the other." The Lord, he felt, was his consolation. "The deepest shades with which earth's tribulations can darken our horizons," he wrote, "are but the shadows which the Sun of Righteousness casts before Him when he is about to rise in our hearts 'with healings in His wings.'"[55] When Mahan recalled the prayer of an acquaintance, who can doubt that he recorded it as the echo of his own deepest feeling?

> Lord, when Thou didst take from me my only child ... I said to Thee that Thou hadst made a great vacancy in my soul, a void which nothing but Thyself could fill, and that I trusted Thee so

> to fill that void with thine own fulness.... I told
> Thee that I must now have far more of Thyself
> than I had ever had before. [56]

In his grief, as we have seen, Brother Asa felt sustained, consoled, and healed by the in-dwelling Spirit of God.
But it is one thing to be sustained, healed, and consoled,
and another to understand why intense grief and suffering,
well nigh unbearable, is necessary in the first place.   In
Baptism of the Holy Ghost Brother Asa asked this question
in a moving way.   Devastating events descend upon us suddenly "as crushing avalanches from the heights above us."

> They seem to drop down upon us immediately from
> His hand, crushing our fondly cherished hopes,
> smiting our persons till all our sensibilities quiver
> with excruciating agony, smiting also those most
> dear to us, and causing our hearts to bleed for
> sufferings we cannot relieve, and then taking from
> us even "the desire of our eyes with a stroke."
> These providences also most frequently, perhaps,
> strike that department of our nature most suscep-
> tible to suffering.   How often do we hear individu-
> als exclaim, "Anything, but this."   "Why did God
> smite me in this one spot?"[57]

Mahan answered his own question, formulated with
such striking vividness, by writing that such suffering, when
endured with submissive trust in God's goodness, may, indeed must, have a salutary effect upon character formation.
Assuming such endurance, Mahan listed some of the uses
of providential suffering: 1) Afflictions render things unseen
and eternal real to the mind.   They are "divine monitors ...
reminding us of God, duty, death, eternity, redemption and
retribution." 2) They discipline a person to subject himself to the divine will.   "Here let the creature learn obedience, here 'let patience have her perfect work.'" 3) They
strengthen and confirm Christian virtue.   "Did days of darkness never come, fulness of bread might induce forgetful-
ness of the Giver." 4) They impart assurance of hope.
"The light of God, in which we now live and walk, sanctifies even the furnace through which we have been conducted,
into [the] state of perpetual quietness and assurance, where
'the days of our mourning are ended.'" 5) They impart
blessed visions of the eternal future, impart soul-satisfying
visions of Christ, and impart power for good to the Christian.   "They fit him, as he otherwise could not be, to com-

fort them who are in any trouble." 6) They enable a person to grow into a spiritually significant human being. They
develop "that meek submission, that subdued quietude of
heart ... that tender sympathy with suffering in others, and
readiness 'to heal the broken-hearted,' that deep and fixed
trust in God, that serenity of hope, that crucifixion to the
world, that yield purity of thought and life, and, above all,
that fixed devotion to Christ." We glory in tribulation,
"knowing that tribulation worketh patience; and patience experience; and experience hope."[58]

Mahan's discussion of the uses of suffering amounts
to a restatement of the character-building solution to the
problem of evil. It is not clear that he here intended a
full scale response to this problem, nor can such a theodicy
be found anywhere in his writings. Certain questions are
left unanswered. Suffering at times simply overwhelms and
defeats a person, quite apart from moral considerations.
Moreover, his discussion leaves untouched the point of the
mass annihilation of character and life that comes in natural
catastrophes. There is evidence that Mahan recognized the
extreme difficulty of such questions, and a reader can only
feel a sense of loss that Mahan's propensity for tackling
tough questions should have failed at this point. The truth
of the matter is that his ultimate response to the problem of
evil, though he never quite admitted it, must have been that
the ways of God pass understanding. That this was not an
adequate response philosophically Mahan was no doubt well
aware.

The Civil War

Even before the deaths of his wife of more than thirty
years and of a son and daughter at early ages, Asa Mahan
was grieved by the ravages of the war and appalled by what
he took to be the bungling of the Union generals which prolonged it. Having been a student of military science and
tactics all his life, he criticized in detail the strategy of
the North and developed an alternative one of his own.
Briefly, the weaknesses of Union strategy included captur-
ing places instead of aiming decisive blows at the Confeder-
ate army; scattering instead of consolidating troops; fighting
at extremities instead of at the vital center of enemy power;
failing to use the artillery, cavalry, and infantry coopera-
tively in battle; using frontal instead of flanking attacks; attacking by single line instead of pincer movements; and so

on.   The plan of attack he developed in late 1862 hinged on
the general idea of breaking Robert E. Lee's line of communications by use of a large force on the south side of the
James River, "while his position at Fredericksburg should
be turned by a flank movement of the army of the Potomac."[59]

Mahan explained his views in detail in letters to Salmon P. Chase, Secretary of the Treasury, Senators Sumner,
King, and Chandler, and members of the Committee on the
Conduct of the War.   They were not unimpressed with his
ideas and urged President Lincoln to consider them.   It may
be the case, as one commentator suggests, that it was his
prestige as a college president that gained a hearing for his
ideas in Washington, but a far more powerful factor was his
friendship with Chase, a friendship which had begun in the
early days in Ohio.   Mahan deluged Chase with letters and
received a letter from the Secretary of the Treasury, dated
October 29, 1862, agreeing with his criticisms of the past
conduct of the war.[60]

Long distance communication was inconclusive at best
and ineffectual at worst, so Mahan journeyed to Washington
in December 1862 intending to call upon the President and
lay before him his plan for more efficient conduct of the
war.   Chase immediately arranged a conference for Mahan
with E. M. Stanton, Secretary of War, who, even among
friends, was noted for his bad manners.   "Where is your
General to carry it out?" he repeatedly demanded, giving
no serious attention to what Mahan proposed.   The president of Adrian, unlikely at any time to respond cordially to
such treatment and at the moment seriously upset by the
terrible wounds of his son at Fredericksburg, replied hotly
to Stanton and either left or was ushered out of the Secretary's office.[61]

Mahan next approached Senators Wade and Wilson who
endorsed his plan, and the three men spent the next evening
with President Lincoln, to whom Mahan explained his plan
in detail.   The President was impressed and asked his visitor to put his plans in writing, which Mahan immediately
did.   Wade, Wilson, and Mahan saw Lincoln a second time
and the President was disposed to accept the plan.   He wrote
on the back of the last sheet of Mahan's document, "The
Secretary of War will examine the enclosed plan with the
view of its being carried into operation," signed "A. Lincoln."[62]   It was thought desirable to have a military opinion
and General Irvin McDowell seemed a likely candidate to

consult. On January 23, 1863, still in Washington, Mahan
wrote Chase that McDowell approved the plan but would not
offer his advice unless asked by the President. Mahan said
he highly approved of McDowell's response and would Chase
kindly ask the President to request McDowell's opinion. [63]

For a moment it seemed that Lincoln intended to use
Mahan's plan and name McDowell the general to carry it out.
However, Stanton and H. W. Halleck, the General-in-Chief
at that time, talked with Lincoln the whole next day, everyone else being denied entrance, with the result that the President shelved the plan. It seemed at first to Mahan that
petty jealousy caused the shelving of his plan, since a major general of the Army of the Potomac reported that Halleck had been heard to say, "It would never do to have a
civilian plan our campaigns." Later, however, he came to
wonder if even baser motives were involved and if the war
were being deliberately prolonged.

> This I know to have been the judgment of the wis-
> est statesmen in Washington, that the men who ac-
> tually controlled matters in the high places of mil-
> itary authority there, had no desire--but an oppo-
> site one--to bring that war to a speedy termina-
> tion. The reason is obvious. The emoluments
> of office were too great and the annual [military
> budget] presented too [many] multiplied opportun-
> ities to amass untold private fortunes, to allow
> controlling minds to be willing that their oppor-
> tunities should pass away by the early termination
> of that war. [64]

Mahan returned to Adrian and continued to press his
views mainly by writing to the Secretary of the Treasury.
On February 27, 1863, he outlined further plans and entreated Chase to lay them before the President and his Cab-
inet. He concluded the letter by saying that the army must
be controlled either by traitors or imbeciles, "the biggest
ones since the world began." On April 15, 1863:

> After I left Washington, this past winter, one of
> the Senators to whom I had revealed my plan of
> the campaign, visited Gen. Burnside, presented to
> him a plan for flanking the army of Gen. Lee.
> Gen. B. chose to adhere to the plan which he had
> previously devised. He tried it and failed.... Af-
> terwards he met this senator and confessed to him

his deep regret that he had not adopted the plan
which said senator had proposed, the very plan
which I had described to that senator. [65]

To Chase's objection that he was Secretary of the Treasury,
not War, and that forms must be observed, Mahan charac-
teristically replied,

My opinion is, Mr. Chase, that the nation has a
right to expect of you, that at this crisis, you
will not heed mere forms of etiquet, but will act
for the nation. Will you not lay the above before
the President? [66]

The day after Theodore died, his father wrote Chase from
Cleveland with still more details. He began by relating the
tragedy to the Secretary but with an iron hand stopped short
--"this, however, is not the object of this note." Remembering Stanton's jibe no doubt, he bitterly wrote,

If you have not generals who can give you the plan
by which all I have named above may now be accomplished, you may say to the President that I
affirm that I can take the American Army as it is,
and make such disposition of it as to render the
utter destruction of the army of Gen. Lee as great
a certainty as did the dispositions of Washington
that of Cornwallis, as I can give the plan by which
generals of adequate capacities can do the same.
Now is the golden opportunity for this nation. [67]

In May 1864 General Butler was dispatched to attack
Lee's line of communications in a way Mahan approved but
with what he considered a totally inadequate force. The president of Adrian publicly denounced the move, and his remarks were highly irritating to the Republicans in the village.
Judge Barbour advised Mahan to refrain from further criticism for his own good, to which the characteristic reply was,
"Please say to the Republicans and Democrats too, Judge
Barbour, that Dr. Mahan will continue to utter what he thinks
on this and other subjects. "[68]

Lest it appear that Mahan was all asperity during
these trying years, it must be added that when he visited
his old friend John Scott, editor of the Methodist Recorder,
at Pittsburgh, on his journey both to and from Washington,
Scott's son was quite favorably impressed with the culture

and charm of the man, a view he continued to hold throughout his long life. W. A. Scott recalled Mahan as a person
"of imposing appearance, refined presence, wide knowledge,
and a most entertaining conversationalist, possessing a mag-
netism which very speedily attracted to himself the admira-
tion and friendship of those who were so fortunate as to make
his intimate acquaintance."[69] Scott's recollections are important since they constitute the only independent corrobora-
tion of Mahan's account of his adventures in Washington nar-
rated in his Critical History of the Late American War. Mahan's letters to Chase and Sumner still exist and confirm,
as far as they go, his account of events in the Critical History, but unfortunately the letters from Chase and Sumner
to Mahan have not survived.

We have not presented Mahan's military plans in detail, or judged them; such matters require a specialist in
the history of military strategy. It should be pointed out,
however, that the publisher of the Critical History, A. S.
Barnes, had Mahan's manuscript evaluated by Lieutenant
General H. W. Smith, United States Army, before publishing it. Smith thought Mahan very knowledgeable about military strategy but was non-committal on his evaluations of
the generals and politicians of the Civil War days.

Otto Eisenschiml, a recent historian of the Civil War,
has used Mahan's Critical History to bolster his own interpretation and evaluation of Stanton and the Radical Republicans in the House and Senate in what seems to us a wholly
unconvincing way. Eisenschiml claims that Stanton and the
Congressional radicals conspired to prolong the war in order to insure the permanent subjection of the South and that
Mahan's Critical History supports his view. According to
Eisenschiml, Mahan "had the rare privilege of witnessing
from a ringside seat, as it were, one of Stanton's unblush-
ing intrigues." "History has been enriched by [Mahan's]
account of how the war was deliberately sabotaged by [Stan-
ton] and the Radicals, and was not brought to a close until
hatred of the South had grown sufficiently to let them per-
petuate themselves in power by depriving the conquered States
of their constitutional privileges."[70] Eisenschiml suggests
that Mahan also came to suspect that Stanton and the Radical
Republicans had conspired to this end. Mahan "shuddered
at what he was discovering and suspecting."

Had the two senators who had sponsored his meeting with Lincoln been sincere? Or had they known

all along that Stanton would kill any plan that might
end the war quickly? Could it be that by inviting
Mahan to Washington, they had done so to discour-
age and silence him? While he did not put these
thoughts into his book, they must have passed
through his mind, as he wondered what was behind the "deliberate intent to prevent" a military
movement which had been endorsed by leading generals, and which Lincoln himself had called the
best that had yet come to his attention. [71]

The author adds that perhaps Mahan's suspicions would have
been multiplied had he known that Senator Wade, a radical,
was deep in the confidence of Stanton and that, according to
one commentator, "differences of aim and opinion [between
them] were exceedingly rare."

It is a hazardous process for an historian to specu-
late what might have been going through a person's mind unless he has significant manuscript sources for such ascrip-
tions. Eisenschiml fails to supply the sources to justify the
ascription. Indeed, he is even mistaken in writing that Wade
and Wilson had invited Mahan to come to Washington. It
was his association with Chase, and the fact that the Secretary shared his doubts about Union strategy, that brought
him to Washington. Hence there is no reason not to accept
at face value Mahan's claim that he believed the war was
prolonged by poor generals and by profiteers (in which group
Mahan did not place Stanton). Something that Eisenschiml
does not mention might seem to tell in favor of his thesis.
As we shall see, Mahan's attitude toward the Republican
Party changed significantly after the Civil War, particularly
as a result of Grant's first term as President. He quickly
disapproved of the course of action pursued by the Radical
Republicans during Reconstruction years. However, it would
be a mistake to project this later disenchantment backward
in time and see it as supporting any conspiracy theory.
Again we have no reason not to take at face value Mahan's
own explanation of why he thought the war had been prolonged.

The Election of 1872

By 1872 the critics of the Radical Republican view of
Reconstruction had become significantly large within the Re-
publican Party itself, and they came to be called "Liberal
Republicans." The Liberals were prepared to leave the party

if necessary in order to avert further punishment of the
South and to introduce reforms into civil service and tariff
policy.   The Spoils System had begun to get out of hand already in President Grant's first administration.   Carl Schurz,
a Senator from Missouri, was one of the outstanding leaders
of the Liberals.   Seeing no hope for reform within the Republican Party, Schurz and the rest of the dissidents met in
Cincinnati in May 1872 and nominated Horace Greeley for
President.   The convention of the Democratic Party accepted
both the candidate and platform of the Liberals.   Greeley
seemed like a reasonable candidate since he had been strongly antislavery before and during the war and after the war
had effectively criticized "Grantism" and Radical Reconstruction in the pages of his influential New York Tribune.

Mahan had just retired as president of Adrian and
used some of his released time in speaking in Greeley's behalf.   One of these speeches was given in Oberlin, where
the committee members who invited him, including Theodore
John Keep, thought he still was a member of the Republican
Party.   Much to their consternation the first president of
Oberlin launched an attack on Grantism and supported universal amnesty and reconciliation. [72]   The Lorain County
News took a dim view of the speech and replied at length,
claiming, among other things, that "if reconciliation means
oblivion of the past, forgetting Andersonville and Libbey
prisons, it means that we cease to walk by the light of experience, that we warm a chilled viper in our bosom."[73]
Oberlin was unmoved by Mahan's talk, but the Liberals were
delighted with it and requested Mahan to become their candidate for Congress in the Michigan second district. [74] Again
something entirely unexpected had turned up and the hand of
God was seen in it.   He was seventy-two years of age but
launched into a vigorous campaign for Greeley and himself.

Greeley toured the country, an unusual action at the
time for a presidential candidate, and did all in his power
to spread "the gospel of understanding" between North and
South.   Speaking at rallies and conferences, Mahan campaigned vigorously for Greeley and the Liberal-Democratic
platform in large areas of Michigan and Ohio.   People well
knew that Asa Mahan had lost the major part of his family
as a direct result of the Civil War and found it difficult to
believe that anyone in such circumstances could avoid a vin-
dictive attitude toward the South.   In a letter to the Chicago
Tribune Mahan acknowledged his bereavement but insisted
that he could not cherish or encourage bitter and vengeful
feelings toward Southerners.

I shall be pardoned here for a single personal rem-
iniscence. In a late political gathering in Cleveland, Ohio, I made the following statements: In
your great city cemetery lie the remains of an
only son, who lost his life from injuries received
--first from a Southern bullet, and then from a
clod of earth thrown against his body by a ball
from a Southern cannon. By his side lie the remains of the wife of my youth, who died from
grief and over-fatigue around the sick and dying
bed of our son. By their side lie the remains of
a blooming daughter, who, as all her physicians
testified, died from no other cause than drooping
heart sickness on account of the death of that mother and brother.... Such are my grievances. What
duties do they impose? Duties to my dead, to
myself, and to the living people of the nation. Do
they call upon me to cherish in myself and excite
in the living around me bitter and vengeful reminiscences? Cannot each Southern man who has been
bereaved, too, excite in himself and the people
around him what are to him and to them remem-
brances equally bitter and embittering? Will such
a policy benefit our dead, ourselves or our country? Does it not tend, while it cannot reach our
dead, and bless God for it, to blight our virtues
and our joys, and to savagize the national heart?
Does not the spirit of amnesty, good will and national brotherhood, on the other hand, tend equally
to perfect our virtues, deepen our joys and consolations, and to purify and to patriotize the national heart? Did not He who is our Supreme Ex-
emplar learn obedience and love amnesty, too,
from the things which He suffered? Shall not our
grievances teach us a similar lesson? Such as I
understand the subject, are the duties of the patriot and the Christian in this crisis of our national existence. [75]

It was an uphill battle for both Greeley and Mahan.
The Radical Republicans appealed to party loyalty and the
old effective slogan "vote as you fought." Both the presidential and congressional candidates were subjected to ridicule. Thomas Nast, cartoonist for the widely read Harper's
Weekly, heaped pictorial insults on Greeley; and George William Curtis, still under the illusion that Grant was serious
about civil-service reform, not only printed Nast's cartoons

but also editorialized in the same vein. [76] On August 22,
1872, the Lorain County News reprinted a scurrilous attack
on Greeley from the June 26, 1871, issue of the Oberlin
New Era:

> All will admit that he lacks courage, and has not
> a moderate amount of stability. Any old woman
> could turn and divert this mind from one thing to
> another.... Something of such an old granny is
> this Greeley. [77]

In the same issue the News has this tidbit, "Greeley buggies
are advertised at Grand Rapids, Michigan. They are so
called because they turn so easily." When he spoke in
Cleveland the Leader responded: "Asa Mahan formerly occupied a high position in church and societies, but we feel
charitable toward him for travelling with such a crowd, seeing as he is about eighty years old and entering his dotage."[78]

Greeley and Mahan never had a chance to be elected:
the former carried only Georgia, Texas, Missouri, Tennes-
see, Maryland, and Kentucky, while the latter lost his bid
for a Michigan congressional seat. It was not a fruitless
effort, however, for it helped set the stage for a Liberal-
Democratic victory in 1884. Along with many others, Curtis
became a convert to the Liberal point of view and joining
forces with Schurz and E. L. Godkin helped elect Grover
Cleveland President in 1884 and thus break the stranglehold
of the Republican Party on American politics.[79] Greeley
never lived to see this outcome, but Mahan did. Greeley,
exhausted by his campaigning, hurt deeply by the one-sided
outcome, and saddened by the death of his wife as well, died
three weeks after the results of the election were known.
Asa, on the other hand, seemed made of granite and returned emotionally and physically quite intact to Adrian,
where he spent the next two years in retirement continuing
to write books on philosophy and religion as he had always
done.

Mahan was now seventy-four and it seemed that he
would continue in his "writing retirement" for a few more
years and then fade away. Fading away, however, was far
from the destiny that awaited Asa Mahan. There were fifteen more years of work and adventure ahead for this already venerable man--years of work and adventure to be
spent far from the shores of his native land. Brother Mahan was no less surprised by this turn of events than were

his family and friends. Before turning to this new chapter
in his life, however, we should review his commitment to,
and defense of, scriptural holiness, the tie that bound all
the chapters of his life into a coherent whole.

In Defense of Holiness

According to Mahan, all evangelicals believe that salvation is obtained only through the grace of God and is never
a matter of man's achievement. Unfortunately, he continued,
Calvinists abandon this Reformation view when it comes to
following the commands of God. They look upon the combatting of sin as a matter of man's effort and, given a sinful nature, expect their constant failures. Against such a
viewpoint Mahan emphasized that holiness, which is simply
loving God and man unreservedly can be attained in the same
manner that salvation is attained. Holiness is obtained by
freely asking for and accepting the gracious gift, promised
in the Bible, of the in-dwelling Spirit of Christ, a presence
that ensures triumph over sin. Mahan was at one with Wesley in saying that a person must pray for Christ to dwell
in his heart and lead him into righteous ways. Mahan emphasized: "To comply with the condition is our part in the
transaction," and "the condition being complied with, our
responsibility in the matter is at an end."[80]

Throughout his Adrian years and the rest of his life,
the good doctor continued to promote and defend the holiness
view first presented in his Oberlin years in The Scripture
Doctrine of Christian Perfection, The True Believer, and
Lectures on the Ninth of Romans and developed in his Adrian
years in Baptism of the Holy Ghost. In the last fifteen years
of his life ink flowed from his pen in torrents as he produced The Promise of the Spirit (1874), Out of Darkness into Light (1875), The Consequences of Neglect (1876), Misunderstood Texts of Scripture (1876), Life Thoughts on the
Rest of Faith (1877), Autobiography: Intellectual, Moral and
Spiritual (1882), The Natural and the Supernatural in the
Christian Life and Experience (circa 1883), as well as innumerable essays and sermons published in The Banner of
Holiness and Divine Life, periodicals which he edited from
1874 to 1889.[81] The holiness viewpoint was given different
labels at different times: Christian Perfection, Scriptural
Holiness, the Baptism of the Holy Ghost, the Higher Life,
the Rest of Faith, Perfect Love, and Full Consecration.
They meant essentially the same thing for Mahan, with the
one exception to be noted later.

Throughout the long period covered by his publications Mahan not only reiterated his central theme but also systematically defended it against what he took to be misunderstandings, and even caricatures, as well as against various criticisms advanced by people who understood the viewpoint and whose intelligence and integrity Brother Mahan respected. We shall examine a variety of criticisms, carefully present Mahan's answers, and, upon occasion, elaborate his responses, not by way of proving that he was right and his opponents wrong, but by way of clarifying issues that are still vitally present in contemporary religious circles. After all, questions cannot be answered in any satisfactory fashion unless they are clearly stated and understood in the first place.

Both Mahan and Finney were often interpreted as presenting an antinomian viewpoint--the doctrine that the in-dwelling Spirit of God displaces human agency and produces perfect acts even when the behavior of the person seems abominable by ordinary standards. To be fair, there are passages in the later Autobiography as well as in the earlier Christian Perfection and True Believer, to name only several cases, which lend themselves to such an interpretation, where the author seems to suggest the absence of human agency in sanctified living. The following are examples from Christian Perfection and True Believer: "However hard your heart may be, he can take it from you, and give you a heart of flesh in its stead. However firmly fixed your habits of sin may be, he can break them all up. However strong the power of your carnal inclinations, he can subdue them all, and give you a perfect victory over them." We receive Christ as Savior "and yield up our whole being to his control, that he may accomplish in us all the purposes of his infinite and special love." There is "the continued assurance that, through the grace of Christ, I am one with God; that my will is lost in the divine will; that I have no will to do what God would not have me do, and that all that he would have me do, I will to do."[82] From the Autobiography: "Christ himself, through the Spirit, enters the citadel of the soul, puts to death 'the lust that was in the members,' 'destroys the body of sin,' sanctifies to Himself 'the whole Spirit, and soul, and body,' and then, under the power of the Spirit, sends the believer into the world."[83]

In spite of misleading quotations, Mahan's view--as a reader who peruses entire sermons and books will agree-- has no antinomian implications whatever. Far from the Spirit's supplanting human agency, the person's free will or free choice is everywhere involved in the spiritual trans-

action called sanctification. To begin with, the in-dwelling
Spirit of God, whenever present, is there only because a
person freely and without constraint sincerely sought its presence through prayer. Moreover, after the advent of the
Spirit, the person is subject to temptation just as before and
the possibility of backsliding is ever present. The continuing presence of the in-dwelling Christ is required to resist
temptation and prevent backsliding, but such continuing presence is wholly dependent upon the constantly renewed decision, wholly uncoerced, to ask for his presence. The
sanctified believer must be ever alert on his own not to become complacent and forget to seek that continuous presence
necessary for triumph over sin. Finally, the in-dwelling
Spirit does not act mechanically by overriding man's sen-
suous nature with its propensities for selfish and evil acts
and by producing virtuous ones instead. Rather its presence entails that a person is endowed with a new nature that
has a propensity toward good rather than evil, and hence
the new acts are consistent with the person's reformed character or nature. Even the new nature, however, is not assured a permanent and unaltered existence. At every minute it is "up to a person" and open to a person to decide,
to choose, what kind of a person to be, what sort of nature
to have. The essence of Mahan's agency theory is that being free entails a divorce between the sensible nature of a
person--the kind of sensibilities that determined what sort
of thing he did, how he acted--and the will, or volitional
faculty, which itself was not determined by the sensibilities
but rather itself determined what sort of sensibilities would
constitute the motives for his acts.[84]

     Not only is it clear that Mahan's view is not anti-
nomian, but a case could be made, with prima facie plaus-
iblity at least, that Old School Calvinist doctrine does have
its own kind of antinomian flavor. After all, antinomianism
is a kind of determinism or necessitarianism, or "cannot-
ism." With the in-dwelling Spirit, according to antinomian
doctrine, a person cannot do otherwise but act perfectly.
But this is simply the converse of the Old School doctrine
that a person is inherently depraved and cannot help but act
sinfully. Even those who are saved in "God's own good
time" are part of the predestined Elect and cannot choose
otherwise than be a part of it. This inverted kind of antinomianism, Finney and Mahan thought, "has been the devil's
most successful means of destroying souls"[85] since it in-
duces the view that there is nothing one can do to combat sin.

     Some New Light advocates held what might be called

a cooperative view of combatting sin. The help of the Holy
Spirit, invoked through prayer, together with the dedicated
and earnest effort of the supplicant will be partially successful
in combatting the sinful tendencies of man. They will be only
partly successful because the sinful nature of man makes complete success impossible. For Mahan, however, man in an unregenerate condition is so basically corrupt and depraved that
his contribution to any cooperative effort in this sense is doomed
to ruin the enterprise wholly from the very beginning. The
kind of cooperation needed, he felt, was of a crucially different kind. The needed cooperation amounts to man's earnest request in prayer for the in-dwelling Spirit which en-
dows him with the power, stemming from a new nature, to
live without known sin since the powerful tendencies toward
sin no longer exist. 86 But beware, for the old nature is
never wholly dead in the sense that it cannot be reinvoked
by an act of free will on the part of the agent.

    "How can anyone act perfectly?" critics asked in-
dignantly. Even Peter and Paul upon occasion acted in ways
that did them little honor indeed. If that can be said of
them, how presumptuous it is to claim that Christians can
act perfectly in the nineteenth century. Mahan answered that
neither he nor Finney claimed that a sanctified person acts
perfectly. The critic confuses a sanctified will and nature,
which characterizes an agent, with objective rightness or
wrongness, which characterizes an act. The person is holy,
or sanctified, or perfect if he is wholly committed to God;
an act is perfect if in addition to the agent's sanctified intention the act itself is just, right, appropriate, and so on.
That the former is attainable seems clear since it would be
odd for a Christian knowingly to consecrate himself to God
only partially. But no person is able to act perfectly since
no one except God is infinitely wise. Given his imperfect
knowledge, a person is bound to produce out of ignorance
acts that are wrong or unjust even though his will and nature is genuinely sanctified. On this view presumably it
would be correct to say that a sanctified person who acted
unjustly had not sinned but acted unfortunately out of ignorance. However, Mahan stressed, unjust acts resulting from
ignorance are sins if the requisite knowledge was available. 87

    Another criticism of Mahan's view was that it did not
allow, or account for, spiritual growth. His answer depended upon the same distinction made in replying to the previous criticism. It is impossible to will partly to do right
and partly not. One either loves God with all his heart and

his neighbor as himself and thus fulfills the whole of the
law, or he does not intend to act justly and he follows the
law not at all.   However, it is possible to have a sanctified
will and still act imperfectly out of ignorance.   Only God
is infinitely wise.   Hence sanctification, he thought, is both
instantaneous and capable of growth.   The presence of the
Holy Spirit sanctifies the will instantaneously, but its continued presence instructs man in God's law and in knowledge
of right acts and hence man grows in holiness. 88

Mahan's distinction between the instantaneous sanctification of the will and the growth in holiness through increased knowledge of the will of God is an important distinction, and the resulting clarity no doubt contributed a
great deal to his significant impact on Methodism.   His distinction, for example, is helpful in clarifying a specific point
in John Wesley's teaching.   Sometimes the latter wrote as
if sanctification was instantaneous while at other times he
seemed to think of it as a gradual process. 89   From Mahan's viewpoint one must first distinguish between the sanctification of the will and the increase in knowledge before
asking whether sanctification is instantaneous or gradual.
Sanctification of the will, then, must be characterized as
instantaneous and the growth in holiness through increased
knowledge as gradual.

Other critics worried about the newness of the doctrine, as if that fact, even if true, should count against it.
In any case, Mahan replied, the doctrine of holiness, far
from being new, and somehow startling, was explicitly held
by the fathers of the Primitive Church.   It was only in later
years that church officials lost sight of the doctrine or, if
aware of it, denigrated it.   "Which came first, Calvinism
or Arminianism?"   Mahan asked, and answered, "To be
sure, Arminius came after Calvin, and Wesley after the
Westminster Confession [but] if we go back to the Primitive
Church the opposite answer must be given."   Moreover, to
some of his contemporaries Mahan's views did not seem
new but essentially in the Wesleyan tradition.   "Though it
is not to be maintained that he expresses himself Methodis-
tically upon all the points of this great doctrine, we are satisfied that the thing we mean by Christian perfection is truly
set forth in that book [Scripture Doctrine of Christian Per-
fection]."   A later reviewer reaffirmed this view, saying
Mahan's views are not new but "essentially Wesleyan," and
pointed out cheerfully that Christian Perfection had been reprinted ten times and had been published in England under
the auspices of John Stevenson. 90

Instead of arguing that Mahan's doctrine demanded too much, critics sometimes claimed that he demanded too little. He had written that a person is responsible only for that degree of perfection in his action commensurate with present ability, not with the perfection commensurate with his ability had he never sinned at all. In his Autobiography Mahan replied: "Where did the idea originate, that God requires of us, not what is now possible to us through grace, but what would be possible, had we never sinned? Nowhere, we answer, but in the bewildered brain of the objector. Not an intimation of any such standard as this can be found in the Bible."[91]

Critics often said that if a believer were entirely sanctified, he would no longer be subject to temptation to sin in any form; after all, being tempted is itself sinful. Mahan replied that according to this argument Christ himself would count as a sinner since He was tempted--certainly a reductio ad absurdum. "The fact that Christ was thus tempted, and 'yet without sin,' absolutely implies that mere temptation to sin is not sin in anyone." Only temptation yielded to is sin. "Temptation promptly resisted and overcome implies the purest and brightest virtues known in the universe of God." Moreover, the imperfectly sanctified believer has his long periods of sleep "with hardly a dream of peril" and as consequence falls to temptation. A fully and wisely sanctified believer, on the other hand, "is perfected in watchfulness ... and, like the prudent general, is never for a moment off his guard."[92]

Quite a common criticism of Christian Perfection and the Higher Life was that if believers were entirely sanctified they would always be in a joyful, uplifted state; but since no one is in such a perpetual state there must be no sanctified believers. Mahan replied that needless to say Jesus was sanctified yet suffered great sorrow and affliction. So it is with ordinary sanctified believers. The believer "who is perfect in love" must often suffer great affliction for the name of Christ, endure great afflictions, and, if need be "may for a season be in heaviness through manifold temptations."

> Yet suffering and sorrow, with such a mind, are always intermingled with such "everlasting consolations, and good hope through grace," as to induce forms of hallowed experience to which others are strangers. Sitting under the shadow of a great sorrow, with "Christ in the soul, the hope of

glory," we naturally exclaim, "Lord, it is good
to be here." Never is the peace of the soul more
perfect than when walking with the Son of God in
the furnace of affliction and sorrow. [93]

As we have seen, Mahan was writing on this topic from the
depths of personal experience, and he filled many pages of
the Baptism of the Holy Ghost and Out of Darkness into Light
with the consolations and upliftings of the Holy Spirit in times
of great sorrow and affliction.

A recent commentator, comparing Christian Perfection and Baptism of the Holy Ghost, concludes that Mahan
changed his views from Christian Perfection, which obtained
in both the old and new dispensations, to a Pentecostalism
that pertains only to believers in the new dispensation. The
phrase "Baptism of the Holy Ghost," he contends, which Mahan had never used before, supposedly signals the new direction of his thought. [94] In fact, there was no new direction to Mahan's thought; there was simply a new dimension
added to the old one, and he continued to defend all strands,
old and new, throughout his career.

To begin with, the phrase "Baptism of the Holy Ghost"
was perfectly familiar to Mahan very early in his Oberlin
days. It was the title of a Commencement dissertation given
by one of the Lane Rebels, and Mahan himself in The True
Believer already had written about "that memorable era of
my existence when, I may say, that I first received the full
baptism of the Spirit,--a baptism in which the Son of righteousness shined out in cloudless light, beauty, sweetness,
and glory, upon my soul." Here the phrase meant identi-
cally the same thing as the in-dwelling of the Spirit of
Christ in a sanctified believer.

There was, to be sure, a Pentecostal dimension added to the phrase in Baptism of the Holy Ghost. Basing his
theory on Paul's interview with the twelve Johannite believers of Ephesus and on Paul's statement in Eph. i, 13, "after that ye believed, ye were sealed with the Holy Ghost of
Promise," Mahan wrote that believers need only wait upon the
Lord in faith and prayer to receive a direct Pentecostal shower
upon themselves. It will lift them to a higher level of spirituality and power than was ever possible before the new dispensation. What are we to make of Brother Mahan's new sense
of "Baptism of the Holy Ghost"? As we shall see, it did
not change the direction of his thought but simply added a
new dimension to it.

Beginning with Christian Perfection and The True Believer, continuing through the myriad of later books, and ending with with his last article, Mahan advocated the same viewpoint. Through the grace of God, the Spirit of Christ as an in-dwelling presence is available through earnest and sincere prayer. The results of this presence are manifold: victory over sin, consolation in affliction, sustainment of heavy burdens, joy and ecstasy in union with God, and an enduement of power to work effectively for Him--to preach beyond one's own power, to be successful in revivals and conversion, and so on. In Christian Perfection he stressed victory over sin; in a letter to his wife, printed in The True Believer, he expressed joy and ecstasy in the fullness of Christ; and in Baptism of the Holy Ghost he emphasized consolation, sustainment, and the enduement of power to do God's work. All of these elements were still present and variously stressed in all of his books and articles that followed Baptism of the Holy Ghost.

Though Mahan's terminology varied a great deal through the years, his concepts remained unchanged. He sometimes used the phrase Christian Perfection, and sometimes Scriptural Holiness, Baptism of the Holy Ghost, the Higher Life, and the Rest of Faith synonymously as referring to the in-dwelling of the Spirit, and the resulting cluster of benefits, without any distinction between what is possible in the two dispensations. At other times he divided what is possible in the two dispensations and called the benefits specific to the new dispensation the result of the baptism of the Holy Spirit. However, the division of benefits specific to the new dispensation varies from place to place. Sometimes victory over sin occurs in both dispensations, while all the other benefits are a function of the Pentecost. At other times victory over sin and joy in the fullness of God come under both dispensations, while remaining ones are Pentecostal. Eventually Mahan lumped all of the benefits together as available in both dispensations except for the enduement of power to do God's work, which remained the unique function of the Pentecost. This view is expressed in his pamphlet, written late in life, entitled The Natural and Supernatural in the Christian Life and Experience and, given the nature of the Pentecost, appears to be the most plausible division. [95] The upshot of our discussion, then, is clear: Mahan never abandoned his views on Christian Perfection in favor of Pentecostalism. He remained loyal to his system of interrelated concepts and simply regrouped them according to what seemed to him at a given time the Pentecostal function.

Chapter 7

LONDON AND EASTBOURNE

The Winding Way to England

After the deaths of Mary Dix Mahan, Theodore, and Elizabeth, Asa was a lonely man. Of course he still had five daughters, but they were grown and making their own ways in the world. Anna and Lucy were long since married; Mary Keep was twenty-nine and soon to marry Charles Reynolds; Sara was twenty-six and working for the Sanitary Commission in Cleveland (overtaxing herself, it seemed to her friends, just as she had when she helped her mother in the vain effort to nurse Theodore back to health); and Almira Barnes was twenty and soon to marry one of the Kimballs in nearby Jackson (her only child was to be the artist Alonzo Kimball).[1]

Where Mahan met Mary E. Chase is difficult to say, but it was probably during the period he spent in Ohio cooperating with the Methodist Protestants in their effort to found a college. Mary was the widow of the Reverend Silas B. Chase, who had practiced medicine in Cincinnati (after the Mahans had left the city) and had been buried in his home town of Bethel, Ohio. Three years had passed since the death of Mary Dix Mahan when Asa and Mary Chase were married in Adrian on May 22, 1866.[2] The second Mary and Asa lived a happy and companionable life together, much of it, contrary to every expectation, in England. Going to England was another one of the dramatic twists in the serpentine career of the indefatigable Dr. Mahan.

The Mahans went to England in search of proof that

192

a highly advertised Townley-Chase Estate existed and if so
to press Mrs. Mahan's claim to part of it in behalf of the
American Missionary Association.   Why they went instead
of other Chase heirs is a long and exciting tale in itself
which can be recounted here only briefly.   There is a large
correspondence concerning the adventures and misadventures
of the Chase heirs in the archives of the American Missionary Association, which is part of the Amistad Collection at
Dillard University. [3]

  In 1846 and again in 1872 there was a rash of articles
in such newspapers as The Salem Gazette and The Yarmouth
Register to the effect that there was a huge estate in England to which various Americans named Chase were legiti-
mate heirs.   The stories conflicted in details and may have
been founded on little if any fact, but the generally agreed
upon outline of the story was as follows: In 1700 a Baronet
named Townley, possessing a large estate in Lancastershire,
had a further fortune bequeathed to him, all of which real
estate and money he bequeathed to his son and grandson.
The grandson had no heirs and the question arose to whom
the estate should go.   The original Baronet had a sister,
and the Court of Chancery decided that the estate belonged
to her descendents.   She had married someone named Chase,
and they had four sons--Richard, William, Aquila, and
Thomas.   Richard remained in England and allegedly his
heirs already had been awarded their share of what had generally become known as the Townley-Chase Estate.   The
three other brothers had emigrated to the United States and
their descendents were supposedly declared the other heirs
by the Court of Chancery.   Mrs. Mary Mahan's first husband had been a descendent of Aquila, and Silas Chase's
will had left all of his property and rights to his wife.
Hence Mrs. Mahan was one of the presumptive heirs to
the Townley-Chase Estate!

  The news of the estate was well advertised in the
East in the early 1870's.   Members of the Chase family,
mainly from New England, New Brunswick, and Nova Sco-
tia, held a convention in Boston in October 1872 and appointed a committee to "sift the matter to the bottom" and
take appropriate action.   The committee had members from
only these areas, and the Chases on the frontier, in Ohio
and Michigan, suspicious of Easterners, complained.   When
the committee met at the Sherman House in Boston on Saturday, July 5, 1873, George W. Chase of Rutland, Ohio,
was added to the roster.   According to a circular distributed by the committee, Dr. John B. Chase of Taunton,

Massachusetts was appointed "the delegate to England" and
should "if practicable, take passage in a Cunard Steamer
leaving New York not later than the 1st. September next."

The Mahans wrote the secretary of the committee,
who advised them not to inform other Chases of the existence of the estate. They were puzzled by this advice and
eventually took a dim view of it. Was the Eastern committee trying to keep the number of heirs at a minimum to
insure as large a share of the estate as possible for the
ones who prepared their genealogies and presented them to
the appropriate authorities in England? Wanting everyone
with a justifiable claim included, Mrs. Mahan immediately
wrote to numerous Chases who she thought might have a
claim, including her brother-in-law, Ira Chase of Delaware
County, Ohio; E. R. Chase, Catherine Chase, Philip W.
Noel, and O. E. Weston of Kingston, Ohio; and I. W. Chase
of Kalamazoo, Michigan. They also corresponded with
George W. Chase, who, though a member of the Eastern
committee, had doubts about it himself.

Though they were by no means prosperous, the Mahans were primarily interested in the estate on religious
grounds. Mahan's friend of Cincinnati and Oberlin days,
George W. Whipple, was still Secretary of the American
Missionary Association, the headquarters of which remained
in New York City. Mrs. Mahan gave Whipple power of attorney to pursue her claim to the estate with the condition
that three fourths of any money recovered would go to further
the work of the Missionary Association among the freedmen
of the South. All of the Ohio Chases with whom the Mahans
corresponded subsequently made the same arrangements with
the Association. Whipple was not sanguine about the likely
success of his effort, but he thought that anything that might
substantially aid the freedmen was well worth the effort.
Furthermore, he was fond of Asa Mahan and was more concerned with his friend's financial security than he was.

The correspondence in Whipple's files reads like a
cloak-and-dagger adventure tale, but we must be content
with only a few episodes. Dr. Chase of Taunton never did
embark for England, and various other members of the committee made unauthorized trips to London. Nothing ever
came of them. The Ohio and Michigan Chases became increasingly suspicious of the Easterners. George W. Chase
tried to touch all bases: he remained a member of the committee, gave Whipple power of attorney, and eventually made

an unpublicized and unsuccessful trip to London himself.
Even Ira Chase, Mrs. Mahan's brother-in-law acted strangely.   He went to Newburyport, Massachusetts to gather and
have notarized the genealogical evidence that was necessary
to substantiate Mrs. Mahan's and his own relationship to
Aquila Chase.   He returned precipitously without the authenticated data and without any adequate reason for his failure.
The Ohio and Michigan Chases wondered if he had suddenly
aligned himself with the Eastern committee members.   As
a result, Asa Mahan went to Massachusetts and Maine and
successfully procured and had notarized the necessary genealogical data.

Meanwhile, Whipple had contacted Shepherd and Son
and Fred Tompkins, solicitors in London, and had received
conflicting reports.   Shepherd reported that no record of
the decision of the Court of Chancery in favor of American
heirs could be found, but Tompkins assured Whipple that
such a record existed.   It seemed desirable to both Mahan
and Whipple to have someone on the scene from the United
States.   A minister friend in Adrian agreed to go to London
on behalf of the A.M.A. and Mahan contributed to a fund to
defray his expenses.   At the last minute the Adrian friend,
for what reason we cannot discover, was unable to go to
London, and at the very last minute Mahan had to go in his
place.   When he arrived in London he was not impressed
with Shepherd and Son, since they had only employed a young
clerk to search the records of the Chancery Court.   He was
much more impressed with Fred Tompkins and so wrote
Whipple.   However, Whipple received a conflicting report
from the Reverend G. D. Pike, representative of the A.M.A.
in Manchester, England.   Shepherd was reliable, he thought,
while Tompkins was not.   Mahan himself became disillusioned with Tompkins when this solicitor said he had the
necessary information but would not release it unless paid
five hundred dollars.   Shocked beyond belief and without the
necessary financial resources, he began himself to search
the files of the Times in the British Museum to find the
issue that supposedly contained the advertisement to the
Chase heirs and in which a reference to the decision of the
Court of Chancery had been made.

Soon after his arrival Mahan became active in the
holiness circles in London.   He could not read continuously
at the British Museum since the bad lighting adversely affected his eyes.   His books were already well known, and
he was cordially received by holiness ministers.   Person-

ally he was a success and was invited to participate in the
Oxford Convention for the Promotion of Scriptural Holiness.
After staying with different friends for several months he
sent for Mrs. Mahan, and they established their first home
in London at 14 Bedford Place, Bloomsbury. It was close
to the British Museum, where Mahan intermittently continued
his research on the Chase estate after the Oxford Convention. Soon, however, he was completely engrossed in the
English Holiness Movement. His move to Kentish Town, a
London suburb, signalled that the Townley-Chase adventure
had come to nothing. However, that mattered little to him
since the Oxford Convention proved to be the spark that ig-
nited the fervor for holiness that swept through the British
Isles and the United States and became a major strand of
evangelical Christianity for many years to come. And Asa
Mahan was at the heart of the movement during its plentiful
years just as he had been during its lean years.

Origins

Americans were largely responsible for preparing
the ground for the holiness harvest that began at Oxford in
1874. The books of Asa Mahan and T. C. Upham of Bow-
doin College (who had adopted the holiness viewpoint in part
as a result of reading Mahan and other Oberlin authors)
first seriously aroused the interest of evangelical Anglicans,
as well as dissenters, though their influence was more among
the learned clergy than the laity. W. E. Boardman's The
Higher Christian Life in 1859 appealed to a wider audience
and helped overcome the prejudices against the topic long in
fashion. Interest was stimulated even to a higher pitch by
Robert Pearsall Smith's Holiness Through Faith, (1870) and
Walk in the Light (1873), and by Mrs. Hannah Whitall Smith's
The Record of a Happy Life (1873), all of which were widely circulated in England. Smith, who had been drawn into the ambit of
holiness by Hannah, was happy to escape working in the New Jersey glass factory of his Whitall in-laws, the handsome profits
of which nevertheless supported the strange, peripatetic
lives of the "transatlantic Smiths." After a much heralded
breakdown in his health Smith and his family journeyed to
England in 1872 for his recuperation. They were warmly
welcomed upon arrival and invited to numerous drawing room
meetings in London. In the spring of 1873 Boardman also
visited England in search of restored health, and he, too,
was warmly received. Evangelical ministers in the spring
of the year invited Smith and Boardman to speak on the topic

of the Higher Life to ministers and lay workers of London,
in groups of thirty or forty, at a series of breakfasts. The
two men spoke altogether to twenty-four hundred pastors in
this fashion. [4]

In the meantime the evangelistic campaign of Dwight
L. Moody and Ira D. Sankey in the United Kingdom during
1873-74 was highly successful and awakened multitudes to
the possibilities of what the evangelists saw as a new Christian life. They converted hundreds of nonbelievers and re-
portedly quickened the spiritual life of those who were already Christians. Interest in missions also mounted as a
result of their work. [5]

In the summer of 1874, W. Cowper-Temple, fathered
by Lord Palmerston, sponsored a six-day Conference on
holiness at his country home "Broadlands." He invited a
hundred people including Smith, who acted as chairman of
the meetings. The purpose of the conference was to "have
a few days of quiet prayer and meditation upon the Scriptural possibilities of the Christian life, as to maintained
communion with the Lord and victory over all known sin."
Other invited guests included Canon Wilberforce, Andrew
Jukes, Theodore Monod, Mrs. Amanda Smith, Ion Keith-
Falconer, and Arthur Blackwood. The issue was raised,
"Should we not have a conference open to a much larger
number of people?" Amidst general agreement that they
should, Blackwood, a Christian layman who was then chief
of the Postal Service in England, proposed that such a conference be held at Oxford at the earliest opportunity. [6] Thus
it was that the Oxford Union Convention came about which
brought together Boardman, Smith, Battersby, and Mahan
with such momentous results.

The Oxford Convention

This convention was held in Oxford from August 29
to September 7, 1874, during the University off-term period,
thereby meeting the desire expressed at Broadlands to meet
at the earliest opportunity. The invitation to the Convention
announced that it was to be a "Union Meeting for the Promotion of Scriptural Holiness" and explained:

> In every part of Christendom the God of all grace
> has given to many of His children a feeling of deep
> dissatisfaction with their present spiritual state, and

a strong conviction that the truths they believe
might and should exercise a power over their
hearts and lives, altogether beyond anything they
have as yet experienced.... They see with deep
distress the grievous gap there is between what
they know of Scriptural truth, and how they live."[7]

The prime mover and principal speaker was, again,
Robert Pearsall Smith. Other speakers included Hannah
Smith (whose Bible readings were very popular); Theodore
Monod, W. Gibson, and George Pearce of Paris; Otto Stock-
mayer of Switzerland; Evan Hopkins, I. E. Page, Thornly
Smith, C. B. Sawday, G. R. Thornton, and Filmer Sulivan
of England; Asa Mahan and W. E. Boardman of the United
States, and others. One of those present at the Convention
was T. D. Harford-Battersby, Vicar of St. John's, Keswick,
in the lake district of England, who was soon destined to
become one of the founders of the Keswick Convention.

I. E. Page reported the Oxford Convention for The
Methodist Recorder, a middle of the road religious periodical, less evangelical, for example, than The Methodist. For
September 4, 1874, he wrote that there was a lack of defin-
iteness in many of the Oxford speakers in contrast to Mahan,
"a noble looking old man," who gave "a strong, homely address, on receiving the Holy Ghost as the source of victory."
For September 11 he wrote: "Next morning a similar gathering took place in the large hall, and Dr. Mahan gave a
powerful address."[8] According to the reporter for The
Methodist, "The Rev. Dr. Mahan, of the United States, presided at the Town Hall, and was assisted by the Rev. Canon
Battersby, Lord Radstock, and others."[9] Nevertheless, already at Oxford Page detected an ominous element in Smith's
demeanor. "The peril of leadership in a religious movement
is self-exaltation.... It was noticed with surprise that while
clergymen who, through Mr. Smith's influence, had recently
come into the light were given prominence, men of spiritual
wisdom like Mr. Boardman and Dr. Mahan were kept in the
background."[10]

There can be little doubt that Smith was not keen on
giving Mahan a prominent role in the Convention. Mahan
was a philosopher and theologian and thus represented too
heavy fare for a person who was mentally as well as spiritually a dilettante, one who thrived on show rather than substance. Moreover, Mahan was a powerful speaker and who
wants to be eclipsed at his own show? In addition, there
can be little doubt that a Canon Battersby would appeal more

in principle to Smith than a Boardman or Mahan.   Smith was
delighted with show and prestige and was much drawn to the
English gentry.   He felt much more drawn to members of
the evangelical wing of the Established Church than to dissenting Protestants, even though the former were only now
accepting the holiness view while the latter, following Wesley, had long advocated and defended this vision.   Smith
definitely was a cathedral-type rather than a chapel-type of
man.   Nevertheless, Mahan was heard and much appreciated,
particularly by members of the clergy, and he continued to
play an important role in the holiness movement in the United
Kingdom long after the dramatic and damaging disappearance
of Smith from the scene. [11]

Mahan's influence was not limited to members of the
clergy; his preaching and teaching at Oxford deeply influenced Admiral E. G. Fishbourne.   Mahan greatly enlarged
his new friend's conception and faith on the subject of entire sanctification.   Like Mahan, the Admiral was an ardent
supporter of the Salvation Army and, unlike Mahan, was in
a position to translate his moral support into significant financial contributions.   Fishbourne, as we shall see, later
provided essential financial support for the journal of scriptural holiness, Divine Life, which Mahan continued to edit
until his death at the age of eighty-nine.

The denominations represented at Oxford were quite
diverse: Wesleyan, Primitive, and Free Church Methodists,
Congregationalists, Baptists, and other dissenting groups,
as well as much of the evangelical wing of the established
Church of England.   Numerous permanent groups such as
the Southport Convention arose within the dissenting ranks,
while Canon Harford-Battersby institutionalized the holiness
movement within the Anglican Church as the Keswick Convention, which still meets annually.   Mahan was not identi-
fied with any denomination during his English years and no
doubt gained some of his effectiveness from that fact.   Harford-Battersby could speak of holiness for the Church of
England, I. E. Page and John Brash for the Wesleyans, Benjamin Fell for the Primitives, H. Codling for Free Church
members, A. Gray Maitland for Congregationalists, but Mahan was one of the few who could speak for anyone and everyone. [12]

The Brighton Convention

Within nine months of the Oxford Convention a much

larger Union Meeting was held at Brighton, on the southern
coast of England, from May 29 to June 7, 1875. While one
thousand people attended the Oxford Meeting, eight thousand
assembled at Brighton to hear about and participate in the
Higher Life. Representatives from twenty-three different
countries were present. On May 29, Dwight L. Moody, just
closing his evangelistic services in London, said to his audience, "Let us lift up our hearts to seek earnestly a blessing on the great Convention that is now being held in Brighton, perhaps the most important meeting ever gathered," and
sent the following telegram to Smith: "Moody and 8,000 persons at the closing meeting at the Opera House have special-
ly prayed for the Convention, that great results may follow."
Smith, addressing the Convention said, "Let us ask an answering blessing upon our beloved brother Mr. Moody, a man
who walks with God."[13]

As at Oxford, the meetings were held in various halls
made available without charge by the Town Corporation.
Some of these buildings--the Town Hall, the Corn Exchange,
the Dome, and the Royal Pavilion--seated several thousand
people, but not one of them was adequate to hold the whole
assembly. Meetings had to be held simultaneously in the
various halls. Robert Pearsall and Hannah Smith again took
a leading part in the speaking. Other important speakers
included Stevenson A. Blackwood, Evan H. Hopkins, Henry
Varley, Theodore Monod, H. W. Webb-Peploe, Asa Mahan,
and E. W. Moore. According to the reporter for The Methodist, June 11, 1875, "Rev. Dr. Mahan ... has been preeminently successful; and his room is always crowded, chief-
ly with ministers." On June 25, the reporter complained of
Smith's arrangement of the Convention: "The same men
were put forward again, and again, and again, which was
the more inexcusable when not one of them, with the exception of Dr. Mahan and Theodore Monod, was able to con-
tribute either logical exactness or thoughtful exposition to
the discussion of the great theme."[14]

In the Record of the Convention we read that a minister from Russia, having read Mahan's Baptism of the Holy
Ghost, decided to go to Brighton for further help. "I have
gathered good things," he wrote, "worth taking away." Another minister reported: "When Dr. Mahan said, in his
sermon, 'Will you fall right into the centre of the will of
God?' I said 'Yes, yes, I will!' and that brought deeper
rest and peace than I had ever known before." Mahan held
meetings day after day in the Drawing Room, at which the

baptism of the Holy Ghost was the central theme of exposition and prayer. Each afternoon the room was crowded to
overflowing. To his overflow crowd Mahan said, "How often
it is that believers make a sort of piety of their weaknesses."15

R. P. Smith was still not eager to feature Mahan or
Boardman. Mahan's Drawing Room meetings were sectional
and not plenary meetings. One contributor to the Record of
the Convention wrote that "we regret that the reporters have
no notes of the addresses delivered by Dr. Mahan." During
a plenary session Smith, apparently under pressure, announced, "I have three names before me, and after we have
heard these gentlemen we shall be happy to hear Dr. Mahan."16

It was not long until the whole course of Smith's conduct came into question. While sitting in the Dome at Brighton, Mahan and G. A. Rogers (Vicar of Christ Church, Dover) were "oppressively impressed" with Smith's "rambling,
unedifying, and inappropriate" remarks.

> At length the speaker, apparently losing self-pos-
> session altogether, gave utterance to some of the
> wildest and most absurd apprehensions conceiv-
> able.... 'Horrible!' exclaimed Dr. Mahan. 'What
> are we coming to?' responded Mr. Rogers, both,
> of course, speaking in a whisper. As soon as
> the meeting closed, Dr. M. sought Admiral Fish-
> bourne, and urged him to expostulate with the speak-
> er for what had been uttered. When this was done,
> the individual positively denied that he had, or could
> have, uttered such sentiments, so foreign were
> they from what he had before entertained. This
> denial he steadfastly adhered to, until the reporter
> was called, and read the remarks as delivered.
> Then the speaker was as much amazed as the two
> individuals above-named had been."17

It will come as no surprise that Smith's remarks,
which so distressed his hearers, were antinomian in nature.
He said things that unmistakably implied that those who are
"in Christ" are no longer subject to the letter of the law as
the rule of their conduct, "that they are lifted to a higher
sphere of life, and thus walk in a freedom unknown to those
who are strangers to the exalted adventure of the new and
better life." As if this were not damaging enough, he was

seen kissing a young woman and all sorts of rumors of mis-
conduct ballooned. It is perfectly true that St. Paul had
told the Romans to "salute one another with a holy kiss,"
but was that all that was involved here? Some people thought
not, and "it was whispered that Pearsall Smith was teaching
privately to some of his feminine followers an extravagant
esoteric doctrine of mystical betrothal with Jesus."[18] It
was well known what that sort of counsel had led to in the
past.

That Smith preached antinomian doctrine there is no
doubt. That he was guilty of anything more than innocent
enthusiasm in kissing the young lady has never been proven.
Even friends suggested that he should confess his sins and
thereby cleanse himself. Hannah stoutly defended her husband and insisted there was nothing to confess.[19] Whatever
the true state of affairs might have been, Smith had become
a decided liability to the spiritual heirs of John Wesley. After the Convention a committee of eight including Blackwood,
Hopkins, Varley, and Lord Radstock (no Americans were included) issued a statement that Smith was being removed
from further participation in the movement. Thinking that
they were being gentle with Smith, they said that they were
convinced that all he had done was free from evil intention,
adding that Smith himself "recognized with deep sorrow the
unscriptural and dangerous character of the teaching and conduct in question."[20] Unfortunately, by not describing what
he had said or done the committee report only fueled the
imagination of the enemies of the movement and certainly
did Smith no good. Unhappy as the incident was for all concerned, it had more detrimental effects on Smith than on
the movement, which continued to have successful conventions throughout the United Kingdom, the Continent, and the
United States for many years to come.

The Banner of Holiness

During the progress of the Brighton Convention various leading speakers seemed to have simultaneously the
idea of establishing a weekly paper which would be devoted
to the doctrine of the higher life. According to Mahan,

> Before the close of the conference the plan was
> matured, and soon after all was arranged and The
> Banner of Holiness was before the public, and I
> was placed in the editorial chair. All was as

independent of my planning and agency as was the
production of Magna Charta.   All, as far as I was
concerned, was of divine appointment and direction. [21]

   The Banner had a short but interesting career.   During and after the Brighton Convention various individuals
pledged and paid one thousand pounds for the support of the
paper.   Mahan efficiently dispatched editorial chores but
showed poor judgment in selecting a business manager for
the periodical.   He later wrote: "By imprudent outlays on
the part of one in a responsible position, this sum was exhausted before the close of the first year, and a meeting
was appointed to wind up the concern and stop the paper."[22]

   The interesting features of the short-lived periodical
were its defense of the holiness movement against theological
criticism, on the one hand, and moral criticism as a result
of Smith's performance at Brighton, on the other.   It must
not be supposed that the evangelical wing of the Established
Church managed to move the body of that inertial institution
into spiritual flight.   Admiral Fishbourne's views, for example, brought much opposition.   "Old friends fell off, and
he came to be regarded, as the faithful few ever have been,
as holding extreme views."[23]   Various members of the Anglican clergy criticized their evangelical brethren, and these
criticisms, Mahan felt, were simply poor re-issues of old
arguments hurled at the Oberlinians years before.   In a collection of essays, published as a book, which were critical
of the doctrine of the Higher Life, Canon Ryle questioned,
"Does Christ so dwell in the believer that the believer has
not hourly need to resist the devil, to take heed to his tongue,
his temper, his employment of time, his conduct in every
relation of life, and to walk circumspectly lest he grieve the
Holy Spirit?"   In The Banner Mahan answered spiritedly and
went straight to the point, not wasting words on what he
thought should already be evident.

   Where in all our writings and teachings can anything be found to justify the asking of such questions?   Such misapprehensions always arise when
   individuals "speak evil of that which they understand not."   Instead of teaching that any believer
   ever does, or can, in this life, attain to a state
   in which all that Canon Ryle here refers to will
   not be necessary, we hold and teach, and that as
   of infinite moment, that no one can become, through

faith, "rooted and grounded in love," without becoming, in the same degree, confirmed in the
habit of watchfulness and prayer, "resisting the
devil," "taking heed to his tongue, his employment
of time, his conduct in every relation of life," and
"walking circumspectly lest he grieve the Holy Spirit." Everywhere all such virtues are, in the strongest terms, insisted upon as absolute essentials to
holy living. [24]

The editors of The Freeman, Baptist, and Christian
World launched an attack on the Holiness Movement as a
result of Smith's speech and conduct at Brighton. Mahan
quoted a piece from The Freeman:

> Rumors of an exceedingly painful character have
> been rife for some time past with respect to a
> noted leader of what is called the "higher Life"
> movement. In times gone by, similar pretensions
> to those identified with this gentleman's name have
> led to Antinomianism, which means that what would
> be sinful to an unbeliever is held to be sinless in
> a believer. We think a time has come ... when
> Christian charity requires that these teachings
> should be strictly examined. [25]

Mahan was appalled: Smith at Brighton had managed
to raise the old spectre of John Humphrey Noyes' Oneida
Perfectionism. So Mahan in the pages of the Banner explained carefully what he had hoped by now were the obvious
differences between the holiness viewpoint and any antinomian
doctrine. The editor of The Baptist, with Christian charity,
referred to Mahan's explanation as "long-winded" and as having absolutely nothing to do with the serious matter now in
hand. He disdained to reply to Mahan. The latter accused
him of the logical fallacy of shifting the issue. Originally
the issue raised was whether the doctrine of Holiness had
antinomian consequences. Mahan had rebutted the charge.
Now the issue was changed to the truth or falsity of the
"painful rumours" concerning Smith. Without naming Smith,
Mahan proceeded to tell what he knew about the painful rumors and, while not defending Smith, to explain that whatever he said or did was the result of ill health. Following
the lead of Hannah and the committee, Mahan wrote that
Smith had suffered a head injury as a result of a fall from
a horse years previously and "his brain was seriously affected." Overwork, he added, caused further problems. He

reported that Smith's physician expressed to Dr. Boardman his "undoubted conviction that the aberrations which gave rise to these rumours were wholly occasioned by an impaired state of the brain, so unlike and opposite were they to any events of his whole rational life." Mahan feelingly concluded:

> Our friend is now "sick, nigh unto death," so sick
> that no visitants are allowed to converse with him,
> and sick because "he would not be persuaded,"
> but "took his life in his hand" and crossed the
> ocean to meet the pressing calls which came to
> him from Central Europe. We have an appre-
> hension that the tear of the Recording Angel has
> wiped out the charges which accusing spirits have
> sent up to heaven, charges of aberrations which
> occurred while the sickness which was induced by
> his over-exertions in the cause of Christ, was
> coming on. [26]

Mahan might not have been so sympathetic had he known the eventual outcome of the celebrated Smith affair. The Smith's younger daughter, Alys, was Bertrand Russell's first wife, and in his recent autobiography the philosopher wrote:

> In the summer of 1889, when I was living with my
> Uncle Rollo at his house on the slopes of Hindhead,
> he took me one Sunday for a long walk. As we
> were going down Friday's Hill, near Fernhurst,
> he said, "Some new people have come to live at
> this house, and I think we will call upon them....
> We found that the family were American, named
> Pearsall Smith, consisting of an elderly mother
> and father [and various children]. The father and
> mother had been in their day famous evangelistic
> preachers, but the father had lost his faith as a
> result of a scandal which arose from his having
> been seen to kiss a young woman, and the mother
> had grown rather too old for such a wearing life. [27]

While Hannah remained in the fold and her later life exhibited some sort of coherency, Robert, after the permanent move to England in 1889, deteriorated into a fatuous individual whose life became an exercise in futility. Eventually no one took him seriously, not even the friends of his family. [28]

The Smith's elder daughter, Mary, became the wife
of Frank Costelloe and later abandoned him and their two
children to accompany Bernard Berenson to Florence. Mary
became the mistress of I. Tatti and followed Berenson's art
interests just as previously she had shared Costelloe's social and political commitments. The Smith's son, Logan
Pearsall Smith, author of Trivia, became not only an An-
glophile but a classic example of the expatriate. The United
States, he never tired of proclaiming, was disgusting--this
while he was living on the profits of the Whitall-Tatum Company. It was too much even for George Santayana, no great
admirer of the United States himself. If it is so disgusting,
he chided Smith, why do you return to Johns Hopkins hospital for a critical operation?[29]

Divine Life

Mahan's second venture in publishing a holiness journal lasted a good deal longer. Immediately after the collapse of The Banner an English friend wrote him asking for
an explanation of several passages of scripture. After explaining the passages in detail Mahan also wrote of the need
for a journal of holiness that could be sent free of charge
to Christian missionaries. The friend replied that Mahan
might draw upon him for a thousand pounds to establish the
new periodical, the name of which became Divine Life. The
name of the friend was never mentioned, but it is likely that
it was Admiral Fishbourne. In the July 1887 issue of the
journal William Smyth wrote of the Admiral: "His purse
was ever open to the work of God," to which Mahan added
that "he is a writer for, and in other ways as few know,
one of the staunchest friends of Divine Life."[30]

The journal began as a weekly in 1876 under the title
Divine Life and Missionary Witness, edited by Charles Graham and George Savage, but in May 1877 it became a monthly with Mahan placed in the editorial chair. In June 1878
it became Divine Life and International Expositor of Scriptural Holiness and the Reverend Asbury Lowrey of the United
States became co-editor. In 1883 "of Scriptural Holiness"
was dropped from the title but this reflected no change in
viewpoint. The Reverend C. G. Moore of England was also
added as a co-editor in 1884. The journal was published in
England and distributed throughout the United Kingdom and
the United States. In June 1889, immediately following Mahan's death, Moore and Lowrey, in that order, are listed as

editors of Divine Life and International Expositor.   By August, Lowrey dissolved the union and under the title Divine
Life and Bible Expositor published a strictly American periodical with Daniel Steele as co-editor.   Moore continued as
editor of the English Divine Life, and the Reverend J. G.
Mantle became his co-editor in 1891, supplanted by E. W.
Moore in 1894.   In the same year Divine Life was incorporated into Evan Hopkins' The Life of Faith.   Divine Life and
Bible Expositor in the United States merged with The Illustrated Christian World in 1896. 31

      The amount of material published in Divine Life
throughout the years was enormous, and we are able at
best only to examine a few of Mahan's many contributions
and only suggest the flavor of the whole.   One prevalent
and recurring theme is Finney and the old days at Oberlin,
where, as far as Mahan was concerned, the holiness movement had begun.   On September 21, 1876, he reviewed favorably Finney's Lectures to Professing Christians, referring
to his old colleague's "constant and earnest prayerfulness
and his deep and unbroken communion with the Lord."   In
the same and other issues he pointed up Finney's influence
on Moody.   In June 1877 he wrote glowingly that Finney had
gone from early ostracism to a standing ovation in later
years when the General Association of all evangelical Congregational Churches of the United States met at Oberlin.
In January 1879:   "Wait upon God, reader, as that man of
God [Finney] did, and such will be your upliftings."   December 1880:   the doctrine of special grace "began in Oberlin about the year 1835."   In 1888 just before his death he
again harked back to Finney and his own entrance into higher
life.   They had formulated and preached the doctrine at Oberlin and elsewhere together as comrades in arms. 32

      Another recurring theme is the work of Dwight L.
Moody.   In the issues of November 23, 1876, December 14,
1876, January 18, 1877, and others, Mahan emphasized that
the evangelist's work became truly remarkable only after he
had received the baptism of the Holy Spirit.   At first Moody
had preached almost exclusively to the impenitent and felt
a lack of power in his efforts.   Having fervently prayed for
the enduement of power and having received it, he always
thereafter first preached to believers about how their low
spiritual life could be elevated.   In May 1890 Moore published posthumously a piece by Mahan concerning the events
which had caused Moody first to go to England.   A tract containing portions from Christian Perfection and Baptism of the

Holy Ghost had been distributed in England, and a Mr. Bainbridge had read one and had been converted to the holiness
viewpoint.   It was Bainbridge, then, upon coming to the
United States, who had convinced Moody to go to England,
a momentous event indeed for evangelical Christianity in
that country. [33]

A specific item of interest concerning Hannah Whitall
Smith appeared in the Correspondence Section of Divine Life
for June 1877.   The Smiths had been shattered by the Brighton Convention.   Hannah Smith had written to Mrs. William
Cowper-Temple in April 1876 that if there was to be any
bearable life for either her or her husband, he must be relieved from the dreadful strain.   However, by 1877 Hannah
Smith, unlike her husband, had recovered her equilibrium.
She wrote a cheerful letter to her friend Mrs. Belle Lowrey,
who asked Mahan to print a portion of it in Divine Life.

> You know that two years ago I came to think the
> baptism of the Holy Ghost was a delusion, or at
> least only a deception, caused to enthusiastic minds
> by peculiar temperaments or states of health....
> I have been forced to examine the subject [again],
> and am convinced at last that the "promise of the
> Father" is as truly bestowed as it was in the Bible
> days, and that it is the church's present greatest
> need....   I want to say now as earnestly as I
> know how, that I believe it to be the very truth
> of God and the one greatest need of all believers,
> and I have noticed this, that the warmth and ear-
> nestness of my Christian life have been altogether
> in proportion to my belief or unbelief in this doc-
> trine....   But for this fresh stirring up on this
> subject I could never have returned into any pub-
> lic work.   It was too utterly distasteful to me.
> But with my return to a belief in this doctrine
> came also my power for service, and I have been
> quite hard at work ever since. [34]

The quality of Hannah's long-term commitment, however,
was not wholly untinged with worldly concerns.   According
to her biographer, her religion concealed a woman of the
world, "shrewd and skillful in establishing enduring friendships with the titled ladies of England."   She was something
of a name dropper, "and her humor was a mixture of flat-
footed common sense ... and unconscious snobbery." [35]

The following sampling of contents will suggest the

wide variety of material that appeared in Divine Life, as
well as the attention paid by its editor to practical as well
as theoretical matters: June 1877--since he is often pic-
tured as a teacher of dangerous error, Mahan reprints a
surprising, positive response to his Out of Darkness into
Light from the (Boston) Congregationalist; January 1878--
"The extent to which the doctrine of the Higher Life is per-
meating religious thought in the United States is clearly indicated by the [rapidly growing] number of periodicals published there ... wholly devoted to this one theme"; February 1878--Mahan happily reports a vestige of holiness teaching in the otherwise recalcitrant Record, an Anglican periodical; December 1880--Mahan attacks Henry Ward Beecher as
accepting "a Rationalism more vague, but not less anti-Chris-
tian, than that of Theodore Parker"; May 1881--"Which came
first, Calvinism or Arminianism?" Mahan asks, and answers,
"To be sure, Arminius came after Calvin, and Wesley after
the Westminster Confession [but] if we go back to the Primitive Church the opposite answer must be given"; July 1881--
he defended faith healing and claimed that his second wife
had thereby been cured of cancer; March 1883--he defended
theism as a reasonable alternative between pantheism and
evolutionary theory; and, finally, sprinkled throughout the
issues are reports on holiness conventions, camp meetings,
Saturday afternoon Y.M.C.A. meetings, Salvation Army activities, and Monday meetings at Rochester Square, to say
nothing of news items of special and general holiness meetings held in various parts of England, Scotland, Ireland,
Mexico, Bulgaria, Spain, Australia, Canada, and the United
States. Finally, there are countless advertisements for
books like From the Curate to the Convent, described by
the publisher as "a very valuable book to mothers and daughters to warn them against Ritualism."[36]

London

    Mahan lived in London from 1874 to 1884 when, for
reasons of health, he moved to Eastbourne on the southern
coast slightly east of Brighton, where he lived until his
death in 1889. His London addresses in chronological order were: 14 Bedford Place, Bloomsbury; 2 Rochester Road,
Kentish Town; Ivy Cottage, Kynaston Road, Stoke Newington;
and 68 Springdale Road, Stoke Newington. The moves probably were made to remain close to friends and colleagues
in the holiness movement.

    Since Mahan never returned to the United States and

eventually became a British citizen, it might appear that he
had become an expatriate. However, the case is far otherwise. No one could have been less an expatriate than he,
as is abundantly clear from his sharp defense of the United
States when it was criticized on what he took to be wrong
grounds or in picayune ways. A letter had appeared in The
English Independent deploring the spate of honorary degrees
showered on English residents by American colleges and suggesting even that they had been "begged-for baubles" (as in
the case of Rev. Clement Clemance). That letter and a
later one took a condescending attitude toward institutions
of higher learning in the United States with the exception of
a few like Yale, Amherst, and Harvard. In two letters of
his own to the Independent in 1878 Mahan responded in detail, giving evidence to show that such opinions were completely misguided. What is important for our purposes, however, is that he had a few brisk rejoinders.

> It would be a slander of American colleges to call
> that degree "a sham decoration." It is a genuine
> "decoration" from an honoured college of a country
> which has no occasion to be ashamed of itself or
> of its colleges.... I deeply regret the rough man-
> ner in which your correspondent speaks upon this
> subject. 37

He concluded his second letter by saying,

> Nor do I believe that an individual in this country
> can be named who has received a diploma from
> an American college whose degrees do not possess
> kindred honour with those of Yale and Amherst.
> But why this abuse? Is it not wise to wait until
> the ... icebergs of diplomas are seen gathering
> on either shore of that continent, and are about
> to move in this direction before all England is
> rendered terror-stricken at the deluge of degrees
> which is about to overwhelm your ministers? 38

It was not because he was disenchanted with his own
country that Mahan remained in England the last fifteen years
of his life. He stayed because he found an audience highly
receptive to the role he was playing in the burgeoning holiness movement in England. He saw it as an unlooked-for
field of service and would stay as long as he could harvest
souls for God's storehouse. The harvest seemed to last,
so Mahan stayed. Soon he was committed to projects he

could not in good conscience leave.[39]   Moreover, he made
many warm friends among his fellow workers and felt a
sense of community.   That he never returned to the United
States for a visit is explained quite simply by the fact that
he never had enough money to do so.

      Financially Mahan's English years were thinner than
usual.   He was swindled out of the money on which he had
depended for a sustenance during his and Mrs. Mahan's later years.   An attorney who held for collection a note of
Mahan's against a wealthy individual collected it and instead
of investing the amount as directed absconded with the money.   More money placed with another attorney for the same
purposes went the same route.   Mahan wrote: "Thus all
the pecuniary means that I had for support in my old age--
I being at the age of eighty--were taken from me by fraud."
Yet the theft "which would have induced untold anguish in
my primal Christian life did not cost me a single pang, nor
induce a single vengeful sentiment toward the wrong-doers."[40]
Even so, matters were bad enough to cause Asbury Lowrey
(writing wholly on his own) to publish the following words in
the January 1883 issue of Divine Life.

> It may appear strange that our octogenarian has
> not accumulated a fortune.   But he has not.   He
> is poor.   He lives plainly in the city of London.
> He has made many rich, both materially and spir-
> itually, while his own supplies scarcely amount to
> a competency.   And yet no man is more contented
> and happy than he....   It would be an honour to
> any man of wealth to endow the residue of this
> apostolic man's life.[41]

Apparently no one was able to accept Lowrey's invitation
since when he died Mahan's personal estate amounted to less
than two hundred dollars.

      The lengthening years in London did not dim Mahan's
affection for his children; far away though they might be,
they were in his thoughts as much as always.   Sarah had
died in 1875 after a chronic illness resulting from her un-
tiring labors in the Sanitary Commission during the Civil
War.   A well-merited editorial tribute appeared in the Cleveland Herald and she was kindly remembered in the columns
of the Oberlin Weekly News.   Lucy Dix Mahan Wyman died
in 1880 at the age of forty-nine, she being the one Asa had
held close to his heart in Cincinnati and with whom he had

a special bond. Mary Dix Mahan, Theodore, Elizabeth, and
now Sarah and Lucy--he had a special place for each one in
his lexicon of love. Anna Jenison, Mary Keep, and Almira
Barnes were still alive, and corresponding with them was a
joyful part of his life. He began his letters to Anna, and
presumably to the other two daughters as well, with the sal-
utation "My dear precious Daughter" and in 1882 sent a copy
of the Autobiography to Anna after inscribing on the flyleaf,
"With your Father's undying Love." In 1884 he wrote her
lamenting the fact that he would never see his children and
grandchildren again. "My daily prayer is that I may meet
you all in the kingdom of Light.... Love to all."[42]

The London years were enormously productive ones
for Mahan. In addition to editing The Banner of Holiness
and Divine Life he preached innumerable sermons in the
city and countryside and regularly participated in religious
conventions. After Oxford and Brighton came Dublin, Cambridge, Dover, Glasgow, Bognor, Falmouth, Nottingham,
Scarborough, and so on. Mahan's preaching was as effective as ever. In October 1875 Gray Maitland affectionately
introduced him to the audience at a Convention of the Congregational Churches, where the merits of the Oxford and
Brighton Conventions were being debated, and Mahan "was
received with much cheering." In November 1875 a reporter for The Methodist under the title "Christian Convention
in Dublin" wrote: "Rev. Asa Mahan, from America, delivered a most stirring speech ... and seemed to carry the
audience entirely with him by the earnestness of his manner." In July 1876 a reporter for The Methodist Recorder
noted that "Dr. Mahan's address [at Cambridge] can never
be forgotten by those who heard it, and it seemed to take
hold on the entire assembly, hundreds of whom rose and
testified that they could trust Jesus as a Saviour from sin."
I. E. Page in his book A Long Pilgrimage, published in
1914, described Mahan as impressive in appearance when
he preached, "a tall, strongly-built man, with massive countenance and shaggy beard." "Deliberate in speech, he felt
the importance of his message, his close-linked argument
marching right on."[43]

It is testimony to Mahan's great energy and commitment that during these London years, in addition to his editing, periodical writing, and preaching, he wrote and published eight books in religion and philosophy. He worked
arduously after the Oxford Convention to finish Out of Darkness into Light so that it would be published and available

at the Brighton Convention. It proved to be a great favorite
in holiness circles not only during the Brighton Convention
but for many years afterward. It was republished in 1882
by the Wesleyan Methodist Book-Room. Other important
works of the London period (a number of which we have already referred to) include: The Phenomena of Spiritualism
Scientifically Explained and Exposed, 1875; Consequences of
Neglect, 1876; Misunderstood Texts of Scripture Explained
and Elucidated, 1876; A Critical History of the Late American War, 1877; A Critical History of Philosophy, 1882; The
System of Mental Philosophy, 1882; and Autobiography: Intellectual, Moral, and Spiritual, 1882. Most of these volumes went through numerous editions. There was also quite
early an English reprint of Baptism of the Holy Ghost. [44]

Mahan's books were equally as effective as his editing
and preaching in promoting the holiness viewpoint in England.
In July 1875 there was a laudatory notice of Out of Darkness
into Light in The Methodist Recorder and in September another one in The Methodist. John Brash wrote in Our Lovefeast that in June 1877 "while reading 'Out of Darkness into
Light,' by Dr. Mahan, I felt deeply conscious of my need of
a renewed baptism of power"--which, he wrote, after much
praying he received. In A Long Pilgrimage Page wrote that
"Out of Darkness into Light is a massive book, which has
helped many." Concerning the English reprint of Baptism of
the Holy Ghost the reviewer for The Methodist Recorder wrote
in 1873: it is "thoroughly scriptural in its teaching" and "if
we are to have a genuine and permanent revival of the work
of God, we know of no means more likely to bring it about
than the earnest and prayerful perusals of such works." In
August 1889 in The King's Highway Page wrote that Baptism
of the Holy Ghost was perhaps Mahan's "best and freshest
work" and in A Long Pilgrimage years later exclaimed, "I
have no hesitation in saying that Mahan's Baptism of the Holy
Ghost is worthy of being placed beside William Arthur's
Tongue of Fire. The pages glow with interest; the reader
is constrained to pray as he reads." The book is clear
in thought and style and is "pervaded with earnestness" that
is heart-warming. In The King's Highway for November 1897
the Reverend Joseph Ogden wrote that "outside the Bible, the
book which gave me most assistance was Dr. Asa Mahan's
'Baptism of the Holy Ghost.'" Mahan's Autobiography also
gathered a number of Christians into the fold of holiness,
though Brash and Page thought it a bit "heavy" compared to
his previous performances. Needless to say, there was also
disapproval voiced from sources that had disapproved of the
holiness movement since the days of Wesley. [45]

Mahan's philosophical writing remained a dominant element in his London years. His Mental Philosophy is not insignificant, though his two-volume Critical History of Philosophy is one of his most significant contributions to philosophical literature. The word "critical" is not to be taken lightly. The History is not a compendium of what previous philosophers had maintained but rather a classification of all philosophies into four types, three of which Mahan rebuts and the fourth, that of commonsense realism, he stoutly defends.

According to Mahan, the commonsense judgments of mankind, what is universally concluded when consciousness is consulted without philosophical presuppositions, must reflect basic truths or they would not be so utterly pervasive--they are unavoidably implicit in our actions and have helped mold the structure of all language. This respect for pervasiveness and communality is more trustworthy in principle than respect for contrived and parochial philosophical arguments that lead to such outlandish views as that only mind exists, or that only matter exists, or that it is impossible to know any statement to be true. When such philosophical arguments and positions violate what we know to be true commonsensically, so much the worse for those philosophies. The mediation of commonsense truths becomes a desideratum or requirement, so to speak, for any adequate or acceptable philosophical system. If a system does not meet this requirement it should be eliminated. [46]

Though his classification of philosophies into four types, plus his specific rebuttals of three and defense of the fourth, is an original contribution to philosophical literature, his overall view that philosophical propositions must not entail the falsity of commonsense propositions known to be true was, of course, not unique to him. It was the common element among all Scottish realists--Reid, Stewart, Beattie, Witherspoon, Wayland, Peabody, McCosh, and others--and, ironically, was an overall attitude toward philosophy that was to be upset by the educational innovations of Eliot at Harvard. Scottish commonsense philosophers became old hat there and were replaced by men like George Herbert Palmer, William James, Hugo Muensterberg, Josiah Royce, and George Santayana who promptly supported views that Mahan had considered the products of bleary-eyed and demented philosophers of the past--objective idealism, materialism, skepticism, and gnosticism. [47] It was only well into the twentieth century that an overall attitude toward philosophy

and commonsense not unlike that of the Scottish realists
came to be a dominant strand in Anglo-American philosophy
once again.

The Calm Within

Mahan's calmness and serenity during his English
years was remarked upon by his many friends.   C. G.
Moore testified that "for four years we had an intimate fellowship in service with our dear and honoured friend, wholly
unmarred, which will ever remain one of life's brightest
memories."[48]   J. Jones wrote that Mahan "is one of the
holiest men I ever met with" and "the holy influence which
I felt whilst in his presence I trust shall never be lost."[49]
Asbury Lowrey wrote that "the crowning characteristic of
Dr. Mahan was his moral goodness, his intimate acquaintance with God."[50]   Mary Chase Mahan stated in a letter to
Mrs. Lowrey that "my dear husband was always in advance
of me, he growing more and more lovely and Christ-like in
all respects day by day."[51]

The portrait of Brother Mahan that has emerged from
his English years--"Christ-like" and a "venerable saint" are
recurring epithets--raises the question whether he had mellowed through the years.   There is a complete absence of
the strife and contention of previous years.   Certainly Homer
Johnson, Horace Taylor, John McEldowney, and Luther Lee
did not describe him as a saint.   What had happened to
change him?   In truth, this question commits the fallacy of
many questions; his change requires no explanation since he
had changed markedly little since the early years at Oberlin.
No doubt he did mellow to some extent during later years,
but no more than occurs naturally through physical causes
with the majority of older people.   What in fact had changed
and had produced a new life so free of strife was his environment.   He had only to preach and write about the doctrine of holiness to multitudes happy to hear his message.
There were no power struggles between president and faculty
and no congregations to challenge his right to speak the truth
as he saw it on any issue whatever from the pulpit.   There
were no longer battles to be fought against slavery and in
defense of co-education--these battles had finally been won.
There was no struggle to establish the new education.   By
some miracle Eliot had been chosen president of Harvard,
and the elective system, and much else, was now an established fact.   There were no political campaigns replete with

insults and calumny. Since Mahan belonged to no denomination no occasion ever arose when he had to defend his orthodoxy. In light of these facts we can understand why Mahan
repeatedly told Mary Chase Mahan that his English years
were the happiest ones of his life. [52]

Mahan indeed remained much the same person he had
always been, and upon occasion he could still land a stout
blow. We have already seen an example of his continued
toughness in his spirited defense of American colleges in
the pages of The English Independent. And in his monumental A Critical History of Philosophy he could not help
expostulating against "crazy" and "blear-eyed" philosophies
that outrageously contradicted what we know to be true in
ordinary experience. There is no claim so preposterous
that it has not been advanced by some "demented" philosopher. [53] He had mellowed a bit but changed significantly,
no. It was his spiritual environment that had changed. He
had always had many warm friends and a smaller number
of bitter enemies. Some of the latter no doubt were caused
by personality clashes but many of them resulted from Mahan's savage fights in behalf of what he took to be necessary
reforms. These duties had been discharged and he was now
free to pursue single mindedly the one that mattered most
to him--spreading the word of what his Salvationist friends
called God's promises of full salvation. And even the pursuit of this goal did not bring him the calumny it had in
previous years. He was experiencing the high tide of holiness and did not live to see it ebb. Since his days the tides
have come and gone, though Christian Perfection, Misunderstood Texts, and Baptism of the Holy Ghost are still reprinted
and read however deep or shallow the water may be along
the strand. [54]

Had the aging minister learned to be more tactful in
later years? The answer again is, no. Here too matters
remained in a steady state throughout his life. As always
he could be charming and avoid stepping on people's toes
unless a moral or religious issue arose that required a
straightforward declaration of principle. "Straightforward"
in such contexts usually turned out to be "blunt" for Mahan.
He still could not refrain from doing things like standing up
and finishing what he thought was an inadequate sermon of
James H. Fairchild. With the heavy hand of old, though with
the best intentions in the world, he wrote Anna in October
1882 that she had been a faithful and successful mother in
training her children for honorable positions in the world.

"My daily prayer is that you may be equally faithful and
successful, as a Christian mother." There was no doubt
in the old father's mind that the younger generation was
losing hold of the Great Vision. "I must close by sending
a Father's blessing to all my children, and their children."[55]

What was the state of Mahan's self esteem during the
English years, exaggerated or normal? The answer to this
question is as complicated as it was before. While he did
not place a low value on himself or his work, his self-esteem did not amount to self-conceit. He gave no indication
whatever of being displeased by Smith's effort to outshine
him at Oxford and Brighton and happily accepted whatever
place he was given in the order of speakers, and place of
speaking, in the later holiness conventions. He never sought
editorial assignments and he worked in utter harmony with
his co-editors. Other evidence could be cited but is already
implied in the emerging portrait of Mahan during his English
years. Still there are episodes that might suggest undue
self-esteem, and in all fairness we must examine them.

As we have seen, Mahan was much impressed by
Dwight L. Moody and linked his name with the evangelists'
by pointing out that his work converted Mr. Bainbridge to
the holiness movement and that Mr. Bainbridge was responsible for Moody's coming to England. To Anna he wrote,
"Woman has a calling and a sphere of influence, in our day,
such as was unknown in centuries past.... I bless God
that he has made me so instrumental in bringing on this
great consummation."[56] Do such examples, which could be
expanded, show self-esteem blown up to self-conceit? We
think not. It is the same issue addressed earlier. Mahan,
like Finney and many other evangelists, when they made such
remarks intended to glorify God, not themselves. Mahan
explicitly wrote that his motives for recounting the Moody
story might be open to misunderstanding. He sincerely believed that his only reason for making it was to give further
evidence that God works in marvelous and mysterious ways--
that what appears trivial and accidental is in reality a part
of providential workings.[57] Again the emphasis in the letter
to Anna is that he was the instrument of God, not that he
was the instrument of God.

It is true that an early issue of Divine Life carried a
notice to the effect that Adrian College on June 21, 1877,
conferred the degree of LL.D. upon the Reverend Asa Mahan, D.D.[58] Was such an announcement undue self-praise

and advertisement? It need not be so construed. To be
sure, we cannot say that Lowrey or Moore did it, since
neither one was on the scene yet. However, there were
others on the editorial board of the journal already at this
early date. Still the notice would not have appeared without
Mahan's consent. But the crucial point is that news items
of this sort were not unusual features of that journal or of
other journals which also contained items concerning their
respective editors. In any case, there is a big difference
between justifiable pride and vaulting self-esteem, and surely the notice, like similar cases, can be construed as an
instance of the former. Justifiable pride should not be a
sin in anyone's lexicon of evil things. There are other
items in the later years that could be discussed in connection with the present question, but they soon start to seem
picayune. Mahan did not hide his light under a basket during his later years, and he appreciated deeply whatever recognition was given to him; but there is no evidence to suggest self-conceit and much evidence to deny its existence.
Page, Brash, Mantle, Maitland, Lowrey, Moore, Mrs. Mahan and many others described him as a model pilgrim on
his journey to the Kingdom of Light and well deserving of
the pilgrim's rest at the end of the road. There is no evidence to suggest that they cannot be taken at their word.

Eastbourne

        Since the climate of Eastbourne was superior to Lon-
don's, the Mahans moved there in 1884. The productive
days were not yet over, but there would be none left to
match the great London years. Asa and Mary Chase Mahan first lived at 27 Ceylon Place but in 1887 moved to
Sandringham House at 55 Grand Parade, a hotel overlook-
ing the English Channel and now known as the Norfolk Hotel.
In his Eastbourne years Mahan became a British citizen and
is listed as a voter in the records of the Town Hall of the
Borough. He and Mary worshipped at Longstone Hall, 98
Longstone Road, attended by people of the holiness persuasion and loosely associated with the Salvation Army. It was
later called the Eastbourne Holiness Mission and eventually
became for a time the Salvation Army Youth Centre.[59] Early
in their Eastbourne years the Mahans read with pleasure what
their fellow townsman Lancelot Middleton had to say in the
pages of The Methodist Recorder:

        It will interest many of your readers to know that

> this venerable saint and minister completes his
> eighty fifth year on Sunday next.... Let them to
> whom Dr. Mahan's name has become endeared by
> the message of his writings, think of him next
> Sunday and pray God still to bless his aged ser-
> vant and to brighten his closing days with yet
> sweeter and clearer visions of "the holy city, the
> new Jerusalem"; towards which his pilgrim steps
> have so long been tending. [60]

Mahan was by no means ready to admit that he was
finished with his work, though he knew he could write no
more books. Both he and his friends were astonished at
his continued good health. He wrote Anna in 1884 that his
posture was as erect as ever, his voice as strong, and his
walk about as elastic, "though I become weary much sooner."
In these respects, he exclaimed, "I am the wonder of all
who know me."[61] He wrote continuously for Divine Life;
so much, in fact, that there was a good store of articles
left for posthumous publication. He also preached occasionally at Longstone Hall.

Mahan lived a few years longer, able to do less and
less but still active. He loved to walk on the Grand Parade
and the esplanade happily greeting friends and making new
ones, to all of whom, without doubt, he still spoke about
the journey out of darkness into light. Haig Miller has described the scene:

> A visitor to Eastbourne of late years might have
> been struck by the venerable figure of a man who
> was to be seen walking along the esplanade.... He
> bears the burden of nearly ninety years; but his
> form is tall, erect and full of manly beauty, and
> an aspect of peace is settled upon his countenance.
> If you are so fortunate as to enter into conversa-
> tion with him, you will find ... that he is in a
> pre-eminent degree devout and godly. You will,
> indeed, fully understand, after meeting him, the
> meaning of a phrase often used when we speak of
> such individuals as John Wesley, or Fletcher of
> Madeley--"an apostolic man."[62]

On Mahan's eighty-ninth birthday C. G. Moore observed that
"although feeble, he was in good health, and his heart was made
glad by loving letters and gifts from numerous friends."[63]

In March 1889 Brother Mahan had a slight attack of

pneumonia which was aggravated by piercing east winds.   In
early April he was very low.   When Mary kissed him, as
she thought for the last time, he said, "Let us praise God,
my dear, for all His goodness today before you go."   When
she said to him, "My dear, you are almost home," he
seemed surprised.   When she explained, his "only response
was one of his bright, happy smiles."   He died at 10:30 p.m.
April 4, and to his host of friends the Grand Parade and the
esplanade no longer seemed the same cheery places. [64]

   The good doctor was buried in Ocklygne Cemetery.
The chapel at the cemetery was packed and a large number
of people remained outside.   The service was conducted by
C. G. Moore, and numerous people gave short memorial
talks.   The usual service was read at the graveside "and
brief addresses were given by the Rev. John Dinnick, Rev.
C. G. Moore, and Colonel Reece [of the Salvation Army]--
the last sent to represent General Booth, who would himself
have been present had he not been too far away in Scotland."
Moore described the scene:

> Few who were present will ever forget that mem-
> orable afternoon on that hillside at Eastbourne.
> The Lord of heaven and earth seemed to calm and
> hush all nature around into perfect harmony with
> that last scene.... The quiet and subdued, but
> intensely cheerful and cheering sunlight, the balmy
> air, the whispering breeze, the bright but not glar-
> ing sky, all seemed commissioned to join with our
> words and songs in testifying to the perfectly calm
> and beautiful ending of the long years of Asa Ma-
> han's walk with God here below. [65]

   C. G. Moore and G. D. Freeman were executors of
Mahan's will, which was probated on June 19, 1889.   The
handwritten will, still at Somerset House in London, reveals
what was closest to his heart as death neared.

> I give and bequeath unto my dear wife Mary E.
> Mahan all my personal property real estate and
> all proceeds on Sales of books in England and
> America and all other forms of income whatever.
> I further direct that should my wife Mary E. Ma-
> han die before me that at my death all income
> from the sale of books in both England and Amer-
> ica with any money on hand in Bank or otherwise
> after my funeral expenses shall have been paid be

devoted to the free distribution of my spiritual
writings such as "The Baptism of the Holy Ghost,"
"Out of Darkness into Light," "My Autobiography"
and "Divine Life" etc. among Foreign and Home
Missionaries in and from this country and the
United States and Canada without any denominational distinctions. [66]

Mahan's personal estate amounted to the sad sum of £83-6-0 d.

In July 1889 Moore invited readers of Divine Life to
donate money to erect a grave stone for Mahan.   The stone,
soon a reality, bears the inscription on the bottom, "Erected
by a few of the friends who were blessed through his life
and words."   Right under his name is inscribed "first President of Oberlin College, U.S.A."   The epitaph begins: "Thy
sun shall no more go down, neither shall they moon withdraw itself...."[67]

Mahan's grave has remained unaccompanied and alone
all through the years.   The graves of his loved ones are
widely scattered--Anna Dana Mahan on the crest of the hill
in Orangeville; the infant Theodore in Pittsford; Mary Dix
Mahan, Theodore, Elizabeth, Sarah, and Anna in Cleveland;
and Lucy, Mary Keep, and Almira Barnes in unknown places.
Mary Chase Mahan, who had unwisely invested her limited
funds in a mission in Bulgaria, returned to the United States,
died shortly after, and was buried at the side of Silas Chase
in Bethel, Ohio.

The unaccompanied grave in Ocklynge is the token of
a life.   Though beloved of many people in diverse denominations, he was a member of none.   Though well remembered
in Cincinnati, Oberlin, Adrian, London, and Eastbourne, he
belonged to none of these places in the unique and singular
way conferred upon a life-long resident.   Though well remembered by his remaining daughters, he was, as a result
of the years in England, only dimly remembered by his grandchildren and by some not at all.   To what community, if any,
did he belong?

Mahan's grave has no caretaker.   F. Haslam, Superintendent of Ocklynge, writes that "the grave [of the late Rev.
Asa Mahan] is not looked after but the grass is cut by my
staff approximately twice a year during the course of general
cemetery maintenance."[68]   Mahan's epitaph ends: "For the
Lord shall be thy everlasting life, and the days of thy
mourning shall be ended."

CHAPTER NOTES

CHAPTER 1. NEW YORK YEARS

1. E. D. Eaton, "Asa Mahan" entry, Dictionary of American Biography (New York: Scribners, 1933), XII, 209; "Asa Mahan" folder, Alumni Records, Bosworth Hall, Oberlin College; Pages from Anna Mahan North's Notebook, Asa Mahan Archives, Asbury College. All the standard histories of Oneida County derive their information about the early period of settlement essentially from Pomroy Jones, Annals and Recollections of Oneida County (Rome, New York: The Author, 1851), and the section on early settlers in Vernon appears on pp. 636-41. Early Church Records of both the Mt. Vernon and Vernon Center Presbyterian Churches, Archives of the Vernon, New York, Presbyterian Church; History of Wyoming County, New York (New York: F. W. Beers and Co., 1880), pp. 229-33; Andrew W. Young, History of the Town of Warsaw, New York (Buffalo: Sage, 1869), pp. 164-83.

2. Asa Mahan, "Reminiscences and Reflections, Part VI," Divine Life, Vol. 13, February 1890, especially 213-15. (These articles were published posthumously by C. G. Moore.)

3. Asa Mahan, Autobiography: Intellectual, Moral, and Spiritual (London: T. Woolmer, 1882), pp. 1-39.

4. Ibid.

5. Ibid., pp. 40-57.

6. Asa Mahan, Out of Darkness into Light (New York: Willard Tract Repository, 1876), p. 11.

7. Ibid., p. 13; Autobiography, pp. 50-55.

8. Ibid., p. 19; Autobiography, pp. 65-66.

9. Mahan, Autobiography, pp. 66-67; Out of Darkness into Light, pp. 19-20.

10.   Out of Darkness into Light, p. 20.
11.   Autobiography, chaps. vi-xi, and Out of Darkness into Light, Part I, are relevant to this section.
12.   Autobiography, p. 120.
13.   Ibid., p. 203.
14.   Ibid., pp. 204-14.
15.   Catalogue of the Officers and Students of Hamilton College, December 1, 1823, Hamilton College Archives.
16.   Walter Pilkington, Hamilton College, 1812-1962 (Clinton, New York: Hamilton College, 1962), pp. 120-25, 158; "Asa Mahan" entry, 19020-75, Treasurer's Book of the Philopeuthian Society, Hamilton College Archives; "Theodore Strong," October 23, 1822, and May 1824, College Library Register, Archives; Mahan's name never appears in the Library Register; Records of the Philopeuthian Society, Archives, especially entry for May 5, 1824.
17.   Minutes of the Theological Society, Hamilton College Archives, especially entries for August 24, October 12, October 24-25, November 1, December 10, and December 27, 1823.
18.   Pilkington, p. 273; Henry Davis, Narrative of the Embarrassments and Decline of Hamilton College (Clinton, New York: Hamilton College, 1833), especially p. 58; Autobiography, pp. 250-58; Pilkington, pp. 99, 103, 104; Minutes of Faculty Meetings 1813-80, Hamilton College Archives, entry for November 19, 1823; Fifty Years Ago, Letters to the Hamilton College Alumni Association, collected by Melvin Gilbert Dodge (Kirkland, New York: Hamilton College, 1900), pp. 60-61.
19.   Minutes of Faculty Meetings 1813-80, Hamilton College Register, Archives, entries under "Second Term, 1822," "Second Term, 1823, March 26," "Third Term, 1823, July 25," "Second Term, 1824, May 11"; "Asa Mahan" in Class Folder of 1824, Archives; Hamilton Literary Monthly, Vol. 4, pp. 154, 200; letter from D. McMaster to Edward North, November 18, 1869, Papers of Professor Edward North, Archives; Hamilton College Commencement Program, August 25, 1824, Archives; and C. G. Moore, "Biographical Notes Concerning the Late Dr. Mahan," Divine Life, Vol. 13, October 1889, p. 106.
20.   Fifty Years, pp. 46-47.
21.   Mahan, "Reminiscences and Reflections, Part VII," Divine Life, Vol. 13, March 1890, 226-27.
22.   Mahan, Autobiography, pp. 140-54; and Out of Darkness into Light, pp. 100-102. Mahan's commencement address was "On the Proper Mode of Treating Religious Affections." The handwritten address is in the ATS Archives, Student Essays, Andover-Newton Theological School. A

copy of the program for the commencement exercises on
September 26, 1827, is also in the archives.

23.   Mahan, Out of Darkness into Light, pp. 100-101.
24.   George W. Gale to C. G. Finney, June 6, 1827,
Finney Papers, Oberlin College Library, microfilm, Roll 1.
25.   Mahan, Autobiography, p. 144.
26.   "Brotherly Love," The Oberlin Quarterly Review, January, 1849, pp. 16-17.
27.   Mahan, "Reminiscences and Reflections, Part VII," Divine Life, Vol. 13, March, 1890, 227-29.
28.   Ibid., p. 228; "Asa Mahan" folder, Alumni Records, Oberlin College.
29.   Mahan, Autobiography, pp. 167-68; "Reminiscences and Reflections, Part VII," p. 228.
30.   Smith Ordway, "History of the Pittsford Presbyterian Church" and "Historical Sermon," First Presbyterian Church, Pittsford, Centennial Celebration, 1909; Robert Wadhams, "Historical Sketch of the First Presbyterian Church, First Seventy-Five Years," TS (1934), and pamphlet for Anniversary Sunday, May 16, 1976, pp. 1-2, all in the Archives of the Presbyterian Church, Pittsford, New York.
31.   R. S. Fletcher, A History of Oberlin College (2 vols.; Oberlin, Ohio: Oberlin College, 1943), I, 17-24; H. Pomeroy Brewster, "The Magic of a Voice, Rochester Revivals of Rev. Charles G. Finney," Rochester Historical Society Fund Series, IV (1925), 279; Charles Grandison Finney, Autobiography (originally entitled Memoirs of Charles G. Finney; Westwood, New Jersey: Fleming H. Revell Co., 1876, 1908), pp. 284-301; Ibid., p. 290; The Craftsman, Vol. 2 (1830), 30-31; Paul E. Johnson, A Shopkeeper's Millennium: Society and Revivals in Rochester, New York 1815-1837 (New York: Hill and Wang, 1978), pp. 95-115, especially p. 108.
32.   Finney, Autobiography, pp. 298-99; Johnson, p. 99; original ms. of Finney's Memoirs, pp. 575, 591, Oberlin College Archives, 1978/35, 2/2/2/, Box 10; Brewster, p. 281; Lewis Morey, "History of the First Presbyterian Church of Pittsford, New York," pp. 17-18, Mss. 340, 31503, Archives of the Presbyterian Historical Society, Philadelphia; Fletcher, pp. 18-19, 19-20; Whitney Cross, The Burned-Over District (Ithaca, New York: Cornell University Press, 1950), pp. 154-56.
33.   Records of the First Presbyterian Church in Pittsford, 1825-1862, Book B, pp. 58, 60, 62, 66, 67, and the entry for February 4, 1831, Church Archives.
34.   Mahan, Out of Darkness into Light, pp. 92, 325.
35.   Smith Ordway, "History of the Pittsford Presby-

terian Church," p. 38, Church Archives; Robert Wadhams, "Historical Sketch of the First Presbyterian Church, First Seventy-Five Years," May 11, 1934, Church Archives.

36. Records of the First Presbyterian Church in Pittsford, New York 1825-1862, Book B, entry for February 4, 1831, Church Archives; Ordway Smith, "Historical Sermon," p. 11, Church Archives.

37. Josiah Bissell to C. G. Finney, February 27, 1831, marked "Confidential," Finney Papers, Oberlin College Library, microfilm, Roll 2.

38. Mahan, "Reminiscences and Reflections, Part VIII," Divine Life, Vol. 13, April 1890, 258-59.

39. Ibid., pp. 259-60.

40. Ibid. Cf. Barbara Zikmund, "Asa Mahan and Oberlin Perfectionism," Diss. Duke University 1970, pp. 23-24.

CHAPTER 2. CINCINNATI

1. John Thompson, Amos Blanchard, F. W. Vail, et al. (ten names), Letter to Finney, July 1831; and David Root, Letter to Finney, Sept. 27, 1831; Finney Papers, Oberlin College Library microfilm, Roll 3.

2. Cincinnati Journal, III (April 15, 1831), p. 62; Vine Street Congregational Church Records, 1831-1953, from beginning through entry for July 20, 1835, MS Cincinnati Historical Society Archives.

3. Manual of the Vine Street Congregational Church and Society (Cincinnati: n.p., 1878), p. 5; Vine Street Church Records; Minutes of the Board of Trustees, Vine Street Congregational Church, MS, Cincinnati Historical Society Archives; R. S. Fletcher, A History of Oberlin College (2 vols.; Oberlin, Ohio: Oberlin College, 1943), I, 45, fn. 4; Barbara Zikmund, "Asa Mahan and Oberlin Perfectionism," Diss. Duke University 1969, pp. 28-29; C. B. Boynton, "Historical Address," Semi-Centennial Celebration of the Vine Street Congregational Church, Cincinnati, Ohio (Cincinnati: n.p., 1881), pp. 10-45. For further evidence supporting the antislavery origins of the church see "Centennial Celebration of People's Church, Hotel Metropole, April 1931, MS, Herbert S. Bigelow Collection, Box 2, Cincinnati Historical Society Archives; M. E. Thalheimer, "History of the Vine Street Congregational Church in Cincinnati," Papers of the Ohio Church History Society, IX (1898), 46; and L. A. M. Bosworth, "A Stormy Epoch," ibid., VI (1895), 17.

4. Mahan, "Letter to Vine Street Church, March 8,

1881," Semi-Centennial Celebration, pp. 71-80, esp. pp. 71-72; Vine Street Church Records, report of the request to the Cincinnati Presbytery, April 5, 1831, to form a new church; and Fletcher, History, I, 45-46.

5. See Cincinnati Standard, I (December 16, 1831), p. 58, I (April 20, 1832), p. 130, I (April 30, 1832), p. 130, I (May 4, 1832), p. 138, etc., a paper under the control of Wilson and presenting the matter from his viewpoint; Zikmund, "Asa Mahan and Oberlin Perfectionism," pp. 28, 30-31, 33-38; Raymond L. Hightower, "Joshua L. Wilson: Frontier Controversialist," Church History, III, (1934), 300-16; Hightower, same title, Diss. University of Chicago 1933; and D. L. Leonard, The Story of Oberlin (Boston: Pilgrim Press, 1898), pp. 345-47.

6. The Autobiography of Lyman Beecher, ed. Barbara Cross (2 vols.; Cambridge: Harvard University Press, 1961), II, 261-72; C. A. Dinsmore, "Lyman Beecher," Dictionary of American Biography, II, 135-36; and Leonard, Story of Oberlin, pp. 339-61.

7. Mahan, "Letter to Vine Street Church," p. 72 and Letter to C. G. Finney, February 26, 1832, Finney Papers, Roll 3.

8. Vine Street Congregational Church Records, entries for November 16, 1831; February 20, March 29, June 18, July 12, September 17, 1832; February 14, April 11, May 30, August 9, October 10, November 14, December 11, December 12, 1833; February 11, April 28, April 30, May 13, July 9, August 20, September 10, October 1, November 23, 1834; Minutes of the Board of Trustees, entries for September 5, 1833, and November 13, 1834; Letters of Theodore Dwight Weld, Angelina Grimke Weld, and Sarah Grimke 1822-1844, ed. G. H. Barnes and D. L. Dumond (2 vols.; New York: D. Appleton-Century, 1934), I, 273; and Mahan Autobiography, pp. 163-64.

9. Mahan, Autobiography, pp. 164-67, 173-74.

10. John Thompson, Amos Blanchard, F. W. Vail, et al., Letter to Finney, July 1831; Asa Mahan, Theodore Weld, et al. (28 names), Letter to Finney, February 1832; Mahan and Weld, Letter to Finney, February 26, 1832; Mahan and Weld, Letter to Finney, March 20, 1832. Finney Papers, Roll 3 and, for the last item, Roll 10.

11. Cincinnati Journal, IV (December 30, 1831), 211; V (January 27, 1832), 15; and V (March 23, 1832), 46; Vine Street Church Records, immediately preceding the entry for April 28, 1834, "Thus far examined and approved by the Presbytery, April 2, 1834, A. Mahan, Moderator."

12. Mahan, Out of Darkness into Light, pp. 90-122; Autobiography, pp. 289-92.

13.   Mahan, "Reminiscences and Reflections, Part
II," Divine Life, Vol. 13 (October 1889), 87-88.
14.   Out of Darkness into Light, pp. 91-92.
15.   Ibid., pp. 119-20.
16.   Ibid., pp. 290-92.
17.   Lawrence Lesick, "The Founding of the Lane
Seminary," Bulletin, Cincinnati Historical Society, Vol. 37,
Winter 1979, 237-48; W. W. Sweet, Religion on the American
Frontier: The Presbyterians, 1783-1840 (Chicago: University of Chicago, 1936), pp. 78-79; Fletcher, History, I, 49-
52.   For the story of Lane, the whole of the Trustee Minutes
(office of the Lane Trustees, Cincinnati) should be consulted.
18.   Fletcher, History, I, 52-53.
19.   Indeed, seminarians like H. B. Stanton, E.
Weed, S. W. Streeter, and C. Waterbury were so mature
that they acted as if they were an official committee for
faculty appointments! See Letters of Theodore Dwight Weld
et al., I, 79, 80, 84-85.   For characterizations of Weld, in
addition to the image that emerges from his Letters, and
that explicitly formulated by the editors, see Benjamin P.
Thomas, Theodore Weld, Crusader for Freedom (New Brunswick, New Jersey: Rutgers University Press, 1950); and
Lawrence T. Lesick, "The Lane Rebels: Evangelicalism
and Antislavery in Antebellum America," Diss. Vanderbilt
University 1979.   In contrast to the above, see Bertram
Wyatt-Brown's Lewis Tappan and the Evangelical War Against
Slavery (Cleveland: Case Western Reserve University Press,
1969), where Weld is given a place subordinate to that of
Garrison--the traditional characterization before Barnes and
Dumond published Weld's Letters.   Cf. Lyman Beecher's
Autobiography, II, 321.   For the latest characterization of
Weld, see R. H. Abzug, Passionate Liberator: Theodore
Dwight Weld and the Dilemma of Reform (New York: Ox-
ford University Press, 1980).
20.   Beecher, Autobiography, II, p. 243; Lesick,
"The Lane Rebels," pp. 86-138, 271; Fletcher, History, I,
150-54.
21.   Beecher, Autobiography, II, 243-44; Fletcher,
History, I, 154-55; Lewis Tappan, Letter to Theodore Weld,
September 29, 1834, New York Historical Society, Slavery
MSS, Box II, T.W. #5, 9.
22.   Lesick, "The Lane Rebels," pp. 139-98; Western Monthly Magazine, II, (May 1834) 266-73; Letters of
Weld, I, 136-45; Cincinnati Journal, VII (May 16, 1834),
p. 79.
23.   Beecher, Autobiography, II, 244-45; Fletcher,
History, I, 156.
24.   Lesick, "The Lane Rebels," p. 159.

25. Mahan, Out of Darkness into Light, pp. 117-19;
Autobiography, pp. 176-78; and Lesick, "The Lane Rebels,"
pp. 149-50.

26. Minutes of the Board of Trustees, Lane Seminary, October 6, 1834, Lane Papers, folder 2, McCormick
Theological Seminary; Lesick, "The Lane Rebels," pp. 160,
63; Mahan, Autobiography, pp. 180-81.

27. Mahan, Out of Darkness into Light, p. 116;
L. A. M. Bosworth, "A Stormy Epoch," Ohio Church History Society, V (1894), 17-18; Mahan, Autobiography, p.
174.

28. Minutes of the Board of Trustees, Vine Street
Congregational Church, entries for November 13, 17, 27,
1834; Mahan, Autobiography, pp. 176, 184. Franklin Vail,
who had been instrumental in bringing Mahan to Cincinnati
(See Minutes of the Board of Trustees, Vine Street Congregational Church, June 23, 1831) and who later was general
agent for Lane Seminary, was the one who approached leading members of the Sixth Presbyterian Church and tried to
persuade them to discharge Mahan. Thalheimer, History of
the Vine Street Congregational Church, p. 47. Neff, who
resigned from Mahan's church, was the member of the Board
of Trustees at Lane who exploded angrily when Mahan had
Melindy say that the Board dare not publish Order 2. In
his Autobiography Mahan refers to him as "Mr. N."

29. Mahan, Autobiography, pp. 172-73 and Out of
Darkness into Light, pp. 118-19.

30. Letters of Weld, pp. 215, 217, 251.

31. Beecher, Autobiography, II, 240-49; Lewis Tappan, Letter to Theodore Weld, September 29, 1834, New
York Historical Society; and Weld, Letter to Tappan, May
21, 1836, New York Public Library Archives, 2419.

32. Tappan, Letter to Weld, ibid.

33. Fletcher, History, I, 161-64; Beecher, Autobiography, II, 246-49.

34. Mahan, Out of Darkness into Light, pp. 120-21.

35. Mahan, Autobiography, pp. 183-84.

36. The founding and early development of the Oberlin Collegiate Institute is fully covered in James H. Fairchild, Oberlin: Its Origin, Progress and Results (Oberlin:
Shankland and Harmon, 1860); Fairchild, Oberlin: The Colony and the College, 1833-1883 (Oberlin: E. J. Goodrich,
1883); D. L. Leonard, The Story of Oberlin; W. H. Phillips,
Oberlin Colony: The Story of a Century (Oberlin: Oberlin
Printing Co., 1933); and R. S. Fletcher, A History of Oberlin College.

37. John J. Shipherd, Letter to Fayette Shipherd,

November 23, 1834, TS, 30/24, Box 13, Robert S. Fletcher
Papers, folder "Shipherd Letters 1834," Oberlin College Archives.

     38. Shipherd, Letter to Nathan Fletcher, November
27, 1834, microfilm, Letters Received by Oberlin College,
1822-1866, Roll 2, September 1834-February 1836. For details concerning Shipherd's journey to Cincinnati and subsequent events, see the accounts in Fairchild, Oberlin: The
Colony and the College, pp. 50-77; Fairchild, Oberlin: Its
Origin, Progress and Results, pp. 17-28; Leonard, The Story
of Oberlin, pp. 28-31, 127-28, 130-46; and Phillips, Oberlin
Colony: The Story of a Century, pp. 45-53.

     39. Lesick, "The Lane Rebels," pp. 205-206; Let-
ters of Weld, pp. 79, 80, 84-85.

     40. Shipherd, Letter to John Keep, December 13,
1834, Oberlin College Archives (hereafter referred to as
OCA), 30/83, Box 1, Shipherd Letters; Shipherd, Letter to
Keep, December 15, 1834, ibid.; Shipherd, Letter to Eliphalet Redington and Addison Tracy, December 15, 1834, ibid.;
Shipherd, Letter to Nathan Fletcher, December 15, 1834,
ibid.

     41. Mahan, Autobiography, pp. 190-96.

     42. Fletcher, History, I, 170-72.

     43. Shipherd, Letter to the Trustees of Oberlin Col-
legiate Institute, January 19, 1835, OCA, 7/1/3, Box 2;
C. G. Finney, Autobiography (Westwood, New Jersey: Fleming H. Revell Co., 1876, 1908), p. 333; H. B. Stanton and
George Whipple, Letter to Finney, January 10, 1835, Finney
Papers, Roll 3; H. Lyman and Stanton, Letter to Weld, January 22, 1835, Letters of Weld, p. 201.

     44. Shipherd, Letter to the Trustees of Oberlin, Jan-
uary 19, 1835, OCA, 7/1/3, Box 2.

     45. Fletcher, History, I, 177-78.

     46. Shipherd, Letter to Sturges, April 10, 1835,
OCA, 30/83, Box 1, Shipherd Letters.

     47. Mahan, Letter to Nathan Fletcher, March 12,
1835, OCA, 2/1, Box 1, Asa Mahan.

     48. C. B. Boynton, "Historical Address," Semi-Cen-
tennial Celebration of the Vine Street Congregational Church,
pp. 10-45; "Centennial Celebration of People's Church, Hotel
Metropole, April 1931," Herbert S. Bigelow Collection, Box
2, correspondence for 1931.

CHAPTER 3. OBERLIN

     1. James H. Fairchild, Oberlin: The Colony and the

College, 1833-1883 (Oberlin: E. J. Goodrich, 1883), pp.
70, 88; Homer Johnson, Letter to George N. Allen, July
15, 1850, TS, OCA, 30/24, Box 2, "Allen Letters-W. C.
Cochran" folder; Mahan, Out of Darkness into Light (New
York: Willard Tract Repository, 1876), pp. 123-25; Mahan
and Rev. and Mrs. John Stevenson of London, Letters to
Mary Dix Mahan, Oberlin Evangelist, XII, January 2, 1850,
p. 3; Fairchild, Oberlin: Colony and College, p. 208; Ma-
han, Out of Darkness, p. 214.
        2.   Philip Doddridge Adams, Letter to his mother,
July 1, 1835, OCA, 28/1, Box 2.
        3.   Oberlin Evangelist, Vol. 6, March 13, 1844, 45.
        4.   Mahan, Science of Moral Philosophy (Oberlin:
James M. Fitch, 1848), p. 316.
        5.   "Asa Mahan" folder, Alumni Office Records,
Oberlin College; pages from Anna Mahan North's Notebook,
Asa Mahan Archives, Asbury College; General Catalogue of
Oberlin College, 1833-1908 (Oberlin: Oberlin College, 1909),
pp. 635-36.
        6.   United States Census 1840, Ohio, V. 15, micro-
film, Roll 409, Logan and Lorain Counties, #163.
        7.   Sally Rudd, Letter to Caroline Mary Rudd, March
28, 1836, TS, OCA, 18/5, Box 6, "Rudd."
        8.   Jesse Hart Lang in The Oberlin News, July 7,
1903, p. 1.
        9.   C. S. Hopkins, "A Severe Storm Nearly Fifty
Years Ago," The Oberlin News, August 13, 1897, p. 8.
        10.   Harry E. Woodcock Papers, microfilm, one box,
frames 69 ff., OCA; Timothy Hudson, Letter to James Monroe, January 1, 1849, TS, OCA, 30/24, Box 7, "Monroe
Papers 1844-66" folder.
        11.   Harry E. Woodcock Papers, frames 69 ff.
        12.   A. Clair Siddall, "Consumer Rebellion Against
Orthodox Medicine at Oberlin - 1833," Ohio State Medical
Journal, Vol. 72 (1976), 330-34; Timothy Hudson, "Popular
Distrust of Regular Physicians," Oberlin Students' Monthly,
Vol. 1 (1858), 41-45; Siddall, "History of Homeopathic Medicine at Oberlin, Ohio, 1833-1933," Ohio State Medical Association Journal, Vol. 74 (1978), 121-24; George C. Jameson,
"Historical Sketch of Medicine at Oberlin," Ohio State Medical Journal, Vol. 33 (1937), 299-306 (quotation from p. 303).
        13.   Homer Johnson, Letter to George N. Allen, July
15, 1850, TS, OCA, 30/24, Box 2, "Allen Letters--W. C.
Cochran" folder; copy of the 1850 document concerning "the
basis of unity and hearty cooperation" between Mahan and
the faculty (Mahan's "Confessions") on stationery with printed
letterhead of Johnson's medical office, OCA, 2/1, Box 1,
"Asa Mahan."

14. Out of Darkness into Light, pp. 119-20.
15. Ibid., p. 125.
16. Ibid., pp. 134-35, 149, 158; The True Believer
(New York: Harper, 1847), pp. 276-77.
17. Autobiography: Intellectual, Moral, and Spiritual,
p. 323. For the full details of Mahan's step-wise approach
to what he described as a higher life, see Out of Darkness,
pp. 123-55 and the Autobiography, chap. xiii. Cf. Timothy
Smith's Introduction to C. G. Finney, The Promise of the
Spirit (Minneapolis: Bethany Fellowship, 1980), pp. 16-17.
18. Mahan, Scripture Doctrine of Christian Perfection (Boston: D. S. King, 1839). In 1849 an English edition was published by Partridge and Company with an Introduction by John Stevenson, in whose church in Southwark,
London, Mahan held a successful revival in 1849. Mahan
added prefatory remarks rebutting several criticisms made
in reviews of previous editions of the book. A new edition
entitled simply Christian Perfection was published in London
in 1875 by F. E. Longley. It contained a prefatory letter
by Mahan in which he endorsed all that he had written thirty-
six years before, and an Introduction by George Warner, one
of Mahan's colleagues in the holiness movement in England.
This edition is still reprinted in the United States at the
present time by H. E. Schmul, Salem, Ohio. Concerning
the difficulties in finding a publisher for the original 1839
edition and its quick success see the Oberlin Evangelist,
August 18, 1841, p. 136.
19. Mahan, Scripture Doctrine, pp. 77-79, 98-104,
129-32, 136-39; Autobiography, pp. 281-364.
20. Scripture Doctrine, pp. 162, 172, 186.
21. Ibid., pp. 70-73, 162, 172, 186; Autobiography,
pp. 293, 372-74, 382-86; The Banner of Holiness, I, September 23, 1875, p. 4; Doctrine of the Will, especially pp.
84-85, 103-104; Divine Life, February 1878, pp. 193-95;
Autobiography, pp. 387-89.
22. Mahan, The True Believer (New York: Harper
and Brothers, 1847), p. 275; Out of Darkness, p. 152.
23. Out of Darkness, pp. 321-22.
24. Henry Cowles, A Sermon, On Being Filled with
the Holy Ghost (Oberlin: J. M. Fitch, 1848), No. 4 in a
series of "Tracts on Holiness"; John Cowles, sixteen letters
attacking Oberlin published in the Cleveland Observer from
November 6, 1839 to April 1, 1840; A. M. Hills, Life of
Charles G. Finney (Cincinnati: God's Revivalist Publishers,
1902), pp. 228-35; A. T. Swing, James H. Fairchild (New
York: Fleming H. Revell, 1907), pp. 92, 210; Sherlock
Bristol, Letter to the Faculty and Resident Trustees of Oberlin, December 21, 1844, and Bristol, Letter to Hamilton Hill,

December 21, 1844, OCA, 7/1/5, Box 7; Bristol, Letter to
Henry Cowles, December 26, 1844, TS OCA, 30/24, Box
3; Samuel D. Cochran et al., letter to the Faculty and Resident Trustees of Oberlin Collegiate Institute, December 30,
1844, 30/24, Box 3; John Morgan, Letter to Finney, January
7, 1850, microfilm, Roll 4, Finney Papers; Uriah Thompson
et al., Letter to Board of Trustees, August 23, 1850, OCA,
Board of Trustees Document File, 1/3/1, Box 2, "1850"
folder.

    25. The True Believer, p. iv. Important sermons
by Mahan published in the Oberlin Evangelist but not reprinted in The True Believer include "Christians Dead to
the Law," II September 23, 1840, 153-56; "The Law of the
Spirit of Life in Christ Jesus," IV January 5, 1842, 1-4;
"Crucified with Christ," IV January 19, 1842, 9-11; "Perfect Love Attainable," V April 26, 1843, 65-67; "Perfect
Love Attained," V May 10, 1843, 73-76; "Objections to the
Doctrine of Perfect Love," V May 24, 1843, 81-83; "The
Work and Effect of Righteousness," VII June 18, 1845, 97-
99; "Simplicity in Respect to Christ," VIII May 27, 1846,
81-84; "The Lukewarm Professor," IX (December 22, 1847),
201-203; "A living and a Dead Faith," X January 5, 1848,
1-3; "Faith Impossible to all Who Seek Honor One of Another," X January 19, 1848, 9-11; "The People of Whom
God is Not Ashamed, and the City Which He Hath Prepared
for Them," X February 2, 1848, 17-19; "The One Thing
Needful," X February 16, 1848, 25-27; "All Things Working
for the Good of the Believer," X March 1, 1848, 33-35;
"Gratitude," X March 29, 1848, 49-51.

    In addition to the Oberlin Evangelist, a scholarly journal,
the Oberlin Quarterly Review, was published but lasted only
a few years. Mahan and Finney again were the major con-
tributors, and Mahan edited the journal for a time. His
major contributions include: "The Book of Job," pp. 24-56,
162-96; "Moses," pp. 415-45; "The Idea of Perfection," pp.
463-80--Vol. I, 1845-1846; "A Philosophical Inquiry Concerning Human Liberty," pp. 68-92; "The Moral Law as Revealed in the Bible, pp. 111-27; "The Book of Ecclesiastes,"
pp. 131-57, 263-83; "Certain Fundamental Principles, together with their Applications," pp. 227-43; "The Confession
of Faith of the Presbyterian Church," pp. 473-89--Vol II,
1846-1847; "The Confession of Faith of the Presbyterian
Church," pp. 121-30, 131-50; "Solomon's Song," pp. 311-
20; "Sanctification," pp. 362-79; "Principles of Church Discipline," pp. 473-87; "The Idea of Retribution," pp. 488-
500--Vol. III, 1847-1848; "Brotherly Love," pp. 3-17; "The
Spiritual Writings of Prof. Thomas C. Upham," pp. 101-27;

"Doctrine of the Resurrection," pp. 178-93; "The Tree of Knowledge of Good and Evil," pp. 240-48--Vol. IV, 1849.

26. Oberlin Evangelist, V, December 20, 1843, 206.

27. Phoebe Palmer, The Way of Holiness with Notes by the Way, 2nd ed. (New York: Lane and Tippett, 1848), the Preface of which carries endorsements by both Mahan and L. L. Hamline, a bishop of the Methodist Episcopal Church; D. L. Leonard, The Story of Oberlin (Boston: Pilgrim Press, 1898), pp. 348-49; Mahan, Autobiography, pp. 170-71; James H. Fairchild, Oberlin: The Colony and the College 1833-1883, pp. 146-47.

28. Oberlin Evangelist, VI, September 11, 1844, 150.

29. James H. Fairchild, Oberlin: Colony and College, p. 148; Fairchild, Oberlin: Its Origin, Progress and Results (Oberlin: Shankland and Harmon, 1860), p. 34; Fairchild in The Oberlin Jubilee, 1833-1883, ed. W. G. Ballantine (Oberlin: E. J. Goodrich, 1883), p. 105; Oberlin Evangelist, IX, February 17, 1847, 30-31. Henry Cowles, editor, reprinted the "remarks on Oberlin from a leading Editorial in the Morning Star."

30. Mahan, Autobiography, pp. 250-80.

31. Fairchild, Oberlin: Colony and College, pp. 263, 266-67. Also Fairchild, Oberlin: Its Origin, pp. 39-42.

32. E. J. Comings in Jubilee Notes of the Oberlin Colony and College (Oberlin: I. W. Mattison, 1883, 1884), no editors listed, p. 38.

33. Mahan, Autobiography, pp. 266-70; Jabez Burns, Notes of a Tour in the United States and Canada in the Summer and Autumn of 1847 (London: Stoneman, 1848), p. 152.

34. Delazon Smith, Oberlin Unmasked, A History of Oberlin or New Lights of the West (Cleveland: S. Underhill and Son, 1837), especially pp. 43, 51, 52-55, 58, 63, 66, 67-75; Fletcher, History, I, 436-41.

35. Oberlin College Faculty Records, 1834-1846, entries for May 13, 14, 1835; January 27, 1836; February 26, 1836; March 4, 1836; October 23, 1837; June 1840; July 28, 1840; October 8, 1840--TS, OCA, 30/24, Box 4. Cf. Fletcher, History, I, 444-47.

36. Faculty Records, April 22, 1843, 30/24, Box 7; Fletcher, History, I, 377-78.

37. Francis Wayland, Thoughts on the Present Collegiate System in the United States (Boston: Gould, Kendall, and Lincoln, 1842); Francis Wayland Jr. and H. L. Wayland, A Memoir of the Life and Labors of Francis Wayland (2 vols.; New York: Sheldon and Co., 1867); Henry James,

Charles William Eliot, President of Harvard University,
1869-1909 (Boston: Houghton Mifflin Co., 1930); Fairchild,
Oberlin: College and Colony, pp. 71-73; Henry O. Brown,
Letter to G. R. Hitchcock, July 4, 1835, OCA, 28/1, Box
32, "Brown, Henry O." folder.
        38. Fairchild, Oberlin: College and Colony, 71-73;
D. L. Leonard's "Notes of Talks with Pres. Fairchild,
1894-97," Notebook 1, p. 70, OCA, 30/24, Box 1; Notebook
1, pp. 137, 141.
        Leonard used his "Notes of Talks with Pres. Fairchild,
1894-97," as the basis of a series of ten articles under the
general title, "A Legacy from President Fairchild," published in the Oberlin News: January 16, 1903, p. 8; January 23, p. 1; January 30, p. 8; February 6, p. 8; February 13, p. 4; February 20, p. 4; February 27, p. 4; March
6, p. 4; March 13, p. 8; March 20, p. 4. In these articles
he made less reverent use of the "Notes" than had been the
case when Leonard published his Story of Oberlin while Fairchild was still alive. There were two protesting responses:
Jesse Hart Lang, Oberlin News, July 7, 1903, p. 1, and
George W. Drake, Oberlin News, March 25, 1904, pp. 6-7.
Both Lang and Drake resented Leonard's "attack on our revered and beloved old teachers." Drake penetratingly remarked, "Mr. Leonard may have received [these views] substantially from President Fairchild, but the coloring is his
own; and from an acquaintance of more than sixty years with
the President, I think I may safely say that he would be the
last one to give his sanction to such coloring," p. 6. Leonard wrote a second series of historical articles appearing in
the December 1904 and January 1905 issues of the Oberlin
News, none of which have much significance or make any
reference to Lang or Drake's comments on the previous series.
        39. Mahan's Inaugural Address at Oberlin, printed
in the Ohio Observer, July 9, 1835; Mahan's Commencement
Address, 1841, in the Oberlin Evangelist, III, November 24,
1841, lead article; Daily True Democrat (Cleveland, Ohio)
August 22, 1851, 3/1-7, text of Mahan's address on the relative merits of the old and new systems of education; "An
Old Vision Taking Form," The Graduate School News, Western Reserve University, January 1, 1935, pp. 1-2.
        40. Ibid.
        41. Mahan, Letter to Finney, July 22, 1837, micro-
film, Roll 3, Finney Papers; Fletcher, History, I, 364-72,
432-33; James H. Fairchild, Letter to Mary F. Kellogg,
February 11, 1840, TS, OCA, 30/24, Box 5, "Fairchild
Letters to Mary F. Kellogg, 1838-41" folder; D. L. Leonard,

"Notes of Talks with Pres. Fairchild, 1894-97," Notebook
1, p. 122, OCA, 30/24, Box 1.

42.   Fletcher, History, I, 372.

43.   See note 39 above; James, Charles William Eliot;
John Barnard, From Evangelicalism to Progressivism at
Oberlin College, 1866-1917 (Columbus: Ohio State University
Press, 1969), pp. 66 ff.

44.   Sherlock Bristol, Letter to Hamilton Hill, Henry
Cowles, and George Whipple, December 9, 1844, "Letters
Reveived by Oberlin College, June 1843-July 1845," microfilm, Roll 9; Fairchild, Oberlin: Colony and College, pp.
293-94; Fletcher, History, I, 493-94.

45.   Fairchild, Oberlin: Colony and College, p. 278.

46.   "Oberlin College Faculty Records, 1834-1846,"
March 23, 1840, OCA, 30/24, Box 4; Leonard, "Notes of
Talks with Pres. Fairchild, 1894-97," Notebook 1, p. 41.

47.   Ibid.; and Trustee Minutes, Annual Meeting, August 18, 1846, OCA, microfilm, Roll 1.

48.   The Oberlin Jubilee, 1833-1883, p. 72 (Parker),
p. 163 (Mrs. Putnam), pp. 48-49 (Barbour), p. 212 (J. L.
Patton).

49.   Fairchild, Oberlin: Its Origin, p. 46; Oberlin,
Colony and College, pp. 255, 278. See also Fairchild, "The
First President of Oberlin College," Oberlin Review, April
30, 1889, p. 217.

50.   A. T. Swing, James H. Fairchild (New York:
Fleming H. Revell, 1907), p. 80. Also Azariah S. Root,
Necrological Report for 1888-1889, OCA, Asa Mahan, 30/57,
Box 17.

51.   Sherlock Bristol, The Pioneer Preacher: An
Autobiography (New York: F. H. Revell, 1887), p. 91. For
an extremely appreciative view of Mahan's relation to students see E. J. Comings' letter to "friends," Sept. 25, 1836,
and letters to Fanny Fletcher, May 1, 1838; June 5, 1838;
and three other undated 1838 letters. OCA 30/52, Box 1.

52.   Bristol, Letter to the Faculty and Resident Trustees of Oberlin, December 21, 1844, OCA, 7/1/5, Box 7.

53.   Charles M. Perry, Henry Philip Tappan: Philosopher and University President (Ann Arbor: University of
Michigan Press, 1933), pp. 108-09.

54.   Jabez Burns, Doctrinal Conversations on Pre-
destination, Free Will, Election (London: Stoneman, 1849),
p. 24.

55.   Mahan, Doctrine of the Will, pp. 75-79, 194-
98; Mahan, Manuscript Notebook, Shipman Library Archives,
Adrian College: "Edwardsian definition of liberty: 1. There
is no freedom at all where he has placed it. 2. It gives

no ground for the distinction between natural and moral power. 3. Men are deceived by it.... As soon as it is shown,
that men cannot chose differently from what they do, and
having chosen cannot but act as they do, all will say, then
we are not free. They suppose that [the] phrase we can do
as we choose really means that we have the power of choice."
(There is pagination at the start in the notebook, but numbers soon disappear.) For restatements and elaborations of
his overall views in Doctrine of the Will, see Mahan's Autobiography, pp. 197-214. Cf. Mahan's Lectures on the Ninth
of Romans (Boston: Charles H. Peirce and Co., 1851), pp.
154-80 and Autobiography.

    56. Mahan, The Science of Moral Philosophy (Ober-
lin: J. M. Fitch, 1848, 1884), pp. 70-93, 94-123 (especially 102-103).

    57. Ibid., pp. 94-123.

    58. Finney to James Morison, January 5, 1851, the
Moir Collection, Mitchell Library, Glasgow.

    59. Mahan, Abstracts of a Course of Lectures on
Mental and Morla Philosophy (Oberlin: Printed by James
Steele, 1840), p. 305. This book is "printed but not published," since Mahan did not read proof. His students paid
for the printing since they were copying the lectures "at
great labor and expense of time," p. ii. Mahan's handwriting is difficult to read at best and that accounts for the
"great labor and expense of time." Fletcher, History, II,
703.

    60. Fletcher, History, I, 254-56, 264; D. L. Leon-
ard, "Early Annals of the Oberlin Church," Ohio Church History Society Papers, Vol 8, 100; E. H. Madden, Civil Disobedience and Moral Law in Nineteenth-Century American
Philosophy (Seattle: University of Washington Press, 1968),
pp. 75-77.

    61. Fletcher, History, I, 386-89, 410; Mahan's ac-
count of the Free Soil Convention appeared in the Oberlin
Evangelist, August 16, 1848; Henry B. Stanton, Random Recollections (New York: Harper, 1887); Theodore C. Smith,
Liberty and Free Soil Parties in the Northwest (New York:
Longmans, Green and Co., 1897); Bertram Wyatt-Brown,
Lewis Tappan and the Evangelical War Against Slavery (Cleveland: Case Western Reserve University Press, 1969), pp.
269-86, 328, 331.

    62. Oberliniana, ed. A. L. Shumway and C. Brower
(Cleveland: Home Publishing Co., 1883), chaps. ii and iii;
Fletcher, History, I, 401-402.

    63. Delazon Smith, Oberlin Unmasked, pp. 63, 66.
What horrified Smith and the large majority of Northerners

as terrible radicalness was regarded by a small minority as
not radical enough. Cf. J. W. Chadwick, A Life for Liberty, Anti-Slavery and Other Letters of Sallie Holley (New
York, 1899), pp. 60-61.

64. Criticism of Garrison is the recurring theme of
Mahan's series of articles on reform printed in the Oberlin
Evangelist, February through August 1844; see also Mahan,
Letter to William Scott (long, two column letter), Glasgow
Examiner, April 24, 1852, p. 6, and the Glasgow Daily
Mail, May 6, 1851, p. 1.

65. Oberlin Evangelist, VIII, September 30, 1846,
158; Henry Cowles wrote that the faculty did not want the
Fosters to speak but acceded to the wishes of students and
townspeople; Abby and Stephen Foster, "Our Cause in Ohio"
(a letter to Parker Pillsbury), The Liberator, October 23,
1846, p. 171.

66. Henry Churchill King, The Oberlin Inheritance
(Oberlin: News Printing Co., 1911), p. 9.

67. Oberlin Evangelist, VIII, September 30, 1846,
158-59; Abby and Stephen Foster, "Our Cause in Ohio," p.
171.

68. Fletcher, History, I, 269-70.

69. Mahan, Letter to William Scott, Glasgow Examiner, April 24, 1852, p. 6; Glasgow Daily Mail, May 6,
1851, p. 1.

70. The Liberator, June 4, 1852, vol. 22, pp. 89,
91; June 25, 1852, p. 202; August 27, 1852, p. 139; May
13, 1853, p. 73; The Glasgow Examiner, June 26, 1852, p.
5; Report of the Bristol and Clifton Ladies Anti-Slavery Society, 1852, footnote running through pp. 47-49.

71. Lucy Stone to Stephen S. Foster and Abby Foster,
March 25, 1846, in Abby Kelley Foster Papers, American
Antiquarian Society; Lucy Stone to Abby Foster, July 3, 1846,
and S. T. Creighton to Abby Foster, August 2, 1846, Abby
Kelley Foster Papers.

72. Fairchild, Oberlin: Colony and College, pp.
176, 178-79; Frances J. Hosford, Father Shipherd's Magna
Charta: A Century of Coeducation at Oberlin College (Boston: Marshall Jones, 1937), pp. 57-58; Fletcher, History,
I, 373-85; cf. A. T. Swing, James H. Fairchild, p. 89.

73. Ronald W. Hogeland, "Coeducation of the Sexes
at Oberlin College: A Study of Social Ideas in Mid-Nineteenth
Century America," Journal of Social History, Vol. 6 (1972-
73), 160-76; Carl N. Degler, At Odds (New York: Oxford
University Press, 1980), p. 310.

74. Mahan, "Reminiscences and Reflections, Part
VIII," Divine Life, Vol. 13 (April 1890), 260; Fletcher, History, I, 380-81; Mahan, Autobiography, p. 267.

75. Hosford, Father Shipherd's Magna Charta, pp.
66, 67, 80, 81, 82-83, 91, 100-101; Fletcher, History, I
290-96; James H. Fairchild, "Women's Rights and Duties,"
Oberlin Quarterly Review, IV (1849), 356; C. C. Foote,
Women's Rights and Duties," Oberlin Quarterly Review, IV,
1849, 383-408; Henry Cowles, Letter to Mrs. Cowles, July
28, 1848, TS, OCA, 30/24, Box 3, Fletcher Papers, folder
"Cowles Papers 1840-50"; item 8 in "paper submitted by the
faculty as the basis of unity and hearty cooperation with
Pres. Mahan," OCA, 7/1/3, Box 8, Treasurer's Office File,
"Misc. Archives," folder "Asa Mahan 1850."

76. Hosford, pp. 81, 82-83, 91.

77. Ibid., pp. 100-101.

78. Proceedings of the Women's Rights Convention,
held at Cleveland, Ohio, on October 5, 6, 7, 1853, especially pp. 74, 80, 84-85, 141-42, 185-88.

79. James H. Fairchild, Women's Right to the Ballot
(Oberlin: George H. Fairchild, 1870), pp. 41, 42, 44, 48,
51, 59.

80. Lucy Stone, "Oberlin and Women," The Oberlin
Jubilee, 1833-1883, ed. W. G. Ballantine (Oberlin: E. J.
Goodrich, 1883), pp. 311-21; Antoinette Brown in Proceed-
ings of the Women's Rights Convention, 1853, p. 74.

81. Antoinette Brown Blackwell, "Reminiscences of
Early Oberlin," February 1918, The Schlesinger Library,
Radcliffe College, A-77, folder 1.

82. Antoinette Brown, Letter to Lucy Stone, September 22, 1847, Schlesinger Library, Blackwell Family Papers,
A77, folder 26.

83. Mahan, Abstract of a Course of Lectures on
Mental and Moral Philosophy, p. 303 (civil government has
right to establish "justice by force"); Mahan, Science of
Moral Philosophy, pp. 409-20; Amos Dresser, Bible Against
War (Oberlin: James Fitch, 1849), a reply to Finney and
Mahan.

84. Fletcher, History, I, 281-82.

85. The Standard of Freedom (London, November 3,
1849, pp. 6-7; seven column "Report of Proceedings of Peace
Congress Meeting held in Exeter Hall"; The Christian Times
(London), January 25, 1850, pp. 53-54, Free Soil Party references.

86. The Nonconformist (London), September 5, 1849,
pp. 700-701; September 19, p. 741; October 3, p. 780; Reports of the Peace Congresses at Brussels, Paris, Frank-
fort, London, and Edinburgh in the years 1848, 1849, 1850,
1851, and 1853 (London: n.p. 1861).

87. The Standard of Freedom, December 8, 1849, p.

11; The National Temperance Chronicle N. S. , March 1850,
p. 33; Christian News (Glasgow), October 11, 1849, p. 190;
The National Temperance Chronicle, N. S. , February 1850,
p. 17.
      88. General Baptist Repository N. S. , March 1850,
p. 139; Mahan and Rev. and Mrs. John Stevenson of London,
Letters to Mary Dix Mahan, Oberlin Evangelist, XII, January
2, 1850, p. 3; Mahan, Letter to Finney, January 5, 25,
1850, Finney Papers, Roll 4; General Baptist Repository,
N. S. , Vol. 12, February 1850, 97; The Christian News
(Glasgow), October 4, 1849, p. 181; October 11, pp. 186, 189.
Returning to London, Mahan gave a "valedictory address"
to a large audience, in a room off Surrey Chapel, on "American Slavery." The Christian Times (London), January 25,
1850, pp. 53-54; The Wesleyan Times, February 4, 1850,
p. 76.
      89. Glasgow Examiner, VI, October 20, 1849, 1.
      90. Ibid.

CHAPTER 4.   LEAVING OBERLIN

      1. Sherlock Bristol, Letter to Henry Cowles, Decem-
ber 26, 1844, TS, OCA 30/24, Box 3, R. S. Fletcher Papers.
      2. Samuel D. Cochran, Sherlock Bristol, John Keep,
and Edward Weed, Letter to the Faculty and Resident Trustees of Oberlin Collegiate Institute, December 30, 1844, OCA,
30/24, Box 3, Fletcher Papers.
      3. Bristol, Letter to the Faculty and Resident Trus-
tees of Oberlin, December 21, 1844, and Bristol, Letter to
Hamilton Hill, December 21, 1844, OCA, 7/1/5, Box 7;
Bristol, Letter to Henry Cowles, December 26, 1844, 30/24,
Box 3. The quotation is from Bristol's letter to the faculty
and resident trustees.
      4. Sherlock Bristol in A. M. Hills, Life of Charles
G. Finney (Cincinnati: God's Revivalist Publishers, 1902),
p. 231; Board of Trustees' Document File, 1845-1870, OCA,
1/3/1, Box 2; Document File, 1845: "List of Notes held
against the Institution, with interest calculated to 1st September 1845--Asa Mahan, 15 October 1842, $850 (present
amount $992.50)"; Trustee Minutes, Annual Meeting, August
15, 1845 (Minutes on microfilm in OCA; also TS, 30/24,
Box 16): "Whereas Asa Mahan holds a note against the Instn.
given by its treasurer for $800 and interest and whereas the
said sum with interest is also secured by a mortgage on the
house now occupied by the Treasurer being the property of

the Instn. , Resolved that said note and mortgage be transferred
to Mrs. Almira Barnes of Troy, N.Y. , she having advanced the
said amount of $800 to said Asa Mahan as a loan to the Instn. ";
Trustee Minutes, August 18, 1846: "Mr. Mahan was credited
$450 [for back salary]": Trustee Minutes, August 22, 1848: Ma-
han allowed $200 for past extra services; Board of Trustees'
Document File, 1851 and 1852 (1/3/1, Box 2): "Notes Against
College with interest ... Asa Mahan: $150, $125, $151.42."
        5.   Trustee Minutes, August 15, 1845; William Dawes,
Letter to Henry Cowles, March 1846, TS, OCA, 30/24, Box
3, "Cowles Papers 1840-50" folder; James H. Fairchild,
Oberlin: The Colony and the College, 1833-1883 (Oberlin:
E. J. Goodrich, 1883), pp. 293-94.
        6.   Fletcher, History of Oberlin College, I, 473-74,
493-94; Dawes' letter of resignation, Board of Trustees Document File, 1846, 1/3/1, Box 2.   For the salary issue and
related financial matters of this period, see Sherlock Bristol, Letter to Hill, Cowles, and Whipple, December 9, 1844,
"Letters Received by Oberlin College, June 1843-July 1845,"
Roll 9; Document Files for 1845, 1846, 1/3/1, Box 2, "Summary of Financial Affairs of the Oberlin Collegiate Institute,"
"List of Notes held against the Institution," and "Balances
due to Faculty"; John Morgan, Letter to Mark Hopkins, May 6,
1845, 30/28, Box 4; James Dascomb, Letter to Prudential
Committee, February 9, 1846, 7/1/3, Box 7, "Miscellaneous
Archives," 1842-1849; "Faculty request to meet with Board
concerning salaries," August 19, 1846 (signed in ink by Finney and Morgan, signed by Cowles with a different pen, and
signed by the remainder of the faculty in pencil), Document
File, 1846 1/3/1, Box 2; G. N. Allen, Letter to Hamilton
Hill, August 21, 1846, ibid.; Trustee Minutes, Annual Meetings for 1842, 1843, 1844, 1845, 1846, 1847, 1848, 1849,
Roll 1; and Morgan, Letter to Finney, May 7, 1850, Finney
Papers, Roll 4.   At other colleges, the faculty was less successful because less powerful.   Cf. Walter Pilkington, Hamilton College, 1812-1962 (Clinton, New York: Hamilton College, 1962), p. 206.
        7.   Henry Cowles, Letter to Mrs. Cowles, July 28,
1848, TS, 30/24, Box 3, "Cowles Papers 1840-50" folder.
        8.   Finney, Mahan, and P. P. Pease testimony at
the Gillett trial concerning Finney's conversation with Pease
and Pease's visit to Mahan asking him not to be counsel for
Gillett, OCA Gillett File D-E, 31/4/1, Box 4, Oberlin Community Churches--First and Second Congregational Churches.
D. L. Leonard observed that church trials seemed more frequent than revivals, Oberlin News, February 13, 1903, p. 4.
        9.   "The Lukewarm Professor," The Oberlin Evange-

list, IX, December 22, 1847, 1.

10. A. T. Swing, James H. Fairchild (New York: Fleming H. Revell, 1907), p. 164.

11. Timothy Hudson, Letter to James Monroe, January 1, 1849, TS, OCA, 30/24, Box 7, "Monroe Papers 1844-66" folder.

12. John Morgan, Letter to Finney, January 7, 1850, microfilm, Roll 4, Finney Papers, May 1839-March 1859.

13. Whipple, Letter to Hamilton Hill, February 12, 1850, and Whipple, Letter to Mahan, February 13, 1850, 7/1/5, Box 9; Whipple, Letter to Hill, March 19, 1850, 7/1/5, Box 10.

14. Faculty, Letter to Asa Mahan, March 5, 1850; Mahan, Letter to Dawes, March 8, 1850; Dawes, Josiah B. Hall, and Isaac Jennings, Letter to Mahan, March 11, 1850, 7/1/3, Box 8, "Misc. Archives," "Asa Mahan 1850" folder. See faculty, Letter to Mahan, February 28, 1850, "Letters Received by Oberlin College, September 1848-June 1850," microfilm, Roll 12.

15. Faculty, Letter to Mahan, March 18, 1850, 7/1/3, Box 8, "Asa Mahan 1850" folder; John Morgan, Letter to Finney, January 7, 1850, microfilm, Roll 4, Finney Papers.

16. Trustee Minutes, Special Meeting, April 18-22, 1850, microfilm, Roll 1; John Morgan, Letter to Finney, May 7, 1850, Roll 4, Finney Papers.

17. The petitions which have survived are to be found in 7/1/3, Box 8.

18. Ibid.

19. Ibid.

20. D. L. Leonard, "Notes of Talks with Pres. Fairchild, 1894-97," Notebook 1, pp. 36 ff., Notebook 2, p. 65, 30/24, Box 1.

21. Trustee Minutes, Special Meeting, April 18-22, 1850, microfilm, Roll 1.

22. Ibid.; John Morgan, Letter to Finney, May 7, 1850, microfilm, Roll 4, Finney Papers.

23. Mahan, Letter to Oberlin Board of Trustees, August 15, 1854, 7/1/4, Box 10, Trustee Papers, "1854" folder; Mahan, The True Believer (New York: Harper and Brothers, 1847), p. 275; Out of Darkness into Light (New York: Willard Tract Repository, 1876), pp. 151-55.

24. Mahan, Letter to Oberlin Board of Trustees, August 15, 1854, 7/1/4, Box 10, Trustee Papers, "1854" folder.

25. Ibid.; and S. D. Porter to Oberlin Board of Trustees, December 2, 1854, 7/1/4, Box 10.

26. Ibid.

27. Mahan, Letter to Oberlin Board of Trustees, August 15, 1854, 7/1/4, Box 10.

28. Ibid.; Alfred Vance Churchill, "Midwestern: The Founding of Oberlin," part of a manuscript in Oberlin history published in installments in Northwest Ohio Quarterly, Vol. 23, 1950-51, 168-69.

29. John Morgan, Letter to Finney, May 7, 1850, Roll 4, Finney Papers; Leonard, "Notes of Talks with Pres. Fairchild, 1894-97," pp. 36 ff., 30/24, Box 1.

30. Fletcher, History, I, 482 (see fn. 34); Caroline Mary Rudd Allen, Letter to George N. Allen, July 23, 1850; W. W. Wright, Letter to Allen, July 28, 1850, TS, 30/24, Box 2, "Allen Letters--W. C. Cochran" folder.

31. Timothy Hudson, Letter to James Monroe, January 1, 1849, TS, 30/24, Box 7, "Monroe Papers 1844-66" folder: "A committee was appointed at an informal meeting held last week at Mrs. P[elton]'s to confer with Br. F[inney] on the whole subject. I have not learned the result. Tho' I fear it will finally be that Mrs. P. will close the tavern"; Trustee Minutes, Special Meeting, April 18-22, 1850, microfilm, Roll 1: Mrs. Pelton's proposal was presented near the end of the meeting; Charles Finney, Letter to C. G. Finney, July 9, 1850, Roll 4, Finney Papers; Charles Finney, Letter to Finney, July 29, 1850, Roll 10.

32. Charles Finney, Letter to C. G. Finney, July 9, 1850, Roll 4; July 29, 1850, Roll 10.

33. Caroline Mary Judd Allen, Letter to George N. Allen, July 23, 1850, TS, 30/24, Box 2, "Allen Letters-W. C. Cochran" folder.

34. W. W. Wright, Letter to Allen, July 28, 1850, 30/24, Box 2.

35. Uriah Thompson et al., Letter to Board of Trustees, August 23, 1850, Board of Trustees Document File, 1/3/1, Box 2, "1850" folder.

36. Mahan, Letter to the Trustees of the Oberlin College, August 26, 1850, Document File, 1/3/1, Box 2.

37. A. M. Hills, Life of Charles G. Finney, pp. 228-29, 234-35.

38. Bristol in Hills' Life of Finney, pp. 230-31, 233.

39. Fairchild, The Doctrine of Sanctification at Oberlin (Oberlin: E. J. Goodrich, 1876), p. 14; Fairchild, Oberlin: Colony and College, p. 93.

40. Homer Johnson, Letter to George N. Allen, July 15, 1850, TS, 30/24, Box 2, "Allen Letters-W. C. Cochran" folder.

41.   Sherlock Bristol, Letter to Henry Cowles, December 26, 1844, TS, 30/24, Box 3; "To the Public" by
"Many Citizens," July 28, 1849, TS [anonymous], 30/24,
Box 3, "Cowles Papers 1840-50" folder; Taylor, Letter to
George Whipple, April 1, 1850, "Letters Received by Oberlin College," Roll 12; Fairchild, Oberlin: Colony and College, p. 294.   Without mentioning him by name but precisely describing him, Fairchild wrote that Taylor never showed
any sign of an essentially reformed character.
42.   Faculty, Letter to Mahan, March 18, 1850, "Letters Received by Oberlin College," microfilm, Roll 12; Finney, Letter to James Morison, January 5, 1851, The Moir
Collection, Mitchell Library, Glasgow.   For the suggestion
of disagreements between Finney and Mahan as early as 1845
see the Oberlin Evangelist, VII, August 14, 1845, 135.
43.   Fletcher, History, I, 472-76, 480, 482, 483.
44.   These ideological and religious disputes, as well
as the power struggle, are described throughout Chapter 3.
Fletcher, of course, was aware of these issues but gave
them no weight in his explanation of why Mahan left Oberlin
and why there was, on grounds other than personality traits,
animosity toward him in various quarters.
45.   The elaboration and documentation of these statements constitutes the bulk of Chapter 7.
46.   Fletcher, History, I, 473, fn. 4; Leonard, "Notes
of Talks with Pres. Fairchild, 1894-97," 30/24, Box 1, Notebook 1, p. 41.
47.   Fletcher, History, I, 480; G. D. Pike, Letter
to Whipple, F1-13629, 13709, American Missionary Association Archives, Amistad Collection, Dillard University.
48.   Oberlin Evangelist, Vol. 5, December 20, 1843,
206.
49.   Mahan, Letter to Oberlin Board of Trustees, August 15, 1854, and S. D. Porter, Letter to Oberlin Board
of Trustees, December 2, 1854, 7/1/4, Box 10, Trustee Papers 1854 folder.
50.   Jaob Seeley, Letter to Hamilton Hill, July 23,
1846, microfilm, Roll 10, "Letters Received by Oberlin College, August 1845-December 1846."
51.   Gillett File D-E, 130-31/4/1, Box 4, Oberlin
Community Churches--First and Second Congregational Churches, Oberlin College Archives; "Records of First Church, 1839-
1856," 31/4/1, Box 17, OCA.
52.   Finney, Mahan, and Pease testimony at the Gillett trial, Gillett File D-E, 31/4/1, Box 4, Oberlin Community Churches.
53.   Ibid.

54. "Records of First Church, 1839-1856," June 27,
1848: "On Motion, that Prest. A. Mahan be Bro. Gilletts
councillor in the case, the motion was put and lost." P.
176, 31/4/1, Box 17. For the testimony of Asa and Mary
Mahan, see Gillett File D-E, 31/4/1, Box 4.

55. Mahan would not even have agreed to be counsel
for Gillett, he wrote, "had I supposed that any considerable
minority of the church objected to my doing it." "Nor should
I have done so, had I been aware of the excited state of the
church at the time on the subject." [He had been asked to
be counsel because of the ill health of Gillett, who had planned
to be, and eventually was, his own counsel.] See Mahan,
Letter to Oberlin Board of Trustees, August 15, 1854, Treasurer's Office File, 7/1/4, Box 10, Trustee Papers, 1854
folder. Mahan defended Gillett, and Henry Cowles was opposed to him; and the two men had a serious disagreement
over the case. On February 7, 1849, Cowles wrote to his
daughter Helen, "... when you were hearing me last summer on the Gillett case you [reportedly] said to Lucy [Mahan]
-- 'I am shocked to hear father speak so against the President,' or words to this effect. Perhaps you will recall pret-
ty nearly what you did say. Don't be afraid of letting it go
as bad as it really was. I should like to know about the
truth.... The state of feeling here about the President is
not pleasant either for him or for me. It puts him upon
saying the worst things about me in self defense, there being apparently no other way for him to sustain himself but
to get me down under the same or a greater condemnation."
(TS, 30/24, Box 3, "Cowles Papers, 1840-50" folder.) Anna
wrote Anna Mahan on November 12, 1848, that "the
Gillett concern has 'separated chief friends' here I am sorry
to say." Asa Mahan Archives, Asbury College.

CHAPTER 5.   CLEVELAND

1. Pilgrim Congregational Church: Our First One
Hundred Years, 1859-1959, (Cleveland: n.p., 1959), pp.
5-7; Pilgrim Church, History and Directory, 1859-1929
(Cleveland: Pilgrim Church and Society, 1930), pp. 7-15,
67-77; Daily True Democrat: February 21, 1850, 2/3; Sep-
tember 14, 1850, 2/1; September 21, 1850, 2/4, Western
Reserve Historical Society Archives.
2. Daily True Democrat: February 18, 1850, 2/3;
September 20, 1850, 3/1; September 26, 2/1 and 3/1, 3;
October 23, 2/2; Cleveland Daily Plain Dealer, October 23,
1850, 3; Daily True Democrat: December 6, 1850, 2/1, 2;
February 15, 1851, 2/4.

3. Daily True Democrat: September 20, 1850, 3/1; September 26, 1850, 2/1 and 3/1, 3; Cleveland Daily Plain Dealer, October 23, 1850, 3; Daily True Democrat: February 7, 1851, 2/3; April 24, 2/1; August 8, 2/5; August 13, 2/2; August 21, 2/1 and 2/2, 4; August 22, 2/1 and 3/1-7; and "An Old Vision Taking Form," The Graduate School News, Western Reserve University, January 1, 1935, pp. 1-2.

4. Daily True Democrat, August 22, 1851, 3/1-7; November 2, 1850, 3/3.

5. "An Old Vision Taking Form," p. 1; Maude E. Holtz, "Cleveland University, A Forgotten Chapter in Cleveland's History," M.A. Thesis Western Reserve University 1930, pp. 41-42; William Ganson Rose, Cleveland, The Making of a City (Cleveland: World Publishing Co., 1950), pp. 237-38. Jack Hutter and John Vacha, in "Let Us Have, Then, Our University," Western Reserve Historical Society News (Vol. 34, 1980), pp. 62-67, give an uneven and unbalanced account of Mahan and Cleveland University.

6. Rose, Cleveland, The Making of a City, pp. 237-38; Daily True Democrat: August 8, 1851, 2/5; August 13, 2/2.

7. Daily True Democrat, August 21, 1851, 2/2, 4.

8. Rose, Cleveland, The Making of a City, p. 238; Daily True Democrat: October 10, 1851, 2/5; Morning Daily Democrat, April 28, 1852, 2/3.

9. Daily True Democrat, November 1, 1851, 2/4.

10. Morning Daily True Democrat, May 29, 1852, 2/2, 3; May 31, 3/1; Weekly True Democrat, June 2, 1852, 3/1.

11. Daily True Democrat: October 10, 1851, 2/5; December 16, 2/3; Morning Daily True Democrat: January 9, 1852, 2/1; January 14, 3/1; Daily True Democrat: October 5, 1850, 3/2, 3.

12. System of Intellectual Philosophy, Revised and Enlarged from the Second Edition (New York: A. S. Barnes and Co., 1855), p. vii.

13. United States Census for Lorain County, 1850; "Asa Mahan" folder in the files of the Alumni Office, Oberlin College; pages from Anna Mahan North's Notebook, Asa Mahan Archives, Asbury College; Out of Darkness into Light, p. 302 (the age factor and elimination of the other sisters makes it clear that the one who died soon after Theodore was Elizabeth).

14. Pilgrim Church, History and Directory, 1859-1929, pp. 7-15, quotation from p. 1.

15. Rose, Cleveland, The Making of a City, pp. 237-

38; Daily True Democrat: October 23, 1850, 2/2; Cleveland,
The Making of a City, pp. 237-38.

16. Holtz, "Cleveland University, A Forgotten Chapter in Cleveland's History," pp. 41-42.

17. Fletcher, History of Oberlin College, I, 484-85;
concerning the quality of students Levi Burnell, secretary of
the university, wrote Hamilton Hill on April 19, 1852, in
response to a query from Hill: "In regard to students from
other colleges we of course expect 'honorable dismissions'
as a condition of honorable admission to membership here."
Letters Received by Oberlin College, microfilm, Roll 13;
"Cleveland University, A Forgotten Chapter," pp. 31-32.
Holtz is mistaken in one point--the June 1852 commencement
was not the first held at the university. As we have seen,
the first one occurred in August 1851.

18. Cleveland Daily Herald: December 13, 1852,
2/1.

19. Cleveland, The Making of a City, pp. 237-38.

20. Pilgrim Church, History and Directory, 1859-
1929, pp. 7, 14. Cf. p. 9. Thirza Pelton's death was not
a factor in the collapse of Cleveland University, as here suggested, since it had already failed before her death. Nor
was the dispute between Mahan and Thirza Pelton a significant factor except insofar as it might reflect the dispute
about selling university land discussed below. The nature
of their dispute remains a mystery.

21. Cleveland Daily Herald: December 13, 1852,
2/1.

22. Cleveland, The Making of a City, p. 227.

23. Out of Darkness into Light, pp. 230-31.

24. Fletcher, History, I, 483. Elsewhere it is said
that "a few brave [Oberlin] spirits," including Thirza Pelton
and Mahan, bought the land on the Heights (Pilgrim Church,
History and Directory, 1859-1929, p. 8).

25. Fletcher, History, I, 485; Hamilton Hill, Letter
to George Whipple, December 25, 1850; Timothy Hudson,
Letter to Hill, January 6, 1851; Hill, Letter to Whipple,
November 7, 1851, "Letters Received by Oberlin College,"
microfilm, Roll 13.

26. Hudson, Letter to Hill, January 6, 1851, "Letters Received by Oberlin College," Roll 13.

27. Letter from Asa Mahan to the Oberlin College
Board of Trustees, August 15, 1854, Treasurer's Office
File, 7/1/4, Box 10, "Trustee Papers, 1854" folder; Fletch-
er, History I, 485-86.

28. Asa Mahan, Letter to the Oberlin College Board
of Trustees, August 15, 1854; Trustee Minutes, Annual Meeting, August 20, 1855, Roll 1; Morgan, Letter to Finney,

May 7, 1850, Finney Papers, Roll 4. (George Whipple felt that if in the future Mahan did not change his ways the faculty could get rid of him quietly since Mahan's sifting things to the bottom would entail making public the April 1850 document. This sentiment, reported by Morgan in his letter, does not contradict Morgan's categorical statement that the document was considered private by both parties. Whipple was addressing a different issue.)

29. Mahan, Letter to Hamilton Hill, October 17, 1850; October 4, 1851; February 24, 1852; April 6, 1852, June 17, 1852--"Letters Received by Oberlin College," Roll 13; Document File, 1851, under heading "Liabilities--Notes Against the College with interest calculated to 24 August 1851" (Mahan held three notes against the college); Document File, 1852, "Liabilities, etc." (Mahan still held one note)--"Board of Trustees Document File, 1845-1870," 1/3/1, Box 2; Prudential Committee Meeting, April 28, 1851; Special Meeting, November 6, 1851; Special Meeting, November 14, 1851; Prudential Committee Meeting, January 5, 1852--30/24, Box 11, TS; Trustee Minutes, Annual Meetings, August 1851, 1852, 1853, 1854; Special Meeting, August 1, 1855; Annual Meetings, August 1855, 1856.

30. Tappan, Letter to Finney (where he reports to Finney what he had told Mahan), December 3, 1854; Tappan to John Keep, January 11, 1855; Tappan to James A. Thome, June 13 and June 21, 1855. Photocopies of these Tappan letters, and those to follow, are in the Oberlin College Archives, 30/24, Box 18, Robert S. Fletcher Papers. Typescripts of the letters are contained in 30/24, Box 14. The originals of Tappan's letters are in the Library of Congress.

31. Tappan, Letter to Mahan, August 12, 1855; Tappan, Letter to Finney, August 12, 1855; Tappan, Letter to Finney, August 19, 1855, 30/24, Box 18 or Box 14, O.C.A.; Theodore Weld, Letter to Tappan, May 21, 1836, #2419, Weld Correspondence, 1834-1845, New York State Historical Society.

32. In addition to the letters in the previous note: Tappan to Finney, August 21, 1855; Tappan to Mahan, September 2, 1855; Tappan to Finney, September 15, 1855; Tappan to Finney, September 21, 1855, 30/24, Box 18 or Box 14, O.C.A.

33. Alfred Vance Churchill, "Midwestern: The Founding of Oberlin," part of a manuscript on Oberlin history published in installments in Northwest Ohio Quarterly, Vol. 23, 1950-51, 161.

34. Tappan, Letter to Thome, October 30, 1855, 30/24, Box 18 or Box 14; Divine Life, June 1877, March

1878, January 1879, December 1880; Finney's handwritten
manuscript of his Memoirs, 2/2/2, Box 10; Lorain County
News, November 11, 1863, p. 2.   See pp. 675-76 of the
Memoirs MS for an amusing deleted incident.   Finney proposed bringing a tabernacle tent when he came to Oberlin
in 1835.   Fearing that the tent would prompt the evangelist
to go too far afield, the Oberlinians declined the offer.   Finney cancelled the order for the tent and the money was used
for another purpose.   Deciding that the tent would be useful
for commencements, the Oberlinians next wrote that they
could not get along without it.   Finney was a bit chagrined
but secured the money for a tent the second time from his
New York patrons.

     35.   W. E. Lincoln, "A Reminiscence of Finney and
Mahan," Oberlin News, February 23, 1910, p. 2.

     36.   Frances E. Willard's recollections of Oberlin
childhood, and Mahan and Finney, in The Woman's Journal,
August 22, 1885, pp. 266-67.   Cf. Mary Earhart, Frances
Willard (Chicago: University of Chicago Press, 1944) p. 29.

     37.   Lincoln, "A Reminiscence of Finney and Mahan,"
Oberlin News, February 23, 1910.

     38.   Out of Darkness into Light, pp. 231, 285-86.

     39.   Daily True Democrat, March 11, 1853, p. 3.

     40.   Cleveland Leader: February 7, 1854, 3/3;
March 12, 3/2; March 14, 3/2; March 28, 3/2; April 3,
3/2; April 19, 3/2; Pilgrim Church, History and Directory,
1859-1929, pp. 9-10.

     41.   Cleveland Leader, April 24, 1854, 2/3.

     42.   Proceedings of the National Women's Rights Con-
vention, held at Cleveland, Ohio, on October 5, 6, 7, 1853,
p. 187.

     43.   Ibid., pp. 80-81, 84-85, 185-88.   Cf. History
of Woman Suffrage, 2nd ed. Elizabeth Cady Stanton, Susan
B. Anthony, and Matilda Joslyn Gage (Rochester, New York:
Charles Mann, 1889, and New York: Source Book Press,
1970), I, 152.   From internal evidence the chapter on the
Cleveland Convention seems to have been written by Gage.
The reference to Mahan on p. 152 is uncomplimentary and
unjust.   From her own description of the convention one ex-
pects her wrath to descend on Dr. Nevin rather than Mahan.
Cf. her account with the Proceedings.

     44.   It is doubtful that Mahan would have agreed with
Stone and Brown that "male ascendency" in the Bible resulted
from mis-translations.

     45.   It is not sufficiently appreciated that Mahan was
Garrison's most systematic and persistent critic.

     46.   Asa Mahan et al., editors, Spiritualism: Or a

Discussion on the Cause and Effect of the Phenomena At-
tributed to the Spirits of Departed Human Beings, Held at
Chapin's Hall, Cleveland O. , Commencing, February 20,
1855 (Cleveland: Gray, Beardsley Spear and Co. , 1855);
Mahan, Modern Mysteries Explained and Exposed (Boston:
John P. Jewett and Co. , 1855); Cleveland Leader: August
18, 1854, 3/2; August 31, 3/2; October 11, 2/2 ("President
Mahan's great work on spiritualism is being reprinted in
London" and "this we consider as the highest compliment
which could be paid to our fellow citizen; for in England,
American literature is at a discount"). Modern Mysteries
was published in Cleveland by Jewett Proctor and Worthing-
ton; in New York by Sheldon, Lamport and Blakeman; in
London, by Trubner and Company.
    47. S. B. Brittan, The Telegraph's Answer to Rev.
Asa Mahan (New York: Partridge and Brittan, 1855); Mahan,
Phenomena of Spiritualism Scientifically Explained and Exposed (London: Hodder and Stoughton, 1875) and (New York:
A. S. Barnes & Co. , 1876).
    48. The Christian Ambassador, N. S. 14 (1876), 59-
72; The Original Secession Magazine, N. S. XII (1875-76)
351-53.
    49. Mahan, Misunderstood Texts of Scripture (Lon-
don: Haughton and Co. , 1876), p. 41; Christian Perfection,
p. 79.
    50. Mahan, Lectures on the Ninth of Romans, pp.
59 ff.
    51. Misunderstood Texts of Scripture, p. 147.

CHAPTER 6.   MICHIGAN

    1. David Rood, "The History of Old First," MS,
Archives of the First Congregational Church (UCC) of Jack-
son, Michigan, p. 2; pp. 1-4.
    2. Mahan, Autobiography: Intellectual, Moral, and
Spiritual, pp. 378-79.
    3. The American Citizen, Jackson, Michigan, May
29, 1856, "Local and Miscellaneous News," Jackson Public
Library.
    4. Records of the Jackson Congregational Associa-
tion, MS, Michigan Historical Collections, Bentley Historical
Library, University of Michigan, entries for April 29, 1856;
October 28, 1856; April 28, 1857; October 27, 1857; April
27, 1858; The American Citizen, July 30, 1857, "Local and
Miscellaneous News"; Adrian Daily Expositor, June 7, 1860,
p. 1, Adrian Public Library.

5.   The Jackson Patriot, March 4, 1857, p. 2,
Bentley Historical Library, University of Michigan;   The
American Citizen, March 12, 1857.
        6.   The American Citizen, March 4, 1858.
        7.   Ibid. , February 28, 1856.
        8.   Ibid. , July 16, 1857, "Local and Miscellaneous
News. "
        9.   Ibid. , August 27, 1857, reprinted from the
Adrian Expositor.
        10.   F. A. Hay et al. , The Story of a Noble Devo-
tion (Adrian: Adrian College Press, 1945), pp. 14-15; Al-
bert W. Kauffman, "Early Years of Adrian College, " Michigan History Magazine, XIII, 1929, 74-90; Margaret B. Macmillan, The Methodist Church in Michigan: The Nineteenth
Century (Grand Rapids: Eerdmans Publishing Co. , 1967),
pp. 195-96.
        11.   Andover Theological Seminary: General Cata-
logue 1808-1908 (Boston: Thomas Todd, n. d.), p. 95.
        12.   Harlan L. Feeman, "'Plymouth Church'--Adrian, "
MS, Archives, Detroit Conference of United Methodist Church,
Adrian College Library; Hay, Story of a Noble Devotion, p.
17.
        13.   Caroline Mary Rudd Allen, Letter to George N.
Allen, May 20, 1858, MS, 30/67, Box 1, "Letters Received
by Allen 1853-58" folder.
        14.   Adrian Daily Expositor, May 3, 1860, p. 1;
June 7, p. 1.
        15.   Kauffman, "Early Years of Adrian College, " p.
89.   That Mahan held no prominent office in the Republican
Party in the crucial spring of 1860 is evident from the news-
paper coverage of county and state Republican conventions
and caucuses: Adrian Daily Expositor, May 2, 1860, p. 1;
May 3, p. 2; May 29, p. 1; June 1, p. 1, Adrian Public
Library.
        16.   Hay, The Story of a Noble Devotion, pp. 18-19;
"Early Years of Adrian College, " pp. 84-87; Macmillan,
The Methodist Church in Michigan: The Nineteenth Century,
pp. 195-96; "Michigan Union College, " The American Citizen,
September 24, 1857; "Report of the Special Committee on
Michigan Union College, " The American Citizen, October 22,
1857; "Michigan Union College, " The American Citizen, No-
vember 19, 1857; "Removal of the Michigan Union College, "
The American Citizen, November 18, 1858; "Michigan Union
College, " The American Citizen, December 9, 1858; Adrian
Evening Expositor, February 2, 1859, p. 2; Adrian Evening
Expositor, February 4, 1859, p. 2.
        17.   Hay, The Story of a Noble Devotion, pp. 18-19,

23-24; W. C. S. Pellowe, "Asa Mahan--Sage of Adrian,"
Michigan Christian Advocate, June 11, 1964, p. 5; Mac-
millan, The Methodist Church in Michigan, pp. 195-96;
Trustee Minutes, Adrian College, 1859-1922, entry for
March 22, 1859, MS, Archives, Shipman Library, Adrian
College.

Ironically soon after becoming president of Adrian College, Mahan sat for his portrait which was to hang in the
halls of Oberlin along with portraits of Finney, Dascomb,
and Fairchild. The Musical Union of Oberlin commissioned
Alonzo Pease, an Oberlin artist, to paint all the portraits.
Pease had a studio in Detroit in 1860 and painted Mahan's
portrait in Michigan. It is that portrait which is still on
display, along with those of the other presidents, on the
main floor of the Oberlin College Library. See Oberlin Students' Monthly, Vol 3, December 1860, 62-63; Detroit Daily
Advertiser, July 12, 1860, 1/4, and December 29, 1860,
1/2; Detroit Weekly Tribune, August 14, 1860, 1/2.

18.   Adrian Daily Watchtower, August 23, 1859, p.
2, Adrian Public Library; Hay, The Story of a Noble Devotion, pp. 24-25.

19.   Adrian Daily Expositor, June 11, 1860, p. 1;
June 12, p. 1.

20.   The Story of a Noble Devotion, pp. 19-20; Adrian
Daily Expositor, June 12, 1860, p. 1; Lucinda H. Stone,
"The Effects of Mental Growth," in The Education of American Girls, ed. Anna C. Brackett (New York: G. P. Putnam's Sons, 1874), pp. 202-203.

21.   Mahan, Autobiography, pp. 269-70.

22.   Hay, Story of a Noble Devotion, p. 46.

23.   Semi-Centennial Souvenir, Adrian College, 1859-
1909 (Adrian: Adrian College, 1909), p. 4.

24.   Mahan, Science of Logic; Or, An Analysis of the
Laws of Thought, (New York: A. S. Barnes, 1857); William
Thomson, An Outline of the Necessary Laws of Thought, 2nd
ed. (London: 1849, 1867), pp. 189 ff. Mahan also followed
Thomson closely in his exposition of Lambert's line diagrams.

25.   Mahan, Science of Natural Theology (Boston:
Henry Hoyt, 1867); Hamilton Literary Monthly, Vol. 2, 1868,
p. 290 (notice of Mahan's Science of Natural Theology); Vol.
21, 1887, p. 352 (review of the Science of Natural Theology
nineteen years later!); The Ingham Lectures on the Evidences
of Natural and Revealed Religion (Cleveland: Ingham, Clarke
and Co., 1873), pp. iii-viii, 109-35.

26.   Mahan, "Manuscript Writings, Miscellaneous,"
Archives, Shipman Library, Adrian College. The manuscript has page numbers at the start but pagination soon

disappears. The pages are written on both sides and amount
to about two hundred and fifty manuscript pages. The manuscript is bound and on the spine is printed "Christian Theology, 2." Presumably it was the binding of some other
book used to protect and preserve Mahan's manuscript.

In addition to the citations in the text from Mahan's
Notebook the following skeleton outline of Lecture 1 on "Constitutional Law" is of interest: "Introduction.... Female
Suffrage 1. Women don't want it. 2. Its absence not felt
oppressive. 3. Those who most loudly advocate it are not
the proper representatives of the sex. 4. Absurd to ask
men to give what women do not want." To such arguments
Mahan replies: "Suffrage in this country has been decided
by demagogues for party purposes and not for the good of
the state." It must not be supposed, however, that Mahan
was a radical on the question of women's rights and roles.
He was far more supportive of women's rights than the Oberlin or Adrian communities but less supportive than Mill and
the Garrisonians. We have seen how he helped advance the
cause of women. For the more conservative estimate of
women's roles in life see Science of Moral Philosophy (Oberlin: James M. Fitch, 1848), pp. 378-80.

27. "Trustee Minutes, 1859-1922, Adrian College,"
MS, Archives, Shipman Library, Adrian College, entry for
June 1, 1859; Adrian College Catalogue 1860-61 (Adrian:
S. P. Jermain, 1861); George B. Manhart, DePauw Through
the Years (2 vols.; Greencastle, Ind.: DePauw University,
1962), I, 22, 25, 57, 59-60.

28. Adrian College Catalogue 1864 (Toledo: Spear,
Johnson and Co., 1864).

29. Hay, Story of a Noble Devotion, p. 40. The
number of students enrolled in each department of the College is given in the Adrian College Catalogues from 1860 to
1872. The proportion of students enrolled in the college
courses decreased through the years, and the enrollment of
the college as a whole decreased after 1867-68 no doubt as
a result of the conflict between the Wesleyan Methodists and
the Methodist Protestants.

30. Hay, Story of a Noble Devotion, pp. 11-15; Macmillan, The Methodist Church in Michigan: The Nineteenth
Century.

31. Adrian Evening Expositor, February 4, 1859, p.
2; Kauffman, "Early Years of Adrian College," pp. 75-77;
Macmillan, The Methodist Church in Michigan: The Nineteenth Century, p. 157.

32. "Trustee Minutes, 1859-1922, Adrian College,"
entries for June 17, 1862; October 27, 1862; June 19, 1863;
July 3, 1863; September 28, 1863.

33. Lorain County News, March 15, 1865, p. 2;
March 29, p. 2; May 31, p. 2; Trustee Minutes, Adrian
College, entries for September 12, 1864; September 26,
1864; January 23, 1865; October 24, 1865; November 1,
1865; January 10, 1866; December 3, 1866; February 15,
1867; February 28, 1867; March 1, 1867; June 25, 1868.

34. "Luther Lee" entry in Dictionary of American
Biography, ed. Dumas Malone (New York: Charles Scrib-
ner's Sons, 1933), Vol. 11, 115-16; Luther Lee, "Woman's
Right to Preach the Gospel," in Five Sermons and a Tract
by Luther Lee, ed., D. W. Dayton (Chicago: Holrad House,
1975), pp. 77-100; Kauffman, "Early Years of Adrian College," p. 78; "Minutes of the Wesleyan Methodist Church,
Michigan Conference," Vol. 2, p. 98 (Bentley Historical Library, University of Michigan).

In this text we follow closely the Trustee Minutes of
Adrian College, 1859-1922, and the Minutes of the Wesleyan
Methodist Church in reconstructing the denominational difficulties which beset the College. Other important sources
which confirm and amplify the dispute in great detail are
long letters published in the Adrian Weekly Times and Expositor by McEldowney and Lee on one side and McElroy
and Mahan on the other. See particularly December 28,
1866, p. 1; January 18, 1867, pp. 1, 2; January 25, 1867,
p. 1; February 1, 1867, p. 1; and under the headings of
"Adrian College" and "College Matters," the following issues: December 31, 1866; January 4, 1867; February 27,
1867. For subsequent references to important events, including the fire that destroyed South Hall, see, under similar headings, March 8, 15, 27, 1867; June 17, 28, 1867;
February 7, 1868; February 4, March 11, July 8, July 29,
September 9, October 28, December 30, 1869; February 17,
July 7, 1870; June 22, July 27, and September 7, 1871.

35. Trustee Minutes, Adrian College, entries for
June 17, 1862; October 27, 1862; June 19, 1863; July 3,
1863; September 28, 1863; September 12, 1864; September
26, 1864; "Minutes of the Wesleyan Methodist Church, Michigan Conference, Vol. 2, "20th Session, October 1, 1862"
(by this time page numbers have been discontinued).

36. Trustee Minutes, Adrian College, entries for
July 3, 1863; September 28, 1863; April 15, 1864; Minutes
of the Wesleyan Methodist Church, Michigan Conference,
21st Session, 1863.

37. Trustee Minutes, Adrian College, entries for
September 12, 1864; September 26, 1864; January 23, 1865;
February 2, 1865; October 20, 1865; Minutes of the Wesleyan Methodist Church, Michigan Conference, 21st Session,
1863; 23rd Session, 1865.

38.   Trustee Minutes, Adrian College, entries for
October 24, 1865; November 1, 1865; January 10, 1866;
March 8, 1866; Minutes of the Wesleyan Methodist Church,
Michigan Conference, 23rd Session, 1865; 24th Session, 1866.

39.   Trustee Minutes, Adrian College, entries for
June 13, 14, 15, November 29, November 30, December 3,
1866; February 2, February 15, February 28, March 1, August 16, October 17, 1867; Minutes of the Wesleyan Methodist Church, Michigan Conference, 25th Session, 1867.

40.   Trustee Minutes, Adrian College, entry for June
25, 1868; Minutes of the Wesleyan Methodist Church, Michigan Conference, 26th Session, 1868, 27th Session, 1869.

41.   Hay, Story of a Noble Devotion, pp. 36, 40.

42.   Mahan, Baptism of the Holy Ghost (New York:
Palmer, 1870); Mahan and Finney, The Baptism of the Holy
Ghost and the Enduement of Power, revised and edited by
John Bate (London: Elliot Stock, 1872); Le Baptême de L'Es-
prit et Le Baptême de Puissance, trans. C. Challand (Péry,
Suisse: Tschan, 1889, 1963); The Baptism of the Holy Ghost
and the Enduement of Power was reprinted recently by J.
Edwin Newby (Noblesville, Ind.: Newby Book Room, 1966);
Mahan, "Reminiscences and Reflections, Part IX," Divine
Life, Vol. 13, May 1890, 292.

43.   Adrian College Catalogue 1869-70 (Adrian: Times
and Expositor Office, 1870).

44.   Trustee Minutes, Adrian College, July 1, 1870.

45.   Ibid.

46.   Manhart, DePauw Through the Years, I, 9, 110.

47.   Trustee Minutes, June 21, 22, 1871. Trustee
Flood proposed Mahan as a member of the Board of Trustees and John McElroy, who eventually succeeded Mahan as
president of Adrian, helped to defeat the resolution.

48.   Leonard, The Story of Oberlin (Boston: Pilgrim
Press, 1898), pp. 274-75; Mahan, Principles of Christian
Union and Church Fellowship (Elyria, Ohio: A. Burrell,
1836), pp. 7, 13.

49.   Trustee Minutes, Adrian College, June 22, 1871.

50.   Hay, Story of a Noble Devotion, pp. 40-41.

51.   Semi-Centennial Souvenir, Adrian College 1859-
1909, pp. 3, 4, full page picture of Mahan opposite p. 4;
Adrian Michigan Telegram, September 25, 1964, p. 1; the
humanities classroom building on Williams Street is named
Mahan Hall "in honor of Asa Mahan, founder of the College";
in the stained glass window "the main figure is Dr. Asa Mahan, Congregational minister and founder of Adrian College
in 1859" and "the flaming torch with broken chains symbol-
izes Mahan's struggle in behalf of freedom of slaves, coed-

ucational higher education, and other issues of his time"
(illustrated brochure on Adrian College Chapel). Mahan is
featured in the description of the Michigan Historical Commission Registered Site No. 227 (the site being Adrian College).

52. Mahan, Out of Darkness into Light, p. 302.
53. Lorain County News, November 11, 1863, p. 2
(reprinted from the Adrian Daily Expositor).
54. Lorain County News, November 11, 1863, p. 2.
55. Out of Darkness into Light, pp. 302-303.
56. Ibid. , pp. 343-44.
57. Baptism of the Holy Ghost (London: Elliot Stock,
1876), pp. 207-27, quotation p. 209.
58. Ibid. , pp. 207-27.
59. Mahan, Critical History of the Late American
War, with an Introductory Letter by Lieut. -General M. W.
Smith (New York: A. S. Barnes, 1877), pp. 236 ff. , pp.
258-59.
60. Pellowe, "Asa Mahan--Sage of Adrian," p. 18;
Critical History of the Late American War, pp. 231-32.
61. Critical History of the Late American War, p.
233; W. A. Scott, Letter to the New York Herald Tribune,
February 12, 1928, Section 2, p. 8.
62. Critical History, p. 233; W. A. Scott, Letter
to the New York Herald Tribune, February 12, 1928, Section 2, p. 8; "Dr. Mahan on the American War," International Review, Vol. 4, 1877, 786.
63. Mahan, Letter to Salmon P. Chase, January 23,
1863, Salmon P. Chase Papers, Historical Society of Penn-
sylvania, Philadelphia. Mahan also wrote frequently to Senator Charles Sumner about the conduct of the war. There
are twenty-one letters of Mahan's in the Charles Sumner Papers, Harvard University. They cover the period from December 19, 1861, to December 29, 1870. In addition to discussing martial matters Mahan also made it clear that he
was a candidate for minister to Haiti. See letters of December 19, 1861, and July 15, 1867.
64. Critical History, pp. 234, 235-36, 350.
65. Mahan, Letter to Chase, February 27, 1863;
April 15, 1863, Salmon P. Chase Papers.
66. Mahan, Letter to Chase, April 15, 1863.
67. Mahan, Letter to Chase, June 26, 1863.
68. Critical History, p. 361.
69. W. A. Scott, Letter to the New York Herald
Tribune, February 12, 1928, Section 2, p. 8.
70. Otto Eisenschiml, The Hidden Face of the Civil
War (Indianapolis: Bobbs-Merrill, 1961), p. 74.

71. Ibid. , p. 60.
72. Lorain County News, August 22, 1872, p. 2;
Wilbur H. Phillips, Oberlin Colony: The Story of a Century
(Oberlin: Oberlin Printing Co. , 1933), pp. 126-27.
73. Lorain County News, August 22, 1872, p. 2.
74. Hamilton Literary Monthly, VII (October 1872),
122, reprints portion of letter from Chicago Tribune.
75. Hamilton Literary Monthly, VII (October 1872),
122-23.
76. John D. Hicks, The American Nation, second
edition (Boston: Houghton Mifflin, 1949), pp. 50-53.
77. Lorain County News, August 22, 1872, p. 1;
August 15, p. 6.
78. Cleveland Leader, August 24, 1872, p. 1. Similar abuse was heaped upon Mahan by the Adrian Weekly
Times and Expositor and by other Michigan newspapers, items
from which were reprinted in the Times and Expositor. See
the editorial comment, correspondence section, and miscellaneous news columns of the following issues, most of which
have multiple Mahan items: August 15; September 5 ("The
Venerable Dr. Mahan Mauled Again"); September 12; September 19 (p. 1 article); September 26; October 3, 10, 17,
24, 31; November 7, 14--all 1872. The editors of the Times
and Expositor, however, must have been elastic people since
in early 1874, when Mahan was deeply involved in a highly
successful temperance crusade he was again referred to with
respect as "President Mahan" and "Dr. Mahan" and his
speeches referred to as "felicitous." Cf. Times and Expositor, March 12, 26, April 16, and May 28, 1874.
79. Hicks, The American Nation, p. 52.
80. Mahan, Scripture Doctrine of Christian Perfection, 2nd ed. (Boston: D. S. King, 1839), pp. 98-104; Autobiography: Intellectual, Moral, and Spiritual (London: T.
Woolmer, 1882), pp. 281-364, quotation p. 293.
81. Mahan, Scripture Doctrine of Christian Perfection, ten editions; The True Believer (New York: Harper
and Brothers, 1847); Lectures on the Ninth of Romans (Boston: Charles H. Peirce and Co. , 1851); The Baptism of the
Holy Ghost (New York: Palmer, 1870); The Promise of the
Spirit (London: Elliot Stock, 1874), a shorter version of
The Baptism of the Holy Ghost; Out of Darkness into Light;
The Consequences of Neglect (London: Longley, 1876); Misunderstood Texts of Scripture (London: Haughton and Co. ,
1876); Life Thoughts on the Rest of Faith (London: Longley,
1877); Autobiography: Intellectual, Moral, and Spiritual; The
Natural and the Supernatural in the Christian Life and Experience (London: Haughton and Co. , n. d.), a copy of this rare
work is to be found in the Bodleian Library, Oxford.

82.   Christian Perfection, pp. 130, 132; The True
Believer, p. 274.
83.   Autobiography, p. 313.
84.   Autobiography, pp. 293, 372-74, 382-86; Scripture Doctrine of Christian Perfection, pp. 70-73; Banner of
Holiness, I, September 23, 1875, 4; Doctrine of the Will,
especially pp. 84-85, 103-104; Autobiography, pp. 197-214;
Lectures on the Ninth of Romans, pp. 154-80.
85.   William G. McLoughlin, Introduction to C. G.
Finney's Lectures on Revivals of Religion (Cambridge: Harvard University Press, 1960), pp. xxviii-xxix.
86.   Autobiography, pp. 290-93.
87.   Mahan, Divine Life, February 1878, pp. 193-95;
Autobiography, pp. 387-89.
88.   Autobiography, pp. 294-96, 391-93; "Growing in
Grace," Oberlin Evangelist, IV, August 3, 1842.
89.   John Wesley, "Christian Perfection," "The Scripture Way of Salvation," "Thoughts on Christian Perfection,"
and "Cautions and Directions ...," pp. 252-305 in John Wesley, ed. A. C. Outler (New York: Oxford University Press,
1964); The Journal of John Wesley, abridged by N. Curnock
(New York: Capricorn Books, 1963).
90.   Divine Life, IV, May 1881, 203-204; Mahan's
"Address of the Author" in John Stevenson's edition of Scripture Doctrine of Christian Perfection, pp. xxii-xxiii; Methodist Quarterly Review, Vol. 23, April 1841, p. 308; Christian
Witness, Vol. 7, January 1850, 139.
91.   Autobiography, pp. 376-77. Cf. pp. 374-82.
92.   Autobiography, pp. 382-86; Banner of Holiness,
Vol. I, September 23, 1875, 4.
93.   Autobiography, pp. 386-87; and a prevailing
theme in Baptism of the Holy Ghost and Out of Darkness
into Light.
94.   Donald W. Dayton, "Asa Mahan and the Development of American Holiness Theology," Wesleyan Theological
Journal, Vol. 9, Spring 1974, 60-69.
95.   Mahan, The Natural and the Supernatural in the
Christian Life and Experience (London: Haughton and Co.
n.d.). That this short monograph was written late in life
is clear from internal evidence. Cf. Out of Darkness into
Light, pp. 356-61 for evidence that Mahan never relinquished
his early views on Christian Perfection.
The criticisms, rebuttals, and reappraisals discussed in
this section are by no means exhaustive. For the above and
other criticisms the most important sources--for different
periods in Mahan's life and more recent ones--are: Nathaniel S. Folsom, "Review of Mahan on Christian Perfection,"
American Biblical Repository, 2nd Series, Vol. 2, July 1839,

143-66; Committee of the Presbytery of Cleveland, An Ex-
position of the Peculiarities, Difficulties and Tendencies of
Oberlin Perfectionism (Cleveland: T. H. Smead, 1841);
A. M. Cowan, Oberlin Theology Contrasted with that of the
Confession of Faith of the Presbyterian Church (Mansfield,
Ohio: J. C. Gilkison, 1841); John C. Lord, "Finney's Ser-
mons on Sanctification and Mahan on Christian Perfection,"
Biblical Repertory and Princeton Review, Vol 13, April 1841,
231-50; Leonard Woods, An Examination of the Doctrine of
Perfection, as held by Rev. Asa Mahan and Others (New
York: W. R. Peters, 1841)--Cf. Oberlin Evangelist, Vol.
3, August 4, 18, 1841; S. G. Winchester, Review of Scripture Doctrine of Sanctification by W. D. Snodgrass, Biblical
Repertory and Princeton Review, Vol. 14, July 1842, 426-
75; W. E. Boardman, The Higher Christian Life (Boston:
Henry Hoyt, 1859), pp. 64-73; R. C. Morgan, "The Out-
pouring of the Spirit," The Christian, December 23, 1875,
pp. 7-9; S. A. Blackwood, Letter to The Christian, March
2, 1876, pp. 15-16 (Cf. March 16, 1876, p. 12); The Christian, January 20, 1876, pp. 12-13; James H. Fairchild, "The
Doctrine of Sanctification at Oberlin," Congregational Quarter-
ly, Vol. 18, April 1876, 237-59; Lyman H. Atwater, "The
Higher Life and Christian Perfection," Dickensons Theological
Quarterly, Vol. 4, January 1878, 31-47; R. W. -G., "Mahan
on the Baptism of the Holy Ghost," Evangelical Repository,
6th Series, June 1878, pp. 258-67; B. B. Warfield, "Oberlin
Perfectionism," The Princeton Theological Review, Vol. 19,
January 1921, 1-63, and Perfectionism (2 vols.; New York:
Oxford University Press, 1931), Vol. 2, 54-63; F. C. Waite,
Western Reserve University: The Hudson Era (Cleveland:
Western Reserve University Press, 1943), pp. 169-70, 208-
209. Waite in 1943 still presented the Oberlin views as an-
tinomian and similar to the views of John Humphrey Noyes.
That such a view should still persist in a recent history of
Western Reserve University suggests that there are some
prejudices which are impregnable.

    Finney as well as Mahan replied to critics of the Ober-
lin view. In addition to his lengthy works, see Finney's
"The Doctrine of Imperfection," Oberlin Quarterly Review,
Vol. 3, 1847-48, 1-22; "Recent Discussions on the Subject
of Entire Sanctification in this Life," Oberlin Quarterly Re-
view, Vol. 2, 1846-1847, 449-72; A Reply to Mr. Duffield's
"Warning Against Error" (Oberlin: J. M. Fitch, 1848). The
"Warning Against Error" was the report of a committee
adopted by the Presbytery of Detroit and approved by the
Synod of Michigan on October 18, 1847.

CHAPTER 7.   LONDON AND EASTBOURNE

1. "Asa Mahan" folder in the files of the Alumni
Records Office, Oberlin College; pages from Anna Mahan
North's Notebook, Asa Mahan Archives, Asbury College;
extrapolations of ages from the U.S. Census 1850, Lorain
County, Ohio.

2. "Adrian (Mich.) papers record the marriage in
that place, on the 22nd of May, of Pres. Asa Mahan, former president of this Institution, to Mrs. Mary E. Chase,
widow of the late Rev. S. H. Chase, M.D. of Cincinnati,"
Lorain County News, June 6, 1866, p. 3.

3. The story of the Mahans' "winding way to England" has been reconstructed from the following manuscripts
in the Archives of the American Missionary Association:
Circulars concerning Townley-Chase estate: 64370, 64502,
66943, 66964, 66965, 117170; Asa Mahan's letters to George
Whipple: 69846, 69854, 69856, 69858, 69899, 69907, 69908,
69916, 69917, 69922, 69929, 69932, 69933, 69937, 69940,
69941, 69944, 64717, 64719, 64722, 64738, 69973, 69974,
69986, 69990, 69993, 69994, 69995, 70009, 70019, 70020,
Fl-13913, 13915, 13916, 13917, 13918, 13919, 13922, 13928;
Mary Mahan's letters to George Whipple: 69851, 69853,
117338, 69955, 70031; Cyris Prindle to Mary Mahan: 117407;
George W. Chase to Mary Mahan: 11723, 117335, 117336,
117341, 117346; R. B. Swing to Mary Chase: 117387; J. B.
Chase to Whipple: 64661; P. W. Noel to Whipple: 117372,
117399; E. R. Chase to Whipple: 117345, 117393, 117619;
Ira Chase to Whipple: 117332, 117378, 119209; I. W. Chase
to Whipple: 69923, 69928, 69939, 69963, 69964, 70010,
70541, 70542; George W. Chase to Whipple: 117328, 117329,
117330, 117334, 117361; Fred Tompkins to Whipple: Fl-13102,
13380; Tompkins to G. D. Pike: Fl-13270; Shepherd and
Sons to G. D. Pike and Pike to Shepherd and Sons: Fl-13700;
Pike to Whipple: Fl-13629, 13709; Whipple's Summary of
Mary Mahan's claim to estate: 96376; and notarized genealogies and family records sent to Whipple by the Chases mentioned above and others: 69943, 96643, 99499, 99450, 99451,
99452, 116950, 117400, 117406, 117551, 117552.

4. Asa Mahan, Christian Perfection, The True Believer, and Baptism of the Holy Ghost; Thomas C. Upham,
Principles of the Interior or Hidden Life (New York: Harper,
1843); Mahan, "The Spiritual Writings of Prof. Thomas C.
Upham," The Oberlin Quarterly Review, January 1849, pp.
101-27; W. E. Boardman, Higher Christian Life (Boston:
Hoyt, 1859); Walter and Phoebe Palmer, Four Years in the

Old World (New York: Foster and Palmer, 1867); Hannah
Whitall Smith, Record of a Happy Life (Philadelphia: Lip-
pincott, 1873); Robert Pearsall Smith, Holiness Through
Faith (London: Morgan and Scott, 1870); Mrs. W. E. Boardman, Life and Labours of the Rev. W. E. Boardman, Preface by M. G. Pearse (London: Bemrose and Sons, 1886),
pp. 48-49; Charles F. Harford, ed., The Keswick Convention: Its Message, Its Method, and Its Men (London: Marshall Brothers, 1907); I. E. Page, A Long Pilgrimage (London: Charles Kelly, 1914), chap. IX; Steven Barabas, So
Great Salvation (London: Marshall, Morgan, and Scott,
1952), chap. 1; John Charles Pollock, The Keswick Story:
The Authorized History of the Keswick Convention (London:
Hodder and Stoughton, 1964); M. E. Dieter, "The Holiness
Revival in Nineteenth-Century Europe," Wesleyan Theological
Journal, Vol. 9 (Spring 1974), 15-27; Robert A. Parker, The
Transatlantic Smiths (New York: Random House, 1959).
     5.   Barabas, So Great Salvation, pp. 15-16.
     6.   Ibid., pp. 19-20; Parker, The Transatlantic
Smiths, pp. 21-26.
     7.   So Great Salvation, p. 21
     8.   The Methodist Recorder, September 4, 1874, p.
527; September 11, p. 537.
     9.   The Methodist, Vol. 1 (September 11, 1874), 6.
    10.   Page, A Long Pilgrimage, p. 154.
    11.   For a detailed description of the decline of R. P.
Smith, see Parker, The Transatlantic Smiths, pp. 3-83. Cf.
Logan Pearsall Smith, Unforgotten Years (Boston: Little,
Brown, 1939), pp. 35-77, and Barbara Strachey, Remarkable Relations: The Story of the Pearsall Smith Family (London: Gollancz, 1980), pp. 36-49, 51.
    12.   For descriptions of the Oxford Convention the
following sources are particularly useful: Account of the
Union Meeting for the Promotion of Scriptural Holiness Held
at Oxford (London: S. W. Partridge and Co., n.d.), especially pp. 49, 82, 102; Page, A Long Pilgrimage, pp. 146-
49; Barabas, So Great Salvation, pp. 20-23; Harford, The
Keswick Convention, p. 30; Advocate of Christian Holiness,
Vol. 5 (November, 1874), 113; and Christian Standard, Vol.
8 (December 19, 1874), 405.
    13.   So Great Salvation, pp. 23-24.
    14.   The Methodist, June 11, 1875, p. 12; June 25,
p. 9.
    15.   Record of the Convention for the Promotion of
Scriptural Holiness Held at Brighton (Brighton: W. J. Smith,
1875), pp. 257, 260, 309.
    16.   Ibid., pp. 383, 384, 447.

17. Banner of Holiness, I (December 16, 1875), 195.
18. Parker, The Transatlantic Smiths, pp. 33-36.
19. Ibid., p. 35; Hannah Whitall Smith, Letter to Mrs. William Cowper-Temple, April 25, 1876, Hampshire Records Office, Winchester, England.
20. Banner of Holiness, I (December 23, 1875), 209; Transatlantic Smiths, p. 34. For further descriptions of the Brighton Convention and Smith's role in it see An Account of the Ten Days Convention Held for the Promotion of Scriptural Holiness at Brighton (London: F. E. Longley, 1875), and So Great Salvation, pp. 23-24.
21. Divine Life, Vol. 13 (May 1890), 294.
22. Divine Life, Vol. 13 (November 1889), 115.
23. Ibid., Vol. 11 (July 1887), 22-23.
24. Banner of Holiness, I (September 23, 1875), 4.
25. Ibid., I (December 2, 1875), 161.
26. Ibid., I (December 16, 1875), 195; December 23, pp. 209 ff.
27. The Autobiography of Bertrand Russell (New York: Bantam, 1968), p. 93.
28. Transatlantic Smiths, p. 83.
29. Ibid., pp. 170-71.
30. Divine Life, Vol. 13 (November 1889), 116; ibid. (July 1887), 22-23.
31. Information procured from mastheads of Divine Life.
32. Divine Life (weekly), Vol. 1 (September 21, 1876), 155; Divine Life, Vol. 1 (June 1877), 24-25; Vol. 4 (December 1880), 106; Vol. 11 (1888), 228-29.
33. Divine Life (weekly), Vol. 1 (November 23, 1876), 264; December 14, 1876, pp. 202-204; January 18, 1877, pp. 353-55; Divine Life, Vol. 13 (May 1890), 292-93.
34. Divine Life, Vol. 1 (June 1877), 36-37.
35. Parker, Transatlantic Smiths, pp. 222-23.
36. Divine Life, Vol. 1 (June 1877), 40; Vol. 1 (January 1878), 180; Vol. 1 (February 1878), 196; Vol. 4 (December 1880), 101, 119; Vol. 4 (May 1881), 203-204; Vol. 5 (July 1881), 19-20; Vol. 6 (March 1883), 164-66; Vol. 1 (June 1877), 41.
37. The English Independent, February 28, 1878, p. 204.
38. Ibid., March 14, 1878, pp. 250-51.
39. Editing the Banner of Holiness and Divine Life and commitments to preach and speak at Holiness Conventions throughout the United Kingdom.
40. Divine Life, Vol. 13 (October 1889), 89.
41. Ibid., Vol. 6 (January 1883), 122.

42. Oberlin Weekly News, February 4, 1875, p. 5;
"Asa Mahan" folder, Alumni Office file, Oberlin College;
Asa Mahan Archives, Asbury College (Anna Mahan North's
inscribed copy of the Autobiography); Mahan, letter to Anna
Mahan North, October 17, 1882; November 10, 1884, TS,
OCA, 30/24, Box 7, "Mahan Letters" folder.

43. Banner of Holiness, I (October 21, 1875), 74;
The Methodist, November 26, 1875, p. 11; The Methodist
Recorder, July 14, 1876, p. 395; Page, A Long Pilgrimage,
p. 155.

44. Out of Darkness into Light (New York, Boston,
and London: Willard Tract Repository, 1875); The Phenom-
ena of Spiritualism Scientifically Explained and Exposed (Lon-
don: Hodder and Stoughton, 1875); Consequences of Neglect
(London: Longley, 1876); Misunderstood Texts of Scripture
Explained and Elucidated (London: Houghton, 1876); A Critical
History of the Late American War (London: Hodder, 1877); A
Critical History of Philosophy (London: E. Stock, 1881); The
System of Mental Philosophy (Chicago: S. C. Griggs, 1882);
Autobiography: Intellectual, Moral, and Spiritual (London: T.
Woolmer, 1882).

In addition to the reviews of Mahan's works referred to
throughout this book, the following reviews and notices should
also be consulted: 1) Christian Perfection (in various editions)--Monthly Miscellany, Vol. 2 (March 1840), 164-65;
Methodist Quarterly Review, Vol. 23 (April 1841), 307-19;
Christian Witness, Vol. 7 (January 1850); Wesleyan Times,
January 28, 1850, p. 60; General Baptist Repository, N.S.,
March 1850, pp. 137-39; British Banner, March 13, 1850,
p. 189; Christian Ambassador, N.S., Vol. 13 (1875), 190-
91; 2) Ninth of Romans--Wesleyan Times, January 28, 1850,
p. 60; 3) System of Intellectual Philosophy, revised and enlarged from second edition (reviewed along with works on Intellectual Philosophy by Francis Wayland and L. P. Hickok)
--New Englander, Vol. 13 (February 1855) 129-44; 4) Baptism of the Holy Ghost (in various editions)--Our Own Fire-
side, Vol. 10 (1873), 640; Evangelical Magazine, September
1873, p. 540; Sword and Trowel, Vol. 10 (1874), 486; Christian's Pathway of Power, Vol. 1 (May 1, 1874), 79; Evangelical Repository, 6th Series, Vol. 1 (May 1875), 232; The
Christian, January 20, 1876, pp. 12-13 (a letter by Mahan
defending his views on the Baptism of the Holy Ghost); Evangelical Repository, 6th Series, June 1878, pp. 258-67; 5)
Out of Darkness into Light--The Sword and the Trowel, Vol.
11 (1875), 402; City Road Magazine, Vol. 5 (1875), 336; The
Christian, June 3, 1875, p. 18 and June 17, pp. 16-17;
Dickinsons Theological Quarterly (London), I (July 1875),
479; 6) Life Thoughts on the Rest of Faith--Dickinsons Theo-

logical Quarterly, Vol. 13 (January 1877), 158; 7) Autobiography: Intellectual, Moral, and Spiritual--King's Highway, XII (1883), 45-49; Dickinsons Theological Quarterly, N.S., II (January 1883), 134; 8) A Critical History of Philosophy--Primitive Methodist Quarterly Review, N.S., Vol. 7 (January 1885), 110-31 and July 1885, pp. 443-57; William Hague, Life Notes on Fifty Years' Outlook (Boston: Lee and Shepard, 1888), p. 113; and King's Highway, Vol. 26 (November 1897), 227.

45.   The Methodist Recorder, July 5, 1875, p. 387; The Methodist, September 3, 1875, pp. 11-12; John Brash, Our Lovefeast, pp. 137-38; Page, A Long Pilgrimage, p. 155; The Methodist Recorder, January 17, 1873, p. 31; The King's Highway, Vol. 18 (August 1889), 285-87; A Long Pilgrimage, p. 155; The King's Highway, Vol. 26 (November 1897), 227.

46.   This motif pervades the whole of the two volumes of A Critical History of Philosophy.   The repetition becomes tedious and detracts from an otherwise excellent piece of work--one that is a genuinely important contribution to philosophical literature.

47.   For an account of the sweeping educational changes at Harvard, including those in philosophy, see Henry James' Charles William Eliot, President of Harvard University, 1869-1909 (Boston: Houghton Mifflin, 1930).

48.   Divine Life, Vol. 14 (1891), 311.

49.   J. Jones to James Morison, November 14, 1873, Moir Collection, The Mitchell Library, Glasgow.

50.   Divine Life, Vol. 13 (December 1889), 142.

51.   Ibid., Vol. 16 (March 1891), 60.

52.   Ibid., Vol. 16 (February 1891), 55-56.

53.   The two-volume Critical History of Philosophy abounds in such epithets.

54.   Christian Perfection (the George Warner 1874 edition) and Misunderstood Texts are currently reprinted by H. E. Schmul, Salem, Ohio, and The Baptism of the Holy Ghost and the Enduement of Power is currently reprinted by J. Edwin Newby, Noblesville, Indiana.

55.   Mahan to Anna Mahan North, October 11, October 17, 1884, OCA, 30/24, Box 7, "Mahan Letters" folder.

56.   Mahan to Anna Mahan North, October 11, 1882.

57.   Divine Life, Vol. 13 (May 1890), 292-93.   This is one in a series of pieces devoted to the ways in which Providence moves in mysterious ways and uses men as instruments in achieving results.

58.   Ibid., Vol. 1 (July 1877).

59.   Mahan is listed as a voter in the Burgess Roll

of the Borough of Eastbourne, Sussex County, East Ward,
Polling District 1 (1885-1886), entry number 333 and (1886-1887), entry number 335, Town Hall, Eastbourne; Borough
Librarian of Eastbourne, Letter to Richard Dupuis, May 2,
1970, photocopy in Asa Mahan Archives, Asbury College.

      60.   Mahan, Letter to Anna Mahan North, November
10, 1884, in which he copied Lancelot Middleton's letter for
his daughter to read (OCA, 2/1, Box 1, "Asa Mahan").

      61.   Ibid.

      62.   W. Haig Miller, "The Late Dr. Asa Mahan,"
Divine Life, Vol. 12 (June 1889), 314.

      63.   Divine Life, Vol. 12 (January 1889), 190.

      64.   C. G. Moore, "Fallen Asleep," Divine Life, Vol.
12 (June 1889), 310-13.

      65.   Ibid., pp. 312-13.

      66.   On June 19, 1889 probate of Mahan's will was
granted to C. G. Moore and G. D. Freeman, the executors.
See probate entry in the catalogue at Somerset House, London: Mahan, Asa, 19 June 1889.

      67.   From personal inspection of headstone.

      68.   Superintendent of Cemeteries, County Borough
of Eastbourne, to Richard Dupuis, May 12, 1970, photocopy
in Asa Mahan Archives, Asbury College.

INDEX

Mahan, Asa (cont.)

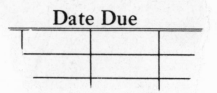

Date Due